Microsoft® Office Word Applications

Pasewark and Pasewark*

For Microsoft Office 2000, Office XP, Office 2003, and Future Versions

With: Business, Career, Personal, and Educational Applications

William R. Pasewark, Sr., Ph.D.
Professor Emeritus, Business Education, Texas Tech University

Scott G. Pasewark, B.S.
Occupational Education, Computer Technologist

William R. Pasewark, Jr., Ph.D., CPA
Professor, Accounting, Texas Tech University

Carolyn Pasewark Denny, M.Ed.
National Computer Consultant, Reading and Math Certified Elementary Teacher, K-12 Certified Counselor

Heather Treadaway Pasewark, B.A.
English/Computer Teacher

Frank M. Stogner, MBA, CPA
International Business

Jan Pasewark Stogner, MBA
Financial Planner

Beth Pasewark Wadsworth, B.A.
Graphic Designer

*Pasewark and Pasewark is a trademark of the Pasewark LTD.

THOMSON
COURSE TECHNOLOGY

Australia • Canada • Mexico • Singapore • Spain • United Kingdom • United States

Microsoft Word Applications

Cheryl Costantini
Executive Editor

Chris Katsaropoulos
Managing Editor

Robert Gaggin
Product Manager

Kim Ryttel
School Marketing Manager

Steven Deschene and Efrat Reis
Cover and Internal Design

Jodi Dreissig
Product Manager

Patty Stephan
Director of Production

Trevor Kallop
Senior Manufacturing Coordinator

Kelly Robinson
Production Editor

CEP Inc.
Developmental Editor

GEX Publishing Services
Compositor

Banta — Menasha
Printer

COPYRIGHT © 2003 Course Technology, a division of Thomson Learning, Inc. Thomson Learning ™ is a trademark used herein under license.

Appendix D, *Keyboarding and Touch System Improvement*, is an excerpt from *Keyboarding Skill Builder for Computers*, Copyright 1996 by William Robert Pasewark, Sr. All rights reserved.

Printed in the United States of America

2 3 4 5 6 7 8 9 BM 05 04 03

For more information, contact Course Technology, 25 Thomson Place, Boston, Massachusetts, 02210.
Or find us on the World Wide Web at: www.course.com

ALL RIGHTS RESERVED. No part of this work covered by the copyright hereon may be reproduced or used in any form or by any means—graphic, electronic, or mechanical, including photocopying, recording, taping, Web distribution, or information storage and retrieval systems—without the written permission of the publisher.

For permission to use material from this text or product, contact us by
Tel (800)730-2214
Fax (800)730-2215
www.thomsonrights.com

Disclaimer
Course Technology reserves the right to revise this publication and make changes from time to time in its content without notice.

Microsoft and the Office logo are either registered trademarks or trademarks of the Microsoft Corporation in the United States and/or other countries. Course Technology/Thomson Learning is an independent entity from Microsoft Corporation and not affiliated with Microsoft Corporation in any manner. This text may be used in assisting students to prepare for a Microsoft Office Specialist exam. Neither Microsoft Corporation, its designated review company, nor Course Technology/Thomson Learning warrants that use of this publication will ensure passing the relevant Microsoft Office Specialist exam.

ISBN 0-619-05528-6

Preface

To Students

Knowing how to use computers will be a valuable asset to help you in the business, career, personal, and school roles in your life—now and in the future.

Welcome to *Microsoft Word Applications*, a book that will help you to be a confident and proficient computer user.

Now, please go to the Introduction Unit, page 1 (Introduction 1), and start learning about your computer.

To Teachers

A New Book for a New Approach to Teaching Computer Applications

The instructional strategies and the funding for computer application courses are changing dramatically. For example:

1. Students now enter computer applications courses with a very wide variety of computer skills acquired from previous computer instruction and from out-of-class computer experiences.

2. Restricted budgets are making it more difficult to purchase new textbooks to upgrade to new versions of Microsoft Office.

To overcome these and other teaching challenges, schools need a textbook with a new approach. *Microsoft Office Applications* (MOA) is just such a book.

Microsoft Office Applications: A Flexible Approach for Teaching Office

1. The Book Contains:

a. <u>What to Do</u>s that are *general* instructions for all Microsoft Office versions. They describe how to create a document or a file.

b. <u>Hot Tips</u> in the margins are *specific* instructions that help students to execute functions or operations, such as how to save, print, and close a document.

Students apply computer skills developed in the <u>Tasks</u> to produce realistic documents for their business, career, personal, and school life skills. There is a model, "Your Application Completed," for each application.

2. The Supplements Are:

Booklets of 150 pages that contain the familiar Step-by-Step, specific instructions for Tasks in the book. There are separate supplements for Office 2000, Office XP, and Office 2003. Supplements will be available for new Office versions so that you can teach with the same MOA book when you upgrade your software, or if you have labs with multiple versions of Office.

Supplements can be used by less experienced students who need the support of version-specific Step-by-Step instructions.

With the adoption of the MOA book, Step-by-Step Supplements are also available without charge on the Instructor Resources CD and from *www.Course.com*.

Origin of the Microcomputer Office Applications Books

At numerous presentations and conferences during the last several years, the authors asked teachers to record their three major problems when teaching computer classes. The problems were compiled into a master list of Top Problems Teaching Computers. The authors wrote Microcomputer Office Applications to help teachers overcome these challenges.

SEVEN Challenges Teaching Computer Applications

ONE Solution: *Microsoft Office Applications*
by Pasewark and Pasewark

Challenge #1. Students have a wide range of computer experiences, learning abilities, and interests.

Solution:

Novice students use the MOA text and the version-specific supplement that contains Step-by-Step instructions.

Competent students use the MOA text and margin notes.

Skilled students use the MOA text with enrichment exercises such as Extra Challenge, Internet, Teamwork, simulations, and Critical Thinking and Problem Solving Projects.

Depending upon their level of computer competencies, students are supported by basic computer information in segments of the MOA book such as Computer Concepts, Windows Basics, Concepts for Microsoft Office Programs, and a Review of Microsoft Office Basics. Computer-assisted assessment programs are available for these computer competency aides.

Challenge #2. Students prefer doing instead of reading.

Solution:

MOA books have an uncluttered, easy-to-read page layout; clear, concise instructions; enumerated Step-by-Step instructions that are easy to follow; and numerous screen captures that help students *see* what they need to do.

Challenge #3. Textbook budgets are limited.

Solution:

Adopt MOA and you no longer have to purchase a new text every time Microsoft releases a new version of Office. An inexpensive, updated, Step-by Step Instruction supplement is available when you change software.

ONE BOOK FOR ALL VERSIONS

2000   XP   2003   **FUTURE VERSIONS**

Challenge #4. Teachers and students want a plentiful supply of interesting, realistic applications.

Solution:

MOA contains more than 300 activities which include an on-going Integrated Simulation at the end of each unit, as well as Critical Thinking and Problem Solving projects that range in length from 15 minutes to 10 hours. There are applications for business, career, personal, and school life-skills.

Challenge #5. Students lack business skills.
Solution:
In addition to business applications, the appendices contain model document formats, succinct guides for writing letters and e-mails, skill building for keyboarding, and the numeric 10-key touch systems.

Challenge #6. Space is limited on the computer desk.
Solution:
The top-spiral, easel-back, standalone MOA text has a smaller footprint, is easy for students to handle, and places the copy at eye-level.

Challenge #7. Teachers want to meet Microsoft Office Specialist requirements.
Solution:
The two texts, when used together, include all of Microsoft Office Specialist competencies at the Core level.

In addition:
1. *Microsoft Office Applications* by Pasewark and Pasewark includes more Microsoft Office software programs than any other high school text on the market: **Word**, **Excel**, **PowerPoint**, **Access**, **Outlook**, **Publisher**, **FrontPage**, **Speech Recognition**, and **Windows**.
2. MOA books are *flexible*. For example, they can be used in schools with labs that have different versions of Microsoft Office; in classes with students who have a wide variety of abilities and instructional patterns; and as the "core" or "extra" applications book.
3. Students must keep "focused on task." An appealing, interesting, easy-to-succeed, user-friendly computer applications book can encourage students to remain "on task." The new learning approach in *Microcomputer Office Applications* can help.
4. Getting Ready activities include these important work traits: Developing Good Computer Work Habits; Help! Where Can I Get It?; and Verifying Your Work.

Teaching Support Materials
The following support materials will help you to teach better, faster, and easier:

Assessment, Testing, and Certification
SAM and TOM
Experience the power, ease, and flexibility of SAM and TOM. These innovative software tools provide the first truly integrated technology-based training and assessment solution for your applications course.

Use SAM to measure your students' proficiency in Microsoft Office applications through real-world, performance-based questions and monitor their success through detailed reports.

TOM works in conjunction with SAM to cultivate the ultimate learning experience. With TOM for Microsoft Office, students learn Office concepts and skills actively through both guided and self-directed instruction. Now you're free to teach the way you want to teach, and students are free to excel!

ExamView®
ExamView® is a powerful objective-based test generator that enables you to create paper, LAN, or Web-based tests from test banks designed specifically for your Course Technology text. Utilize the ultra-efficient QuickTest Wizard to create tests in less than five minutes by taking advantage of Course Technology's question banks, or customize your own exams from scratch.

Microsoft Office Specialist Program

This Introductory book, with its companion Advanced book, will prepare students for the Microsoft Office Specialist Core exam for **Word**, Excel, Access, PowerPoint, Outlook, and FrontPage.

To learn more about Microsoft Office Specialist, visit *www.mous.net*.

Start-Up Checklist

For the Start-Up Checklist, see Appendix M.

Teaching Schedule and Resources

These charts in the Annotated Instructor Edition will help you plan your course and facilitate reports to your school administration.

The headings of the charts for the Units in the book are: Days, Activities, Resources on CD, Microsoft Office Specialist Objectives, and TEKS objectives.

Acknowledgments and Author's Credentials

Acknowledgments

The authors gratefully thank Rhonda Davis for coordinating the preparation of the manuscript and for using her business experiences to write the Access unit and several other segments of this book.

We also thank Billie Conley, a Lubbock High School computer teacher, for reviewing the manuscript and preparing the Business Students Association simulation that is in the Advanced book.

All of our books are a coordinated effort by the authors and scores of professionals working with the publisher. The authors appreciate the dedicated work of all these publishing personnel and particularly those with whom we have had direct contact:

Course Technology: Jodi Dreissig, Chris Elkhill, Chris Katsaropoulos, Robert Gaggin, Dave Lafferty, Kelly Robinson, and Kim Ryttel. We particularly want to recognize Tom Tyner, Regional Sales Manager, for his valuable advice about this book.

Custom Editorial Productions Inc.: Anne Chimenti, Jan Clavey, Jean Findley, Rose Marie Kuebbing, Betsy Newberry, and Megan Smith-Creed.

Many professional Course Technology sales representatives make educationally sound presentations to teachers about our books. We appreciate their valuable work as "bridges" between the authors and teachers.

Dedication

This book is dedicated in memory of Warren Caster and Diann Corbin. Their thoughtful acts of kindness and service as sales representatives have earned them the respect, admiration, and friendship of countless teachers and many authors. — *Bill Pasewark, Sr.*

Authors' Commitments

In writing this book, the authors have dedicated themselves to creating a comprehensive and appealing instructional package to make teaching and learning an interesting, challenging, and rewarding experience for students and teachers.

With these instructional materials, teachers can create realistic learning experiences so learners can successfully master concepts, knowledge, and skills that will help them live better lives — now and in the future.

The authors' commitment to students and teachers is a successful pedagogical formula for writing textbooks as evidenced by their award-winning books.

Award-winning Books by the Pasewarks

The Text and Academic Authors Association recognizes the best textbooks of the year in eight academic disciplines. The Pasewarks won a Texty Award for their following computer books:

2002, *Microsoft Office XP, Introductory Course*

2001, *Microsoft Works 2000*

2000, *Microsoft Office 2000, Introductory Course*

1994, *Microsoft Works 3.0, Macintosh*

In 1994, their book, *The Office: Procedures and Technology*, won the first William McGuffey Award for Textbook Excellence and Longevity and a Texty Award for the best business book of the year.

About the Authors

Pasewark LTD is a family-owned business. We use Microsoft Office in our business, career, personal, and family lives. Writing this book, therefore, was a natural project for the eight authors in our family who are identified on the title page of this book.

The authors have written more than 100 books about computers, accounting, and office technology.

Pasewark authors are members of several professional associations that help authors write better books and have been recognized with numerous awards for classroom teaching.

Other Microsoft Office Applications Books in this Series

Microsoft Office Applications, Introductory
Varied applications, projects, and simulations introduce students to the Microsoft Office Suite of software programs. Along with the Advanced book, prepares students for Microsoft Office Specialist Core exams for Word, Excel, Access, PowerPoint, and FrontPage.

Microsoft Office Applications, Advanced
Applications are more challenging than in the Introductory book. Along with the Introductory book, prepares students for Microsoft Office Specialist Core exams for Word, Excel, Access, PowerPoint, Outlook, and FrontPage.

Microsoft Excel Applications
Combines the Excel units from the Introductory and Advanced books. Prepares students for the Microsoft Office Specialist Excel Core exam.

Contents

Introduction to Microsoft Office Unit IN-1
Introductory Microsoft Word Unit IW-1
Advanced Microsoft Word Unit AW-1
Appendix A Windows Basics A-1
Appendix B Computer Concepts B-1
Appendix C Concepts for Microsoft Office Programs C-1
Appendix D Keyboarding Touch System Improvement D-1
Appendix E Ten-Key Numeric Touch System Improvement E-1
Appendix F Models for Formatted Documents F-1
Appendix G Task Filenames and Descriptions G-1
Appendix H Application Filenames and Descriptions H-1
Appendix I E-Mail Writing Guides I-1
Appendix J Letter Writing Guides J-1
Appendix K Proofreader's Marks K-1
Appendix L Microsoft Office Specialist Program L-1
Appendix M Start-Up Checklist M-1
Glossary GL-1
Index IX-1

Introduction to Microsoft Office Unit

Part 1 - Review of Microsoft Office Basics
Part 2 - Using the Internet
Part 3 - Getting Ready

Introduction Unit

Introduction Unit Contents

Part 1 - Review of Microsoft Office Basics

Tasks
- 1 - Start an Application 4
- 2 - Menus, Toolbars 5
- 3 - Open Existing Document 7
- 4 - Save, Close 9
- 5 - Preview, Print 10
- 6 - Get Help 12
- 7 - Use Office Assistant 15
- 8 - Quit an Application 16

Applications
- 1 - Open, Save, Preview, Print, Close 17
- 2 - Get Help 18

Part 2 - Using the Internet

Tasks
- 1 - Access, Search 21
- 2 - Use URLs, Print 23
- 3 - Add Favorites 24

Applications
- 1 - Access, Search, Print, Add Favorites 25
- 2 - Access, Print, Add Favorites 26

Part 3 - Getting Ready

- Urgent and Important Notice Before You Start 28
- Terminology 28
- Tasks and Applications 28
- Type Styles 28
- Developing Good Computer Work Habits 29
- Review Pack CD 29
- Help! Where Can I Get It? 30
- Verify Your Work 30
- Sample Pages 30
- Sample Page from this Book 31
- Sample Page from the Step-by-Step Instructions, Supplement ..32
- Learning Boxes 33

Part 10 - Working with Long Documents

Application 3 - Insert Subdocuments, Insert Bookmark, Create Table of Contents

Complete the IT Security Manual.

What To Do

1. The Security Manual document should be open from the previous Application. Change the document to Outline View if necessary.
2. Insert the **Company Policies** document, the **Computer Virus Procedures** document, and the **Disaster Restart and Recovery** document, located in the Security Manual Master folder, in the appropriate location in the manual.
3. Preview the document. Insert page breaks if necessary.
4. Create a bookmark for the Program and Data File Backup section in the Disaster Restart and Recovery Plan subdocument. Name the bookmark **Backup**.
5. Create a table of contents for the manual.
6. Preview the document. Save, print, and close the document.

Your Application Completed

Figure 10-12 Security Manual master document

- Table of Contents
- Introduction   1
- Company Policies   2
- Procedures to Detect and Repair Computer Viruses   3
- Disaster Restart and Recovery Plan   4

  - C:\Norton Laboratories\Security Manual Master\Introduction.doc

  - C:\Norton Laboratories\Security Manual Master\Company Policies.doc

  - C:\Norton Laboratories\Security Manual Master\Computer Virus Procedures.doc

  - C:\Norton Laboratories\Security Manual Master\Disaster Restart and Recovery.doc

Extra Challenges

- Read the Company Policies document for Norton Laboratories. Norton emphasizes the importance of keeping computerized information secure. Research laws concerning electronic security breeches. What are the consequences of breaking these laws?
- Create and apply styles for the headings and text of the manual.
- Create a title page for the manual.

Teamwork

- Read the Disaster Restart and Recovery Plan for Norton Laboratories. With a classmate, create a restart and recovery plan for your computer lab. Have the class vote on the best plan and implement it in the lab.

Part 1

Review of Microsoft Office Basics

Objectives

After completing this Part, you should be able to:
- Start an Office application from Windows.
- Use menus and toolbars.
- Open an existing document.
- Save and close a document.
- Preview and print a document.
- Use the Help system.
- Use the Office Assistant.
- Quit an application.

Part 10 - Working with Long Documents

Application 2 - Create Master Document, Create Subdocument

Your boss, Harold Hastings, has asked you to work on the company's IT security procedures. Your staff has completed their assignments and saved their work to the shared file you designated. Now you must integrate their work into a single report to present to your boss.

What To Do

1. Select the **Security Manual Data Files** folder and copy it to the solution file designated by your teacher. Rename the folder **Security Manual Master** followed by your initials.

2. Open a new Word document. Change the document to Outline View if necessary.

3. Key the outline shown in Figure 10-10.

Figure 10-10 IT Security Manual outline

> - **Introduction**
> - **Policies**
> - **Viruses**
> - **Disasters**

4. Save the outline in the Security Manual Master folder as **Security Manual**, followed by your initials.

5. Create a subdocument for the Introduction heading. Key the text as shown in Figure 10-11.

Figure 10-11 IT Security Manual introduction

> The continuation of business functions and accessibility of information is crucial to the operation and profitability of the company. This manual identifies the procedures for protection of information systems and recovery plans should there be a disaster.

6. Save the document and leave it open for the next Application.

Advanced Word 80

Part 1 - Review of Microsoft Office Basics

Task 1 - Start an Application

What To Do

1. Click the **Start** button to open the Start menu. Point to **Programs** (if using Windows 2000), or **All Programs** (if using Windows XP), and click **Microsoft PowerPoint** (you may need to click **Microsoft Office** first). PowerPoint starts, and a blank presentation appears. See Figure 1-1.

Figure 1-1 A blank presentation (in Office XP)

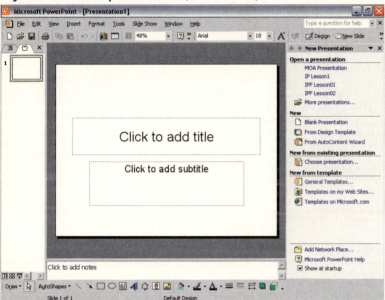

2. Click the **Close** button on the right side of the menu bar to close the blank presentation. The PowerPoint program will remain open.

3. Open the **Start** menu again.

4. Point to **Programs** (Windows 2000), or **All Programs** (Windows XP), and then click **Microsoft Word** (you may need to click **Microsoft Office** first). Word starts and a blank document appears. Leave Word and PowerPoint open for the next Task.

Computer Concept

- You can also open a new file from within an application by choosing **New** on the **File** menu. The New dialog box appears.

Web Site

- For more information on Microsoft Office and other Microsoft products, visit Microsoft's Web site at *http://www.microsoft.com*.

Hot Tip

- If the Microsoft Office Shortcut Bar is installed, you can use it to open an Office application and create a blank document at the same time.

Introduction 4

introduction unit - part 1   task 1

Part 10 – Working with Long Documents

Application 1 – Create, Reorganize Outline

Your supervisor is interested in redesigning the office space. She is interested in improving the work environment by designing ergonomically correct workspaces. Create an outline for a report for your supervisor about ergonomics.

Extra Challenge

- Use the Internet to find more elements of an ergonomically-sound work environment. Design a home office. Make a list of the requirements you considered in designing the office.

What To Do

1. Open a new Word document. In Outline View, create the outline shown in Figure 10-9.

Figure 10-9 Ergonomics outline

> ✧ **Ergonomics**
> ✧ *Definition – Ergonomics is the study of how the workplace environment affects the health and productivity of employees. A comfortable work area increases the employee's efficiency and job satisfaction.*
> ✧ **Workstation**
> - Chair – The employee should be able to adjust the chair to fit his height. His feet must be flat on the ground and his back should be supported by the back of the chair.
> - Desk – The work surface of the desk should be elbow height. It should be large enough to arrange objects logically.
> ✧ **Lighting**
> - Overhead Lighting – Overhead lightning or natural lighting should provide light for the entire work area. There should not be a glare on the computer screen, keyboard or the documents.
> - Task Lighting – Task lighting provides light for the work surface. The light should be adjustable to prevent glare.
> ✧ **Equipment**
> - Monitor – To reduce headaches and neck pain, the monitor should be just below eyelevel at a distance of 30 to 40 inches from the employee.
> - Computer – The keyboard should be at elbow height. The mouse should be convenient to the keyboard to limit strain on the arm.

2. Collapse the outline to show only the headings.
3. Move the *Equipment* heading above the *Lighting* heading.
4. Expand the outline.
5. Move up the *Desk* heading with its text.
6. Save the document as **Ergonomics** followed by your initials. Print and close the document.

Part 1 - Review of Microsoft Office Basics

Task 2 - Menus, Toolbars

What To Do

1. Your screen should display the opening screen for the Word program. See Figure 1-2, which shows the opening screen for Word 2002. Look carefully at the parts of this screen labeled in Figure 1-2. These basic parts of the screen are similar in all of the Office programs and are discussed in Table 1-1.

Figure 1-2 Word opening screen (in Office XP)

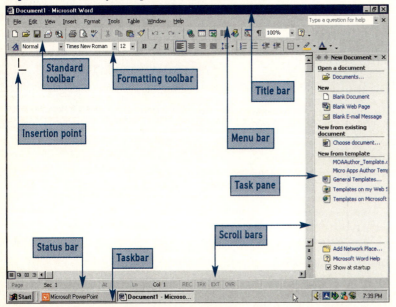

Table 1-1 Understanding the opening screen

Item	Function
Title bar	Displays the names of the Office program and the current file.
Menu bar	Contains the menu titles from which you can choose a variety of commands.
Standard toolbar	Contains buttons you can use to perform common tasks.
Formatting toolbar	Contains buttons for changing formatting, such as alignment and type styles.
Insertion point	Shows where text will appear when you begin keying.
Scroll bars	Allow you to move quickly to other areas of an Office document.
Status bar	Tells you the status of what is shown on the screen.
Taskbar	Shows the Start button, the Quick Launch toolbar, and all open programs.
Task pane (Office XP and later versions)	Opens automatically when you start an Office application. Contains commonly used commands applicable to each application.

(continued on next page)

Hot Tip

- If you do not know the function of a toolbar button, move the mouse pointer to the button, but do not click. The name of the button will appear.

Computer Concepts

- In Office XP and later versions, the task pane opens automatically when you start an Office application. It is a separate window on the right side of the document window. It contains commonly used commands to help you work more efficiently. To close the task pane, click the **Close** button. To view the task pane, open the **View** menu and choose **Task Pane**.
- As you work, the program adjusts the menus to display the commands used most frequently. It adds a command when you use it and drops a command when it hasn't been used recently.
- Toolbars are a quick way to choose commands. The toolbars use *icons*, or small pictures, to remind you of each button's function. Toolbars can also contain pull-down menus. Unless you specify otherwise, only the Standard and Formatting toolbars are displayed, but many more are available. To see a list of the toolbars you can use, right-click at any location on a toolbar.

Part 10 - Working with Long Documents

Task 8 - Create Table of Contents, Insert Index

What To Do

1. The Employee Handbook master document should be open from the previous Task. Change the document to **Outline** View.
2. Place the insertion point in the blank page above the Message from the President. Key **Table of Contents**. Insert a Table of Contents.
3. Place the insertion point to the end of the document. Key **Index**.
4. In the Benefits subdocument, mark the following headings to be included in the index:

   Equal Opportunity

   Insurance

   Cafeteria Plan

   Retirement

   Holidays

   Vacations

   Sick Leave

5. Format the index with one column and right-align the page numbers.
6. Insert a Next page section break above the Index heading.
7. Preview the document. Save, print, and close the document.

Your Task Completed

Figure 10-7 Table of Contents

```
Table of Contents
A Message from the President..................................................2
Philosophy..................................................................3
The History of Norton Laboratories........................................4
Norton Benefits...........................................................5
Your Responsibilities.....................................................7
Norton Laboratories Product List..........................................8
```

Figure 10-8 Index

```
Index
Cafeteria Plan.............................................................5
Equal Opportunity..........................................................5
Holidays...................................................................5
Insurance..................................................................5
Retirement.................................................................5
Sick Leave.................................................................6
Vacations..................................................................6
```

Hot Tips

- To create a table of contents, open the **Insert** menu and click **Reference**. Click **Index and Tables** on the submenu. Click the **Table of Contents** tab.
- To create an index, open the **Insert** menu and click **Reference**. Click **Index and Tables** on the submenu. Click the **Index** tab.
- To mark an entry for the index, click the **Mark Entry** button on the Index tab. Select the text to be marked and click to place the insertion point in the *Main entry* box.

Extra Challenges

- Create and apply styles for the heading, sub-headings, and text in the Employee Handbook.
- Create a title page for the Employee Handbook.

Advanced Word 78

Part 1 - Review of Microsoft Office Basics

Task 2 - Menus, Toolbars, continued

2. Locate on your screen each of the items listed in Table 1-1. Read the function for each item. **Office 2000 users:** The task pane does not exist in Office 2000.

3. Locate the menu bar and click **Edit** to open the Edit menu. A list of basic editing commands displays. See Figure 1-3.

4. Click the arrows at the bottom of the Edit menu. An expanded menu of commands displays. See Figure 1-3 (the options on the Edit menu vary slightly between the Office programs).

Figure 1-3 Basic menu vs. expanded menu

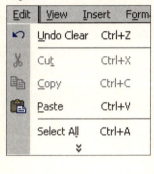
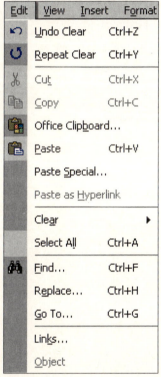

Did You Know?

- As with the menus, toolbars initially display buttons only for basic commands. To see additional buttons, click the down arrow on the right end of the toolbar and choose from the list that appears. When you use a button from the list, it is added to the toolbar. If you haven't used a button recently, it is returned to the More Buttons list.

5. Move the insertion point to any location on a toolbar and right-click. A list of the toolbars is displayed.

6. Click **Drawing**. The Drawing toolbar is displayed at the bottom of the screen.

7. Right-click again on any toolbar and choose **Drawing**. The Drawing toolbar is removed from the screen. Leave Word and PowerPoint open for the next Task.

Part 10 - Working with Long Documents

Task 7 - Create Cross-References

What To Do

1. The Employee Handbook master document should be open from the previous Task. Expand the subdocuments if necessary.

2. In the subdocument **The History of Norton Laboratories**, place the insertion point at the end of the last paragraph. Key **For more information see**. (Do not key the period, but do insert a space after the word **see**.)

3. Insert a cross-reference for **Norton Laboratories Product List**. In the *Reference type* box, select **Heading** and in the *Insert reference to* box, select **Heading text**. Select **Norton Laboratories Product List** from the *For which heading* section and click the **Insert** button and then click **Close**. Key a period after the text *Norton Laboratories Product List*.

4. Place the insertion point on the text *Norton Laboratories Product List*. Strike **Ctrl** and click the text. The insertion point is moved to the Product List document.

5. Save the document and leave it open for the next Task.

Key Term

- Cross-reference — Text that refers you to another part of the document for further information.

Hot Tip

- To insert a cross-reference, place the insertion point where you want the cross-reference to be inserted. Open the **Insert** menu and click **Reference**. On the submenu, click **Cross-reference**.

Part 1 - Review of Microsoft Office Basics

Task 3 - Open Existing Document

What To Do

1. With Word on the screen, open the **File** menu and choose **Open**. The Open dialog box appears. See Figure 1-4. **Office XP (and future version) users**: You can use the task pane to open a document. With Word on the screen, choose **More Documents** in the Open a document section of the task pane. The Open dialog box appears. See Figure 1-4. (You may have to select **Document** in the Open a document section of the task pane if it is the first time this program has been opened.)

Figure 1-4 Open dialog box

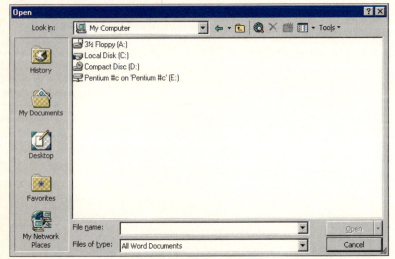

2. Click the down arrow to the right of the **Look in** box to display the available disk drives.

3. Click the drive that contains the data files for this course and locate the **Employees** folder. See Figure 1-5.

Figure 1-5 Employees folder

4. Double-click the **Employees** folder. The folders within the Employees folder appear.

Hot Tips

- Office offers you three shortcuts for opening recently used files. (1) The first shortcut is to choose My Recent Documents or Documents (Windows 2000) from the Start menu. A menu will open listing the most recently used documents. Open the file you wish to display. (2) The second shortcut can be found on the bottom of the File menu, which lists the filenames of the four most recently opened documents. Choose the file you wish to open. (3) The third shortcut is for Office XP (and future version) users only. The four most recently opened documents are also listed at the bottom of the Open a document section of the task pane.
- If the file you wish to open is on a floppy disk, be sure that you have the correct disk and that it is inserted properly into the disk drive.

Computer Concept

- In all of the Office applications, you open and close the files the same way.

(continued on next page)

Introduction 7

Part 10 - Working with Long Documents

Task 6 - Insert Bookmarks

What To Do

1. The Employee Handbook master document should be open from the previous Task. Expand the subdocuments if necessary. Change the document to Normal view.

2. Place the insertion point in front of the heading *Insurance* in the *Norton Benefits* subdocument. Insert a bookmark named **Insurance**.

3. Place the insertion point in front of the heading *Holidays* in the *Norton Benefits* subdocument. Insert a bookmark named **Holidays**.

4. Place the insertion point at the beginning of the document. Go to the **Holidays** bookmark.

5. Return to the beginning of the document. Save the document and leave it open for the next Task.

Key Term

- Bookmark — A place marker that identifies text for future reference.

Hot Tips

- To insert a bookmark, place the insertion point where you want the bookmark to be inserted. Open the **Insert** menu and click **Bookmark**. In the Bookmark dialog box, key a name for the bookmark.
- To use a bookmark, open the **Edit** menu and click **Go To**. On the Go To tab, click **Bookmark** in the *Go to what* box. Click the bookmark name and click **Go To**.

Part 1 - Review of Microsoft Office Basics

Task 3 - Open Existing Document, continued

5. Double-click the **Perez** folder. The names of all files in the Perez folder are displayed. If necessary, click the down arrow at the right of the **Files of type** box and select **All Files** to display all the files.

6. Click **Schedule Memo** to select it. Click **Open** to open the file.

7. Open a second Office document by clicking the **Start** button. Point to **Programs** (or **All Programs**), and click **Microsoft Excel**. (You may need to click **Microsoft Office** first.)

8. Open the **File** menu and choose **Open**. The Open dialog box appears. Click the down arrow at the right of the **Look in** box. If necessary, click the drive that contains the data files.

9. Double-click the **Employees** folder, and then double-click the **Perez** folder.

10. Double-click **April Schedule** to open the file. The April Schedule appears on the screen. Leave the files open for the next Task.

Part 10 - Working with Long Documents

Task 5 - Create Subdocument from Existing Document

What To Do

1. The Employee Handbook master document should be open from the previous Task. Expand the subdocuments if necessary. Select the heading **Message**.
2. Insert the **Norton Letter** document located in the Handbook Master folder as a subdocument.
3. Collapse the subdocuments. Click **OK** if prompted to save the changes to the **Employee Handbook** master document.
4. Double-click the **Message** subdocument icon. A window opens containing the **Norton Letter** document.
5. Close the new document window. Expand the subdocuments.
6. Insert the **Norton History** document, **Norton Benefits** document, **Your Responsibilities** document, and **Norton Products** document from the Handbook Master folder in the same manner you inserted the **Norton Letter** document. Collapse the subdocuments. Click **OK** if prompted to save the changes to the document. Your document should look similar to Figure 10-6.

Figure 10-6 Master Document

- C:\Norton Laboratories\Handbook Master\Norton Letter.doc
- C:\Norton Laboratories\Handbook Master\Philosophy.doc
- C:\Norton Laboratories\Handbook Master\Norton History.doc
- C:\Norton Laboratories\Handbook Master\Norton Benefits.doc
- C:\Norton Laboratories\Handbook Master\Your Responsibilities.doc
- C:\Norton Laboratories\Handbook Master\Norton Products.doc

7. Use Print Preview to preview the master document. If prompted, click **Yes** to open the subdocuments. Scroll down to view each page. Each subdocument should begin on a new page.
8. If necessary, insert a Next page section break at the end of a subdocument to place it on a separate page. Use the Show/Hide button to view the page breaks.
9. Save the Employee Handbook master document, and leave it open for the next Task.

Hot Tip

- To insert a Word document as a subdocument, select the heading where you want to insert the document. Click the **Insert Subdocument** button on the Outlining toolbar.

Computer Concept

- When you save a master document, Word saves it and all of the subdocuments to the same location. Be sure to make any changes to the file name or file location by first opening the subdocument from within the master document and then using the **Save As** command on the **File** menu.

Did You Know?

- To move or delete a subdocument, you must first remove it from the master document. Select the subdocument and click the **Remove Subdocument** button. Removing a subdocument from the master document does not delete the subdocument from your computer.

Advanced Word 75

Part 1 - Review of Microsoft Office Basics

Task 4 - Save, Close

What To Do

1. The April Schedule workbook should be on the screen from the last Task. Open the **File** menu and choose **Save As**. The Save As dialog box appears. See Figure 1-6.

Figure 1-6 Save As dialog box

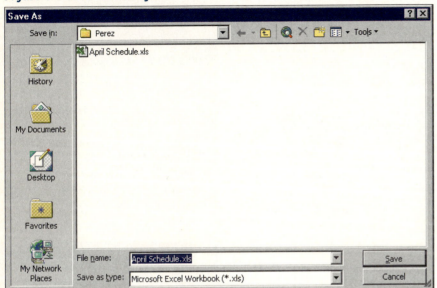

2. In the File name box, key **April Work Sched**, followed by your initials.

3. Click the down arrow to the right of the **Save in** box and choose the **Employees** folder. Double-click the **Garner** folder.

4. Choose **Save** to save the file with the new name in the Garner folder.

5. Open the **File** menu and choose **Close**. April Work Sched closes.

6. Click the **Microsoft Word** button on the taskbar to make it active. Schedule Memo should be displayed. Leave the document open for the next Task.

Did You Know?

- After you close a file, the application will still be open and ready for you to open or create another file.

Hot Tip

- When naming a file, choose a descriptive name that will remind you of what the file contains, such as *Cover Letter* or *First Quarter Sales*. With Windows, a filename may contain up to 255 characters and may include spaces.

Computer Concepts

- Saving is done two ways. The Save command saves a file on a disk using the current name. The Save As command saves a file on a disk using a new name. The Save As command can also be used to save a file to a new location.
- The AutoRecover feature automatically saves a copy of your document every 10 minutes. The saved copy will open automatically when you start Word after a power failure or similar problem. To change how often your files are saved, open the **Tools** menu and choose **Options**. Click the **Save** tab and then click the **Save AutoRecover info every** check box. In the minutes box, choose how often you want your files to be saved.

Introduction 9

Part 10 - Working with Long Documents

Task 4 - Create Subdocument from Outline Heading

What To Do

1. The Employee Handbook master document should be open in Outline View from the previous Task. Select the heading **Philosophy**.

2. Create a subdocument. Place the insertion point beneath the heading *Philosophy* and key the text from Figure 10-5.

Figure 10-5 Norton Philosophy

> **Philosophy**
> The character of a company reflects the character of the people who work there. We are proud of our associates and trust in their integrity. At Norton Industries, a core set of beliefs guides us. At the center of these beliefs is the Golden Rule: "Do unto others as you would have them do unto you." It is a simple but timeless idea. Other beliefs are:
> Treat others with respect and dignity.
> Do what you say you will do.
> Be helpful to others.
> Do not be wasteful.
> Tell the truth.
> Be on time.
> Smile.

3. Collapse the subdocuments. If prompted to save the changes to the Employee Handbook, click **OK**. Notice the hyperlink created for the subdocument.

4. Expand the subdocument.

5. Save the document and leave it open for the next Task.

Key Terms

- **Collapse subdocuments** — Hides the contents of the subdocuments and displays them as hyperlinks.
- **Expand subdocuments** — Displays the contents of the subdocuments.

Hot Tips

- To create a subdocument, select the heading where you want to create the document. Click the **Create Subdocument** button on the Outlining toolbar.
- To collapse a subdocument, click the **Collapse Subdocuments** button on the Outlining toolbar.
- To expand a subdocument, click **Expand Subdocuments** button on the Outlining toolbar.

Did You Know?

- You must expand the master document view in order to create or insert a subdocument.
- The **Collapse Subdocuments** button and the **Expand Subdocuments** button are in the same location. Click to toggle between **Collapse Subdocuments** and **Expand Subdocuments**.

Advanced Word 74

Part 1 - Review of Microsoft Office Basics

Task 5 - Preview, Print

What To Do

1. The Schedule Memo document should be on the screen from the last Task. Open the **File** menu and choose **Print Preview**. Schedule Memo displays on the screen for you to preview. The Print Preview toolbar is also displayed. See Figure 1-7. The Print Preview toolbar buttons are discussed in Table 1-2.

Figure 1-7 Print Preview toolbar

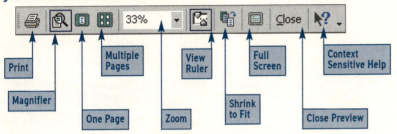

Table 1-2 Print Preview toolbar buttons

Button	Function
Print	Prints the document using the default settings.
Magnifier	Lets you zoom in and out on a section of the document.
One Page	Shows one page in Print Preview.
Multiple Pages	Shows up to six pages in Print Preview.
Zoom	Controls the percentage of magnification in which to view the document.
View Ruler	Displays rulers along the left and top of the Print Preview screen.
Shrink to Fit	Changes the font size of a document so that more text will fit on a page.
Full Screen	Maximizes the window so you can view an entire page on the screen at a larger percentage of magnification.
Close Preview	Closes the Print Preview window and returns you to your document view.
Context Sensitive Help	Displays the formatting of selected text.

2. Click on the text part of the displayed page with the plus sign magnifying glass. Notice how the page is enlarged. (If the plus sign magnifying glass is not displayed as the pointer, click the **Magnifier** button on the Print Preview toolbar.)

Hot Tips

- You can also preview a document by clicking the **Print Preview** button on the toolbar.
- You can also print by clicking the **Print** button on the Standard toolbar or on the Print Preview toolbar, but the Print dialog box won't appear. Clicking the button causes Word to skip the Print dialog box and begin printing immediately using the default settings, which are to print all pages.
- You can change the orientation of a document by opening the **File** menu and choosing **Page Setup**. The Page Setup dialog box appears. Click the **Margins** tab, or the **Paper Size** tab (Office 2000). In the Orientation section, choose either **Portrait** or **Landscape**, and click **OK**.

(continued on next page)

Part 10 - Working with Long Documents

Task 3 - Create Master Document

What To Do

1. Select the **Handbook Data Files** folder from the data files, and copy it to the solution file designated by your teacher.

2. Rename the folder **Handbook Master** followed by your initials. You will create your master document in this folder. The Handbook Master folder also contains files that will be linked to the master document as subdocuments.

3. Open a new Word document. Change the document to Outline View. Key the text from Figure 10-4. This outline will be the basis for the master document.

Figure 10-4 Employee Handbook outline

- Message
- Philosophy
- History
- Benefits
- Responsibilities
- Products

4. Save the document in the Handbook Master folder as **Employee Handbook**, followed by your initials. Leave the document open for the next Task.

Key Terms

- Master document — A file containing links to separate document files.
- Subdocument — A separate file contained in a master document.

Computer Concept

- Master documents allow you to manage working with long documents easily. You can create a table of contents, insert cross-references, or include an index for all of the subdocuments by using a master document.

Did You Know?

- The largest work of nonfiction is the *Yung-lo ta-tien* (Great Canon of the Yung-lo Era). It consisted of 22,937 chapters and 11,095 volumes.

Part 1 – Review of Microsoft Office Basics

Task 5 - Preview, Print, continued

3. Click again with the minus sign magnifying glass. The page returns to full-page view.

4. Click the **View Ruler** button. The ruler appears (or disappears).

5. Click the **Full Screen** button. The window is maximized.

6. Click the **Close Full Screen** button. You are returned to full-page view.

7. Click the down arrow on the **Zoom** box. Click **50%**.

8. Click the down arrow again and click **150%**.

9. Click the down arrow again, and click **Whole Page**. You are returned to full-page view.

10. Open the **File** menu and choose **Print**. The Print dialog box appears.

11. Click **OK** to print the document using the default settings. Your printed document should appear similar to Figure 1-8.

12. Click the **Close** button in the right corner of the title bar to close the Print Preview page. Open the **File** menu and choose **Close** to close Schedule Memo. Leave Word open for the next Task.

Computer Concept

- By default, Word is set to print pages in portrait orientation. Documents printed in portrait orientation are longer than they are wide. Documents printed in landscape orientation are wider than they are long.

Your Task Completed

Figure 1-8 Schedule Memo

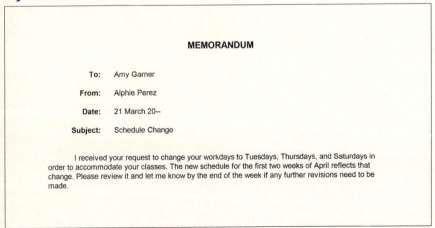

Part 10 - Working with Long Documents

Task 2 - Reorganize Outline

What To Do

1. The Exercise document should be open from the previous Task. Place the insertion point in front of the heading *Why Exercise?*
2. Collapse the outline to show only the headings. It is easier to reorganize an outline when it is collapsed.
3. Select the heading **Look better**.
4. Drag the heading and place it between the headings *Why Exercise?* and *Feel better*.
5. Place the insertion point in front of the heading **Why Exercise?**. Expand the outline. Notice the text underneath the *Look better* heading moved with it.
6. Place the insertion point on the text *Lower High Blood Pressure*. Click the **Move Up** button to move the text up one line.
7. Preview the document. Save, print, and close the document.

Your Task Completed

Figure 10-3 Exercise outline

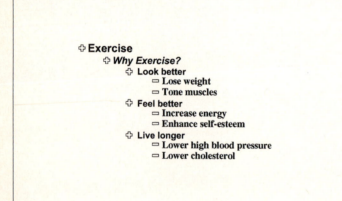

Hot Tips

- To collapse an outline so only the headings show, click the **Collapse** button on the Outlining toolbar.
- To expand an outline, click the **Expand** button on the Outlining toolbar.
- To move a heading up or down in the outline, click the **Move Up** and **Move Down** buttons on the Outlining toolbar or click the headings outline symbol and drag it to the new location.

Computer Concept

- The outline symbols on the screen in Outline View show the document's structure. They will not appear when the document is printed.

Advanced Word 72

Part 1 – Review of Microsoft Office Basics

Task 6 – Get Help

What To Do

1. Open the Word Help program by clicking the **Help** menu and choosing **Microsoft Word Help**. The Microsoft Word Help screen should appear similar to Figure 1-9. If the Office Assistant appears, click the **Options** button, deselect the **Use the Office Assistant** option, and click **OK**. You may need to select the **Microsoft Word Help** option on the **Help** menu again.

Figure 1-9 Microsoft Word Help in Office XP

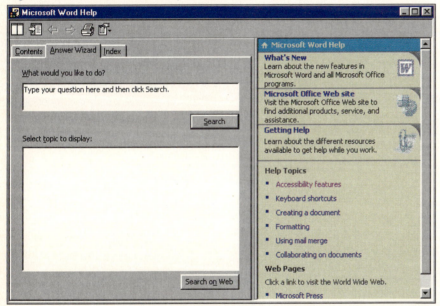

2. If you are using Office 2003, skip to Step 10 and continue.

3. If the left frame is not displayed, as shown in Figure 1-9, click the **Show** button on the toolbar to display.

4. Click the **Answer Wizard** tab in the left frame.

5. Choose one of the links in the right frame and read the contents of the Help window.

6. Click the **Index** tab.

7. Key **print** in the Type keywords box and click **Search**.

Computer Concept

- Use the Office Help system as a quick reference when you are unsure about a function. You can access Help from the Help menu on the application's menu bar. You can choose to see a table of contents with general topics, key a question, or search the Help system.

Hot Tip

- If the Office Assistant appears, turn it off by clicking **Options** in the balloon, clearing the **Use the Office Assistant** check box, and clicking **OK**.

(continued on next page)

Part 10 - Working with Long Documents

Task 1 - Create Outline

What To Do

1. Create a new Word document, and switch to Outline View.
2. Notice the Outlining toolbar is displayed. Take time to study the Outlining toolbar. See Figure 10-1.

Figure 10-1 Outlining Toolbar (Office XP)

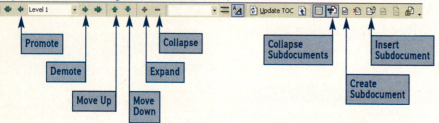

3. Key **Exercise** next to the minus symbol. Strike **Enter**.
4. Click the **Demote** button to move in one level. Key **Why Exercise?**.
5. Continue keying text as shown in Figure 10-2. Use the **Demote** and **Promote** buttons to move up and down levels.

Figure 10-2 Exercise outline

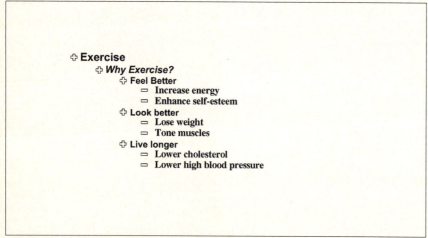

6. Save the document as **Exercise** followed by your initials. Leave the document open for the next Task.

Hot Tips

- To switch to Outline view, open the **View** menu and click **Outline**. You can also click the **Outline View** button at the lower-left of the document menu.
- To move a heading down a level in the outline, click the **Demote** button. Striking **Tab** will also demote a heading to the next lowest level.
- To move a heading up a level in the outline, click the **Promote** button. Striking **Shift+Tab** will promote a heading to the next highest level.

Did You Know?

- A plus symbol (+) before a heading indicates that subheadings or body text are below the heading. A minus symbol (-) indicates that no subheadings or body text are below the heading.

Advanced Word 71

Part 1 – Review of Microsoft Office Basics

Task 6 – Get Help, continued

8. In the choose a topic box, search through the list until you find **Print a Help topic**. Click it to display information in the right frame. **Office XP users:** In the right frame, click **Print the current topic** and then **Print a collection of topics**. The information on both topics will display. Your screen should appear similar to Figure 1-10.

Figure 1-10 Index tab of the Help system in Office XP

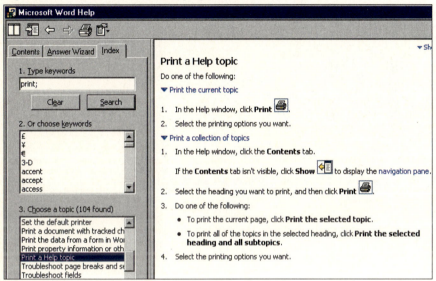

Did You Know?

- Many topics in the Help program are linked. A link is represented by colored, underlined text. By clicking a link, the user "jumps" to a linked document that contains additional information about that topic.

9. Skip to Step 14 and continue.

10. The Microsoft Word Help task pane should be displayed in the right margin. In the task pane, click the **Table of Contents** link to display a list of topics. Click the topic **Working with Text**, then click **Copy and Paste**, and then click **Move or copy text and graphics**. A list of topics display in the right frame. Click **Move or copy a single item** and read the contents that display in the right frame.

11. When finished, double-click the green back arrow at the top of the left frame (Table of Contents) to redisplay the Search box.

12. Key **print** in the Search box and click the green (Start searching) arrow.

(continued on next page)

Part 10

Working with Long Documents

Objectives

After completing this Part, you should be able to:
- Create an outline.
- Reorganize an outline.
- Create a master document.
- Create subdocuments.
- Insert cross-references.
- Insert bookmarks.
- Create a table of contents.

Part 1 - Review of Microsoft Office Basics

Task 6 - Get Help, continued

13. Search through the list of results until you find **Print a Help topic**. Click it to display information in the right frame.
14. Read the information, then print the information by following the instructions you read.
15. Click the **Back** button at the top of the right frame to return to the previous help item.
16. Click the **Forward** button to advance to the next help item.
17. Close the Help program by clicking the **Close** button(s). Leave Word open for the next Task.

Part 9 – Tables and Graphics

Application 4 – Bullet Lists, Insert Clip Art, Wrap Text, Insert WordArt, continued

Your Application Completed

Figure 9-13 Hampton Hills Newsletter

HAMPTON HILLS NEWSLETTER

June
Welcome New Tenants

The staff of Hampton Hills wishes to welcome the following new tenants:
- ☺ Jose Franco
- ☺ Bob and Sue Ming
- ☺ Don Peters
- ☺ Patsy O'Malley

Tenant Joseph Moore will receive $100 off his rent because he recommended Hampton Hills to Don Peters. Remember to tell your friends about Hampton Hills.

Hawaiian Luau Planned

Management will host our annual summer party on August 1. This year's theme is Hawaiian. You and your guest will receive a flower lei donated by Flowers for You.

The party will begin at 7 p.m. near the pool and clubhouse. Refreshments will be served.

Amusement Park Discount Tickets Now Available

Hampton Hills and the Parks of Peoria are offering discount tickets to Safari Park. You can pick up tickets and a map in the office during business hours. Limit five tickets per person please.

New Laundry Machines

Our laundry facility manager has purchased three new washers and three new dryers for the laundry room. There is no additional expense to use these new machines.

Don't Forget to Pay Your Rent!

There is a $25 late charge for rent paid after the fifth of the month.

Clubhouse Reservations

Several local businesses have requested the use of our clubhouse and pool for small company parties. The management has decided to rent the pool area and clubhouse to businesses after pool hours.

As always, tenants have first choice in reserving the property for personal get-togethers. Reservations should be made up to 30 days in advance.

Independence Day Parade

The Peoria Independence parade will pass down Dover Avenue directly in front of Hampton Hills. We'll have the best seats in the city. Because the route passes so close to Hampton property, management asks you to observe the following precautions so that no one will be injured.

- ★ Keep children and animals on Hampton property. Make sure they don't wander into the street during the parade.
- ★ Remember that no fireworks are allowed inside the city or on Hampton property.
- ★ Keep your animal on a leash. This is a city law that will keep them safe.
- ★ Don't park on Dover Street on Saturday. The street needs to be clear for the parade. Cars parked on the street will be towed.

Bicycle Safety Class

Learn safety procedures that could save your life. Plan to attend the Bicycle Safety Class sponsored by the city. The class will be Saturday June 24th at 2:00 p.m. at Cunningham Park Center.

Part 1 - Review of Microsoft Office Basics

Task 7 - Use Office Assistant

What To Do

1. Choose **Show the Office Assistant** from the Help menu. The Office Assistant appears. If necessary, click the **Office Assistant** to display the text box.
2. Key **How do I use the Office Assistant?** in the text box.
3. Click **Search**. A list of Help topics is displayed. Your screen should look similar to Figure 1-11.

Figure 1-11 Default Office Assistant in Office XP

4. Click the down arrow next to the **See more...** option, and choose one of the items listed. The Microsoft Word Help box appears.
5. Read and print the information.
6. Click the **Close** box to remove the Help window from the screen.
7. Right-click on the Office Assistant and choose **Hide**. Leave Word on the screen for the next Task.

Computer Concept

- The Office Assistant is a feature found in all of the Office programs that offers a variety of ways to get help. The Assistant is an animated character that offers tips, solutions, instructions, and examples to help you work more efficiently. See Figure 1-11.

Hot Tip

- You can change the way the Office Assistant provides help by clicking **Options**, choosing the **Options** tab, and making selections.

Did You Know?

- The default Office Assistant character is a paper clip. A default setting is the one used unless another option is chosen.

Part 9 - Tables and Graphics

Application 4 - Bullet Lists, Insert Clip Art, Wrap Text, Insert WordArt

You are a tenant at the Hampton Hills Apartments. You and two other tenants decide to create a newsletter for the apartment complex.

What To Do

1. Open **AW App9-4** from the data files. Save the document as **Hampton Hills Newsletter** followed by your initials.
2. Select all text except for the title *Hampton Hills Newsletter*. Format the text into two columns.
3. Select the list of new tenants. Bullet the list with a character of your choice. Select the list of precautions after the *Independence Day Parade* heading. Bullet the list with a character of your choice.
4. Place the insertion point on the blank line after *Hawaiian Luau Planned*. Insert appropriate clip art. Key **palm tree** in the Search text box. Format the text with the square wrap style and left horizontal alignment.
5. Place the insertion point before the first paragraph under *Independence Day Parade*. Insert appropriate clip art. Key **flag** in the Search text box. Format text with wrap style square and horizontal alignment left.
6. Select the title **Hampton Hills Newsletter**. Format the title with WordArt of your choice. Change the color of the headings to compliment the colors of the WordArt. Your newsletter should look similar to Figure 9-13.
7. Adjust the spacing in the first column so that the heading *Don't Forget to Pay Your Rent!* is at the top of the second column.
8. Save, print, and close the document.

Computer Concept

- If you find that you are using the same commands often, you can add the corresponding buttons to the toolbars (or even create a custom toolbar). Open the **Tools** menu, click **Customize**, then select a category from the Categories box. A list of commands corresponding to the selected category will appear in the Commands box on the right. Click and drag the icons of the commands you use most often to a toolbar.

Extra Challenge

- Create a newsletter for an organization to which you belong. Insert clip art and WordArt to make the newsletter more exciting.

(continued on next page)

Part 1 - Review of Microsoft Office Basics

Task 8 - Quit an Application

What To Do

1. Open the **File** menu. Notice the files listed toward the bottom of the menu. These are the four most recently used files.
2. Choose **Exit**. Word closes and Excel is displayed on the screen.
3. Click the **Close** button in the right corner of the title bar. Excel closes, and the desktop appears on the screen. The taskbar shows an application is still open.
4. Click the **PowerPoint** button on the taskbar to display it on the screen. Exit PowerPoint. The desktop appears on the screen again.

Computer Concept

- The **Exit** command on the **File** menu provides the option to quit any of the Office applications. Exiting an Office application takes you to another open application or back to the Windows desktop.

Part 9 - Tables and Graphics

Application 3 - Insert Table, Paste Special, Draw, Copy, Group Objects, continued

Your Application Completed

Figure 9-12 Shipping Letter

Primary Shipping Company
5402 Highway 437
Dallas, Texas 75201
214-555-9990

November 14, 2006

Norton Laboratories, Inc.
1235 Brookhaven Avenue
Dallas, Texas 75201

To our valued customer Norton Laboratories:

We at Primary Shipping Company are proud that we have not had a price increase for over four years. However, due to increases in fuel costs and landing rights at some of our international destinations, we are forced to increase rates on our services in several regions.

The table below details the new rates, which will go into effect beginning next month. These rate adjustments will help ensure the same top quality express delivery service you have come to expect from us.

We value your business and are happy to answer any questions you may have. You can call us at 1-800-555-3890.

Origin	Destination	Size	Old Rate	New Rate
Dallas, TX	New York, NY	< 1lb	$12.50	$15.00
		1 lb < 5 lbs	$25.00	$30.00
		Over 5 lbs	$6.00/lb	$7.50/lb
	Chicago, IL	< 1lb	$10.50	$13.00
		1 lb < 5 lbs	$22.00	$25.50
		Over 5 lbs	$5.00/lb	$6.00/lb
	Los Angeles, CA	< 1lb	$11.50	$13.00
		1 lb < 5 lbs	$24.00	$26.50
		Over 5 lbs	$6.00/lb	$7.00/lb

Part 1 - Review of Microsoft Office Basics

Application 1 – Open, Save, Preview, Print, Close

As manager of the Coffee Haus, you need to save a copy of April's work schedule into each of the employee's folders.

What To Do

1. Open a new Word document.
2. Locate the **Employees** folder in the data files supplied with this course. Open the **April Schedule** Excel file from the **Perez** folder.
3. Use the **Save As** command to save the file as **April Work Sched**, followed by your initials, in the **Abbott** folder.
4. Repeat the process to save the file in the **Bolten**, **Gibson**, **Kamnani**, **Reid**, and **Wunneberger** folders.
5. Preview and print **April Work Sched**. Your printed solution should appear similar to Figure 1-12. Close **April Work Sched**.
6. Exit Excel. The blank Word document should be displayed.
7. Use the **File** menu to open the **Schedule Memo** Word file from the **Perez** folder.
8. Save the file with the same name in the **Garner** folder.
9. Close **Schedule Memo**. Close the blank Word document without saving and exit Word.

Your Application Completed

Figure 1-12 April Work Sched

 Computer Security

- The 9/11 terrorist attack made everyone more conscious about computer security and safety.

Coffee Haus

Work Schedule for April 1-15, 20--

	M 1	Tu 2	W 3	Th 4	F 5	Sa 6	Su 7	M 8	Tu 9	W 10	Th 11	F 12	Sa 13	Su 14	M 15	Total hrs:
Abbott, Ashley	8	8	8	8	8			8	8	8	8	8			8	88
Bolten, Sam						8	8						8	8		32
Garner, Amy		4		4		8			4		4		8			32
Gibson, Josh	4		4		4		8	4		4		4		8	4	44
Kamnani, Dee	4	4	4	4	4	8	8	4	4	4	4	4	8	8	4	76
Perez, Alphonso	8	8	8	8	8			8	8	8	8	8			8	88
Reid, Katie					4	4							4	4		16
Wunneberger, Brent	4	4	4	4	4			4	4	4	4	4			4	44

Part 9 - Tables and Graphics

Application 3 - Insert Table, Paste Special, Draw, Copy, Group Objects

You work as an assistant for Primary Shipping Company. You have been asked to prepare a letter for Norton Laboratories explaining upcoming price increases.

What To Do

1. Open **AW App9-3** from the data files. Save the document as **Shipping Letter** followed by your initials.
2. Open **AW App 9-3a** from the data files. Save the document as **Shipping Table** followed by your initials.
3. Copy the table into the Shipping Letter document. Use **Paste Special** to link the two tables. (Shipping Table is a Word document.)
4. In the Shipping Table document, change St. Louis, MO to Chicago, IL. Notice the city has been changed in the Shipping Letter document as well. Close the Shipping Table document.
5. In the Shipping Letter document, place the insertion point in the upper-left corner.
6. Draw a perfect square. Copy the square twice. You should have three squares.
7. Position the squares as shown in Figure 9-12.
8. Fill the square in the front with yellow. Fill the square in the middle with blue. Fill the square in the back with Red.
9. Group the squares. Position the logo as shown in Figure 9-12.
10. Preview the document. Save, print, and close the document.

Computer Concept

- To place three or more drawing objects at an equal distance from each other, click **Draw** on the Drawing toolbar. Click **Align** or **Distribute** on the submenu, then **Distribute Horizontally** or **Distribute Vertically**.

Extra Challenge

- Create an original logo for an organization to which you belong. Create a letterhead template for the organization using the logo you created.

(continued on next page)

Advanced Word 66

Part 1 – Review of Microsoft Office Basics
Application 2 – Get Help

Use the Help system in Word to search for some information.

What To Do

1. Open Word and access the Help system.
2. Search on the word **tip**.
3. Choose from the list of topics to find out how to show the tip of the day when Word starts.
4. Print the information displayed in the right frame. Your printed solution should appear similar to Figure 1-13.
5. Search on the question **What should I do if the Office Assistant is distracting?**
6. Choose from the list of topics to find out how to troubleshoot the Office Assistant.
7. In the right frame, choose the option to find out what to do if the Office Assistant is distracting.
8. Print the information displayed in the right frame. Your printed solution should appear similar to Figure 1-14 on the next page.
9. Close the Help system and exit Word.

Ethics & Etiquette
- Helping others learn about computers can enrich their lives.

Your Application Completed

Figure 1-13 Help information on the tip of the day (in Office XP)

▼ Show All

Show the Tip of the Day when an Office program starts

1. Open a Microsoft Office program.
2. Make sure that the Office Assistant is displayed.
   ▶ How?
3. Right-click the Office Assistant.
4. Click **Options**.
5. On the **Options** tab, select the **Show the Tip of the Day at startup** check box.

(continued on next page)

Part 9 - Tables and Graphics

Application 2 - Add Clip Art, Wrap Text

The marketing director of the bank has asked you to add clip art to the Your First Checking Account document.

What To Do

1. Open **AW App9-2** from the data files. Save the document as **Checking Account2** followed by your initials.
2. Select the title. Change the format to Rockwell (or other appropriate font), 26 point, bold, center.
3. Select the headings. Change the format to Rockwell (or other appropriate font), 16 point, bold.
4. Select the address at the bottom of the page. Change the format to Rockwell (or other appropriate font), 14 point, bold, center.
5. Place the insertion point before the title. Insert appropriate clip art. Use the keyword *lighthouse* in the search text box.
6. Format text with wrapping style Behind text and Horizontal alignment Center.
7. Save, print, and close the document.

Your Application Completed

Figure 9-11 Checking Account2 document

Part 1 - Review of Microsoft Office Basics

Application 2 - Get Help, continued

Figure 1-14 Help information on when the Office Assistant is distracting (in Office XP)

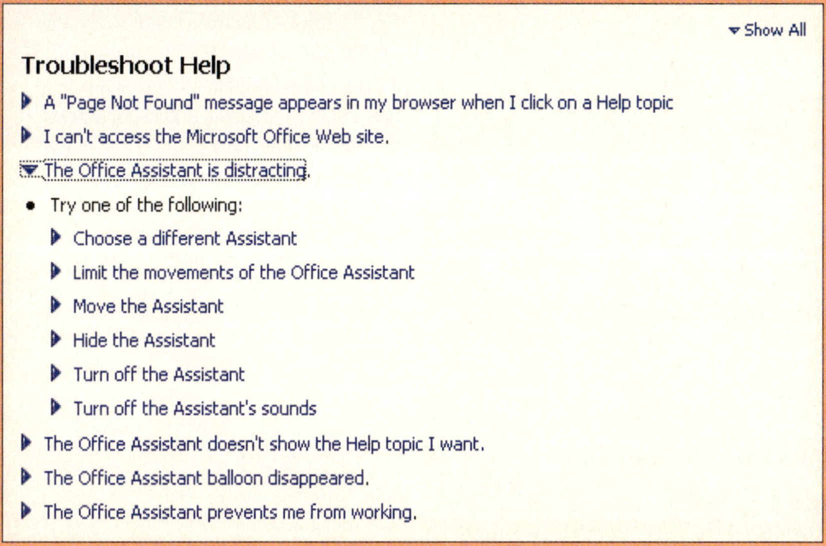

▼ Show All

Troubleshoot Help

▶ A "Page Not Found" message appears in my browser when I click on a Help topic
▶ I can't access the Microsoft Office Web site.
▼ The Office Assistant is distracting.
- Try one of the following:
    ▶ Choose a different Assistant
    ▶ Limit the movements of the Office Assistant
    ▶ Move the Assistant
    ▶ Hide the Assistant
    ▶ Turn off the Assistant
    ▶ Turn off the Assistant's sounds
▶ The Office Assistant doesn't show the Help topic I want.
▶ The Office Assistant balloon disappeared.
▶ The Office Assistant prevents me from working.

Part 9 - Tables and Graphics

Application 1 - Create Table

Marcus Sullivan would like to create a list of references using a table.

What To Do

1. Open a new Word document.
2. Create a table with two columns and four rows.
3. Key the text from Figure 9-10 into the table.
4. Merge the top row into one cell. Change the font size to 18 point, bold.
5. Resize the table to fit the contents of the cells.
6. Preview the document. Save the document as **Sullivan References** followed by your initials.
7. Save, print, and close the document. This will be a part of Marcus Sullivan's personal portfolio for employment.

Your Application Completed

Extra Challenge

- Create your own list of references. Print a copy of the resume, letter of application, list of references, and list of achievements. You have now created a your own personal portfolio for employment.

Figure 9-10 Sullivan References

Marcus Sullivan References	
Dr. Liz Matthews, Chairperson	State University Department of Computer Science Santa Fe, NM 87501 (505) 555-4806
Rafael Cárdenas, President	Sierra Computer Consultants 8086 Ruidoso Boulevard Santa Fe, NM 87505
Gary Williams, Manager	San Juan Electronics 4217 Cimarron, Suite A Santa Fe, NM 87509

Part 2

Using the Internet

Objectives

After completing this Part, you should be able to:
- Access the Internet.
- Search the Internet for information on a topic.
- Access a Web site using an URL.
- Print a Web page.
- Add a Web site to your Favorites list.

Part 9 - Tables and Graphics

Task 10 - Insert Word Art, Customize Bullets

What To Do

1. The Norton Poster document should be open from the previous Task. Click the **Insert WordArt** button on the Drawing toolbar.
2. Select a WordArt style similar to Figure 9-9. Click **OK**.
3. Key **STOP and THINK** in the Edit WordArt Text dialog box. Click **OK**. Adjust the WordArt size and position if necessary.
4. Key the text from Figure 9-9. Format the headings in Rockwell (or other appropriate font), 24 point, bold, Red. Format the lists in Rockwell (or other appropriate font), 16 point, bold, Green.
5. Bullet the lists under each heading. Customize them with a bullet of your choice.
6. Save, print, and close the document.

Hot Tips

- To insert WordArt, click the **Insert WordArt** button on the Drawing toolbar. Choose the WordArt style of your choice in the WordArt Gallery and click **OK**.
- To customize a bulleted list, select the bulleted list. Open the **Format** menu and choose **Bullets and Numbering**. On the Bullets tab, click the **Customize** button.

Extra Challenge

- You have created a poster that lists characteristics for successful working relationships with supervisors and coworkers. Can you think of other characteristics to add to the poster?

Your Task Completed

Figure 9-9 Norton Poster

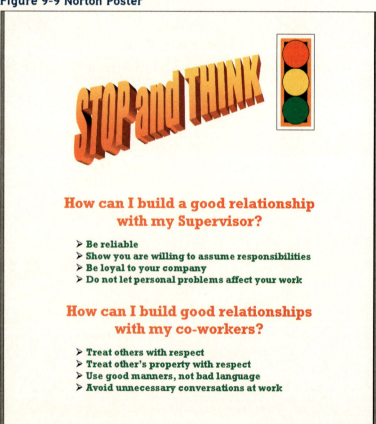

Advanced Word 63

Part 2 – Using the Internet

Task 1 – Access, Search

What To Do

1. Connect to your Internet Service Provider if you're not connected already.
2. Open **Word**. To display the Web toolbar, open the **View** menu and choose **Toolbars**. Select **Web** from the submenu and the Web toolbar displays, as shown in Figure 2-1. The Web toolbar buttons are discussed in Table 2-1.

Figure 2-1 Web toolbar in Office XP

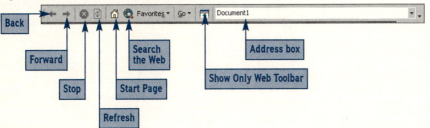

Table 2-1 Web toolbar buttons

Button	Function
Back	Takes you to the previous page.
Forward	Takes you to the next page.
Stop or Stop Current Jump (Office 2000)	Stops loading the current page.
Refresh or Refresh Current Page (Office 2000)	Reloads the current page.
Start Page	Loads your home page, the first page that appears when you start your browser.
Search the Web	Opens a page in which you can type keywords and search the Web.
Favorites	Displays a list of your favorite sites so that you can return to them easily.
Go	Displays a menu of Web commands.
Show Only Web Toolbar	Hides all the toolbars except the Web toolbar.
Address box	Jumps to an address keyed into the box. If not displayed, see Hot Tip for instructions.

3. Locate on your screen each of the buttons listed in Table 2-1. Read the function for each one.
4. Click the **Start Page** button on the Web toolbar. The start page begins loading. Wait a few moments for the page to load. See Figure 2-2. (Your start page may be different from the one shown.)

(continued on next page)

Key Terms

- **Internet** — A vast network of computers linked to one another. It allows people around the world to share information and ideas through Web pages, newsgroups, mailing lists, chats, e-mail, and electronic files. Connecting to the Internet requires special hardware, software, and an Internet Service Provider.
- **World Wide Web** — A system of computers that share information by means of hypertext links on "pages." The Internet is its carrier.
- **Web browser** — Software used to display Web pages on your computer monitor. Microsoft's Internet Explorer is a browser for navigating the Web that is packaged with the Office software.

Part 9 - Tables and Graphics

Task 9 - Rotate, Flip Objects

What To Do

1. The Norton Poster document should be open from the previous Task. Select the grouped signal light object if necessary.
2. Rotate the signal light to the right. The red light is on the right side.
3. Flip the signal light horizontally. The red light is on the left side.
4. Rotate the signal light to the left. The signal light is upside down.
5. Flip the light vertically. The signal light is right side up.
6. Save the document and leave it open for the next Task.

Hot Tip

- To rotate or flip an object, click the **Draw** button and **Rotate or Flip** on the submenu. Click Rotate Right, Rotate Left, Flip Horizontal, or Flip Vertical.

Did You Know?

- To rotate an object in small increments, hold down the **Shift** key and drag the rotate handle (the yellow circle at the top of the diagram).

Part 2 - Using the Internet

Task 1 – Access, Search, continued

Figure 2-2 Start page

Hot Tips

- If the Address box does not display on the Web toolbar, click the **More Buttons** arrow on the Web toolbar, click **Add or Remove Buttons**, and then click **Address:**.
- When you click the Start Page button, Search the Web button, or key an URL in the Address box of the Web toolbar, Microsoft Office automatically launches your Web browser. Depending on your type of Internet connection, you may have to connect to your Internet Service Provider first.

Did You Know?

- You can display the Web toolbar in any Office application and use it to access the World Wide Web.

5. Close your start page by clicking its **Close** button, and return to Microsoft Word.

6. Click the **Search the Web** button on the Web toolbar. The Internet Explorer program opens and displays the MSN Search screen. You may also need to click the **Search** link to display the MSN Search screen.

7. Key **pets** in the Search the Web for box.

8. Click **Search** and a list of pet-related Web sites appears.

9. Click one of the Web sites to display more information on pets.

10. Click the **Back** button to return to the previous page. Click another Web site to display.

11. Click the **Home** button to return to the Start Page for Internet Explorer. Leave Internet Explorer on the screen for the next Task.

Introduction 22

introduction unit - part 2   task 1

Part 9 - Tables and Graphics

Task 8 - Change Order of Layered Objects, Group Objects

What To Do

1. The Norton Poster document should be open from the previous Task. Select the red circle.
2. Move the red circle behind the black rectangle.
3. With the red circle still selected, move the red circle in front of the black rectangle.
4. Group the objects in the signal light drawing using a selection box. Your drawing is now grouped into one object instead of five separate objects.
5. Select the signal light and drag it to the right side of the document.
6. Save the document and leave it open for the next Task.

Key Terms

- **Grouping** — Working with several objects as though they were one object.
- **Selection box** — Box placed around a group of objects so that all objects included in the box will be selected.

Hot Tips

- To move an object behind another, click the **Draw** button and choose **Order** on the menu. Click **Send to Back** on the submenu.
- To move an object in front of another, click the **Draw** button and choose **Order** on the menu. Click **Bring to Front** on the submenu.
- To group objects using a selection box, click the **Select Objects** button on the Drawing toolbar. Draw a selection box around the objects you want to group. Click the **Draw** button on the Drawing toolbar. Choose **Group** from the submenu.

Computer Concept

- Another way to select objects is to shift-click. To shift-click, hold down the **Shift** key and click each object you want to select. Use shift-click when selecting objects that are not close to each other.

Advanced Word 61

Part 2 - Using the Internet

Task 2 - Use URLs, Print

What To Do

1. With Internet Explorer on the screen, click in the Address bar to select the current URL, and then key the following URL (Web address): **www.collegeview.com**.

2. Click the **Go** button at the end of the Address bar. The CollegeView Web site opens and displays on the screen.

3. Move the pointer to **Career Center** and choose **Career Planning** from the menu.

4. In the *Getting Started* section, click the **Getting Started** link. A Web page containing an article titled *Getting Started On Planning Your Career* is displayed.

5. Click the **Back** button to return to the previous page.

6. Click the **Forward** button to return to *Getting Started On Planning Your Career*.

7. Open the **File** menu and choose **Print** to print the Web page. The Print dialog box displays.

8. Click **Print** and the Web page will print.

9. Click the **Home** button to return to the Start Page for Internet Explorer. Leave Internet Explorer on the screen for the next Task.

Key Terms

- URL (Uniform Resource Locator) — Internet address that identifies hypertext documents or "pages."
- Hyperlink or Link — Words or graphic objects that you click to move from page to page within a Web site, to jump to another Web site, or to go to a different location within a document.

Hot Tip

- Be sure to key URLs exactly as they are printed. If you get an error, check your keying.

Part 9 - Tables and Graphics

Task 7 - Add Fill Color, Line Color

What To Do

1. The Norton Poster document should be open from the previous Task. Select the top circle on your drawing of a traffic light.
2. Fill the circle with the color Red.
3. Select the second circle on your drawing and fill it with the color Yellow.
4. Select the third circle on your drawing and fill it with the color Green.
5. Select the second rectangle you drew—the one containing the three colored circles.
6. Change the color of the rectangle (line) to Light Orange, and the line style to 6 point.
7. With the rectangle still selected, fill the rectangle with the color Black. Your drawing of the signal light is complete. See Figure 9-8.

Figure 9-8 Completed drawing of signal light

8. Save the document and leave it open for the next Task.

Hot Tips

- To fill an object with color, click the **Fill Color** button on the Drawing toolbar.
- To change the color of a line, click the **Line Color** button on the Drawing toolbar.
- To change the style of a line, click the **Line Style** button on the Drawing toolbar.

Part 2 - Using the Internet

Task 3 - Add Favorites

What To Do

1. With Internet Explorer on the screen, key the following URL, or another URL provided by your teacher, in the Address bar: **www.weather.com**.

2. Click the **Go** button located to the right of the Address bar. The Weather Channel Web site opens and displays on the screen.

3. Open the **Favorites** menu and choose **Add to Favorites**. The Add Favorite dialog box opens with the weather Web site in the Name box. See Figure 2-3. The Web site in the Name box may not include **Index**.

Figure 2-3 Add Favorite dialog box

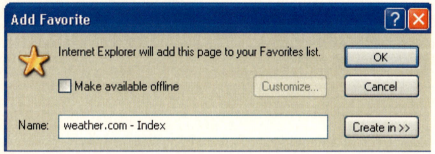

4. Click **OK** and the Web site is added to your Favorites list.

5. Click the **Home** button to return to the start page.

6. Click the **Favorites** button on the toolbar. The contents of the Favorites folder will display on the left side of the screen.

7. Choose **weather.com - Index** (or **weather.com**) from the list. The Weather Channel Web site displays.

8. Click the **Close** button in the right corner of the screen to close Internet Explorer. Close Word. If a message appears asking you if you want to save changes, click **No**.

9. If necessary, disconnect from your Internet Service Provider.

Hot Tips

- You can also right-click on a Web page or link and choose to add it to your Favorites list.
- If the Favorites button does not display on the Standard Buttons toolbar, open the **View** menu, click **Toolbars**, and then click **Customize**. In the Customize Toolbar dialog box, select the **Favorites** button from the Available toolbar buttons list box, click **Add**, and then click **Close**.

Computer Concept

- There are two basic types of Internet connections. Dial-up access uses a modem and a telephone line to communicate between your computer and the Internet. Most individual users and small businesses have dial-up access. Direct access uses a special high-speed connection between a computer network and the Internet. This access is faster but more expensive than dial-up access. Many businesses and institutions have direct access.

Introduction 24

Part 9 - Tables and Graphics

Task 6 - Copy, Paste, Resize Objects

What To Do

1. The Norton Poster document should be open from the previous Task. Click on the circle you drew if not already selected. Click the **Copy** button to copy it.

2. Click the **Paste** button twice. Two copies of the circle appear. You now have three circles.

3. With the last circle you pasted still selected, drag the circle to the top of the smaller rectangle. Resize the circle by dragging the handles until the circle fits snugly in the rectangle.

4. Drag the second circle into the middle part of the rectangle, just below the top circle.

5. Drag the remaining circle into place below the second circle. Your screen should look like Figure 9-7. If necessary, adjust the size of your rectangles so that all three circles fit in the rectangle.

Figure 9-7 Signal light

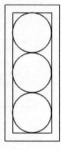

6. Save the document and leave it open for the next Task.

Hot Tips

- To drag an object, place the pointer in the center of the object. Press and hold down the mouse button. Drag the object to the position you want.
- To copy an object, select the object. Click the **Copy** button on the Standard toolbar.
- To paste an object, select the object. Click the **Paste** button on the Standard toolbar.
- To resize an object, select the object. Drag the sizing handles inward and outward to make the object smaller and larger.
- To deselect an object, click anywhere in the window. To delete an object, select the object and press **Delete** or **Backspace**.

Part 2 – Using the Internet

Application 1 – Access, Search, Print, Add Favorites

The owner of the Coffee Haus has asked you to search the Internet for some ideas on expanding and improving the business.

What To Do S

1. Connect to your Internet Service Provider if you're not already connected.
2. Open Internet Explorer as your Web browser.
3. Search for information on the Internet about coffee.
4. Choose one of the Web sites to display more information on coffee.
5. Print the Web page that displays.
6. Add the Web site to your Favorites list.
7. Return to the home page and leave Internet Explorer on the screen for the next Application.

Ethics & Etiquette

- It is wrong to gossip about others via e-mail messages.

Part 9 – Tables and Graphics

Task 5 – Use Drawing Tools

What To Do

1. Open a new Word document. You will be drawing a signal light for a poster to be hung in the Norton Laboratories break room.
2. Position the insertion point in the upper-left corner of the document.
3. Open the Drawing toolbar. Take time to review the buttons on the toolbar. See Figure 9-5.

Figure 9-5 Drawing toolbar

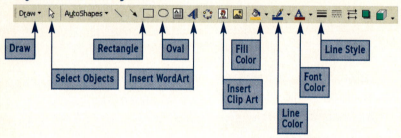

Hot Tips

- To open the Drawing toolbar, open the **View** menu and click **Toolbars**. Click **Drawing** on the submenu. You can also click the **Drawing** button on the Standard toolbar.
- To draw a rectangle, change to Print Layout View if necessary. Click the **Rectangle** button on the drawing toolbar.
- To draw a circle, change to Print Layout View if necessary. Click the **Oval** button on the drawing toolbar.

Computer Concept

- To create a perfect circle or square, hold down the **Shift** key as you drag.

4. Draw an upright rectangle about 2.5 inches tall and 1 inch wide.
5. Draw another rectangle inside the one on your screen.
6. To the right of the rectangles, draw a perfect circle with a diameter of about 0.75 inch. Do not be concerned at this point that the circle is not positioned correctly in the signal light. See Figure 9-6.

Figure 9-6 Drawing for signal light

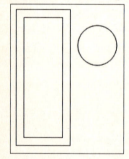

7. Save the document as **Norton Poster** followed by your initials. Leave the document open for the next Task.

Advanced Word 58

Part 2 - Using the Internet

Application 2 – Access, Print, Add Favorites

You decide to search a Web site that contains ideas on starting and managing a small business.

What To Do

1. With Internet Explorer on the screen, key the following URL, or another URL provided by your teacher, in the Address bar: **www.ideacafe.com**.
2. Click **Go** and the IdeaCafe Web site displays.
3. Add the Web site to your Favorites list.
4. Use the scroll bar to view the entire page. Locate and then click the link to display books on business.
5. Locate a book that seems interesting. Click on the book to display more information.
6. Print the information.
7. Return to the start page and display your **Favorites** folder.
8. Choose to display the IdeaCafe Web site.
9. Close Internet Explorer and disconnect from your Internet Service Provider.

Ethics & Etiquette

- Plagiarism is to express thoughts using another person's words without citing the source. Plagiarism is morally and legally wrong.

Part 9 – Tables and Graphics
Task 4 – Insert Clip Art, Wrap Text

What To Do

1. Open **AW Task9-4** from the data files. Save the document as **Norton Expectations2** followed by your initials.
2. Place the insertion point at the beginning of the first paragraph under the heading *Regular Attendance*.
3. Insert appropriate clip art. Use the key word **calendar** in the search text box. Resize text so it is similar to Figure 9-4.
4. With the clip art still selected, format text with wrapping style square and horizontal alignment left.
5. Place the insertion point at the beginning of the first paragraph under the heading *Time Clock*.
6. Insert appropriate clip art. Use the key word **clock** in the search text box. Resize text so it is similar to Figure 9-4.
7. With the clip art still selected, format the text with wrapping style square and horizontal alignment left.
8. Save, print, and close the document.

Your Task Completed

Figure 9-4 Norton Expectations with clip art

Hot Tips

- To insert clip art, open the **Insert** menu and choose **Picture**. Choose **Clip Art** on the submenu. In the search text box, key a word or words that describe the kind of clip art you wish to insert.
- To wrap text, open the **Format** menu and click **Picture**. Click the **Layout** tab and choose a wrapping option. Align the clip art on the page by choosing an alignment in the Horizontal Alignment section. You can also click the **Draw** button on the Drawing toolbar to open the format picture dialog box.

Extra Challenge

- Insert other appropriate clip art in the Norton Expectations2 document.

Part 3

Getting Ready

Objective
Prepare you for a successful, challenging, and pleasant experience while you learn about computers.

Part 9 - Tables and Graphics

Task 3 - Copy Excel Worksheet into Word, Paste Special, continued

Your Task Completed

Figure 9-3 Product Sale

Norton Laboratories, Inc.
Industrial Division
Sales department

It's time for our annual Inventory Reduction Sale! This year sales management has gone completely crazy. They are putting our TOP SELLING products on SALE! The table below lists our sale items.

PSST! Don't tell the accounting department!

Product	Size	List Price	Discount	Sales Price
CeraClear Floor Wax	10 gal.	$40.00	25%	$30.00
CeraClear Floor Wax	5 gal.	$25.00	25%	$18.75
CeraClear Floor Wax	1 gal.	$8.00	25%	$6.00
CeraStrip Wax Remover	10 gal.	$35.00	25%	$26.25
CeraStrip Wax Remover	5 gal.	$20.00	25%	$15.00
CeraStrip Wax Remover	1 gal.	$6.00	25%	$4.50
CrystalClear Window Cleaner	10 gal.	$28.00	25%	$21.00
CrystalClear Window Cleaner	5 gal.	$18.00	25%	$13.50
CrystalClear Window Cleaner	1 gal.	$4.25	25%	$3.19
NoGermz Disinfectant	10 gal.	$23.00	25%	$17.25
NoGermz Disinfectant	5 gal.	$15.35	25%	$11.51
NoGermz Disinfectant	1 gal.	$3.85	25%	$2.89

Part 3 - Getting Ready

Urgent and Important Notice Before You Start
Please read this Getting Ready, Part 3, before starting work. The few minutes you spend now will save you much time later and will make your learning faster, easier, and more pleasant.

Terminology
This book uses the term keying *to mean entering text into a computer using the keyboard. Keying is the same as "keyboarding" or "typing."*

Text *means words, numbers, and symbols that are printed.*

Tasks and Applications
Tasks *introduce computer commands with very brief instructions for basic, simple tasks. Most tasks include a "Your Task Completed" illustration.*

Applications *cover the commands and features you learned in previous tasks, with more steps and considerably more work. Each application is introduced with a realistic scenario.*

Type Styles
The different type styles used in this book have special meanings. They will save you time because you will soon automatically recognize from the type style the nature of the text you are reading and what you will do.

WHAT YOU WILL DO	TYPE STYLE	EXAMPLE
Text you will key	**Bold**	Key **Don't litter** rapidly.
Individual keys you will strike	**Bold**	Strike **Enter** to insert a blank line.

WHAT YOU WILL SEE	TYPE STYLE	EXAMPLE
Filenames in book	**Bold upper- and lowercase**	Open **IW Task2-1** from the data files.
Words on screen	*Italics*	Click beside the word *pencil* on the screen.
Menus and commands	**Bold**	Choose **Open** from the **File** menu.
Options/features with long names	*Italics*	Select **Normal** from the *Style for following paragraph* text box.

ICONS
C means that a Microsoft Office Specialist Certification skill is on this page.

S means that a SCANS (Secretary's Commission on Achieving Necessary Skills) skill is on this page.

Part 9 – Tables and Graphics

Task 3 - Copy Excel Worksheet into Word, Paste Special

What To Do

1. Open the Word document **AW Task9-3** from the data files. Save the document as **Product Sale** followed by your initials. This will be the destination file. Minimize the document.
2. Open Excel. Open **AW Task9-3a** from the data files. Save the document as **Product Spreadsheet** followed by your initials. This will be the source file.
3. Copy the worksheet data in the Product Spreadsheet.
4. Switch to the **Product Sale** document. Place the insertion point on the second blank line after the text.
5. Use Paste Special to link the worksheet data copied from the Product Spreadsheet document to the Product Sale document. Link the information as a Microsoft Excel Worksheet Object.
6. Double-click in the table in the Product Sale document. The Product Spreadsheet table opens.
7. Make the following changes to the spreadsheet:
   a. Format the List Price column and the Sales Price column data as Currency.
   b. Change the percent of discount from 10% to 25%.
8. Save the changes and close the spreadsheet.
9. Switch to the **Product Sale** document. Notice that the changes made in the Excel worksheet are reflected in the Word document.
10. Center the table. Preview the document. Your document should be similar to Figure 9-3.
11. Save, print, and close the Product Sale document.

Key Terms

- Source file — The origin or source for information inserted into a destination file.
- Destination file — The recipient file that receives information from a source file.
- Linked object — An object created in a source file and inserted into a destination file. Changes made in the source file are reflected in the destination file.

Hot Tip

- To link information as a Microsoft Excel Worksheet object, copy the data you want to link. Open the **Edit** menu and click **Paste Special**. In the Paste Special dialog box, choose Microsoft Excel Worksheet object in the *As* box. Click the **Paste Link** option button.

(continued on next page)

Part 3 – Getting Ready

Developing Good Computer Work Habits

Before starting work:

1. Arrange your workstation so you can work effectively.
2. Turn on all equipment or log on to the network.

While working:

1. Use correct posture and proper keyboarding techniques.
2. Save often—about every 10 minutes.
3. Organize your files logically.
4. Use meaningful filenames.
5. Take regular breaks from looking at the screen—stretch.
6. Be a good student, citizen, and classmate.

After finishing work:

1. Save the document.
2. Exit the software.
3. Remove your CD from the computer.
4. Follow your teacher's directions about shutting down the computer.

Review Pack CD

All data files necessary for the tasks, applications, and simulation jobs are on the Review Pack CD supplied with this text. Data files are named according to the first exercise and the unit in which they are used. A data file for a task exercise in the Introduction to Microsoft Word *unit, for example, would have the filename* **IW Task1-1**. *This particular filename identifies a data file used in the first task in Part 1. A data file for the first task exercise in Part 8 of the Advanced Microsoft Excel unit would have the filename* **AE Task8-1**. *Other data files have the following formats:*

Applications: **IW App2-1**, **AE App8-1**

Simulation Jobs: **IW Job2-1**

Part 9 - Tables and Graphics

Task 2 - Format Table, Insert Formula

What To Do

1. Open **AW Task9-2**. Save the document as **Sales Leaders** followed by your initials.
2. Insert a row at the top of the table. Key the following headings: **Last Name, First Name, Region, Manager**, and **Year-to-Date Sales**. Center and bold the headings.
3. Sort the table by year-to-date sales in descending order.
4. Insert a row at the bottom of the table. Key and bold the word **Total** in the first column.
5. Insert the formula **=Sum (above)** in the *Year-to-Date Sales* column to total the data. Bold the total.
6. Use the **Table AutoFormat** command to format the table in a way that improves its presentation.
7. Center the table.
8. Preview the document. Your document should be similar to Figure 9-2.
9. Save, print, and close the document.

Hot Tips

- To sort data in a table, select the table. Open the **Table** menu and click **Sort**.
- To add a formula to a table, place the insertion point where you want the formula to go. Open the **Table** menu and click **Formula**.
- To center the table, select it. Click the **Center** button on the Formatting toolbar.

Your Task Completed

Figure 9-2 Sales Leaders

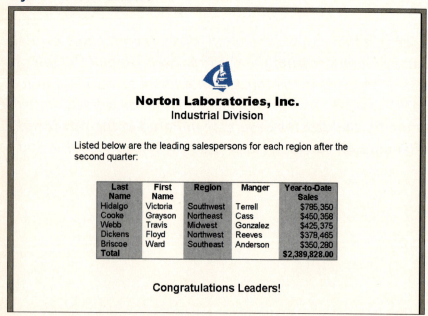

Part 3 - Getting Ready

Help! Where Can I Get It?

You can get help from:

1. The instructions for the task and the learning boxes in the right margin
2. The Software Specific Instructions that may be provided by your teacher
3. The software program's Help system
4. The user's guide for your software program
5. A software specific textbook
6. A classmate sitting next to you
7. Your teacher

Verify Your Work

A competent worker always makes sure finished tasks are complete and accurate. Before printing, reread the instructions and, when available, compare your document with the "Your Task Completed" figure to verify your work. Run the spell check and then proofread the document while it's still on the screen to find errors that the spell check misses. You will then be able to submit your work with pride and experience the satisfaction that goes with work that is done well.

Sample Pages

The next two pages are maps for your learning trip in this book. As you do when traveling by car, study these learning maps before starting your trip so you will understand the features of your book. Using these features to the fullest will help make your learning trip productive and enjoyable.

Part 9 - Tables and Graphics

Task 1 - Create Table

What To Do

1. Start Word and open a new Word document.
2. Insert a table with two columns and three rows.
3. Key the information from Figure 9-1. Key only the information about the companies. Do not key the title yet.
4. Add a row at the top of the table. Key the following:
   Marcus Sullivan
   Achievements
   Change the font to 18 point, bold.
5. Insert a blank line after the word *Achievements*.
6. Merge the cells in the top row. Center the title.
7. Resize the table to fit the contents of the cells.
8. Format the table so the cell borders do not print.
9. Save the document as **Sullivan Achievements** followed by your initials. Print and close the document.

Your Task Completed

Figure 9-1 Sullivan Achievements

Hot Tips

- To insert a table, open the **Table** menu and click **Insert**. Click **Table** on the submenu. You can also click the **Insert Table** button on the Standard toolbar.
- To insert a row, open the **Table** menu and click **Insert**. Click **Rows Above** or **Rows Below** on the submenu.
- To merge cells, select the cells to be merged. Open the **Tables** menu and click **Merge Cells**.
- To resize a table, select the table. Open the **Table** menu and click **AutoFit**.
- To hide the gridlines of a table, select the table. Open the **Table** menu and click **Table Properties**. In the Table Properties dialog box, click the **Table** tab. Click the **Borders and Shading** button, then the Borders tab. In the Setting areas, select **None**.

Extra Challenge

- Create your own list of accomplishments for your personal portfolio for employment.

Part 3 - Getting Ready

Sample Page from this Book

These sample pages will help you to learn about computers quickly and easily. Study these pages before you start reading the book and using your computer.

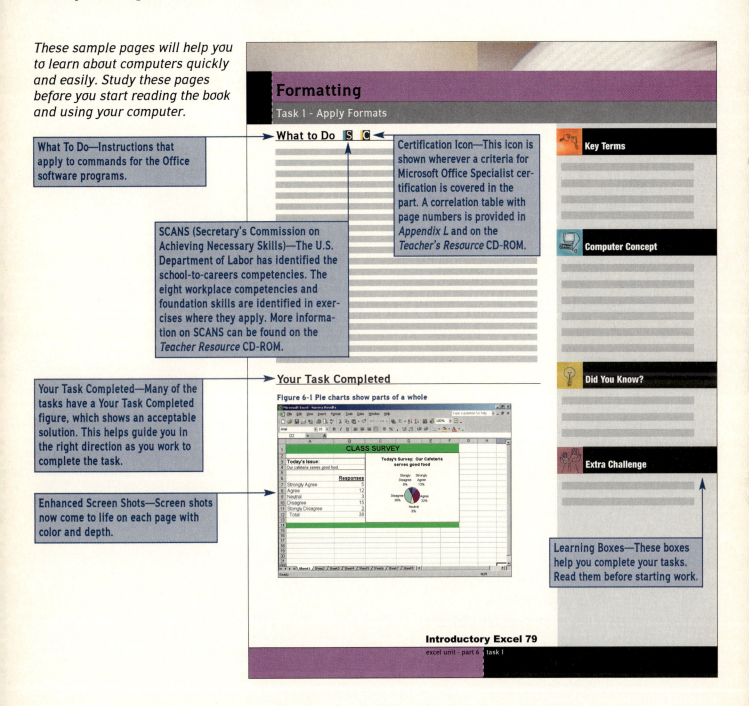

What To Do—Instructions that apply to commands for the Office software programs.

SCANS (Secretary's Commission on Achieving Necessary Skills)—The U.S. Department of Labor has identified the school-to-careers competencies. The eight workplace competencies and foundation skills are identified in exercises where they apply. More information on SCANS can be found on the *Teacher Resource* CD-ROM.

Certification Icon—This icon is shown wherever a criteria for Microsoft Office Specialist certification is covered in the part. A correlation table with page numbers is provided in *Appendix L* and on the *Teacher's Resource* CD-ROM.

Your Task Completed—Many of the tasks have a Your Task Completed figure, which shows an acceptable solution. This helps guide you in the right direction as you work to complete the task.

Enhanced Screen Shots—Screen shots now come to life on each page with color and depth.

Learning Boxes—These boxes help you complete your tasks. Read them before starting work.

Introduction 31

introduction unit - part 3   getting ready

Part 9

Tables and Graphics

Objectives

After completing this Part, you should be able to:

- Create and format a table.
- Copy an Excel worksheet into a Word document.
- Use Paste Special.
- Insert clip art and wrap text.
- Use the Drawing tools.
- Copy, paste, and resize objects.
- Add fill and line color to objects.
- Change order of layered objects and group objects.
- Rotate and flip objects.
- Insert WordArt.

Part 3 - Getting Ready

Sample Page from the Step-by-Step Instructions, Supplement

Separate step-by-step supplements are available for Microsoft Office 2000, Microsoft Office XP, and future versions of the Office program.

Detailed instructions to complete the task.

Screen Shots—Screen shots that help to illustrate the detailed instructions.

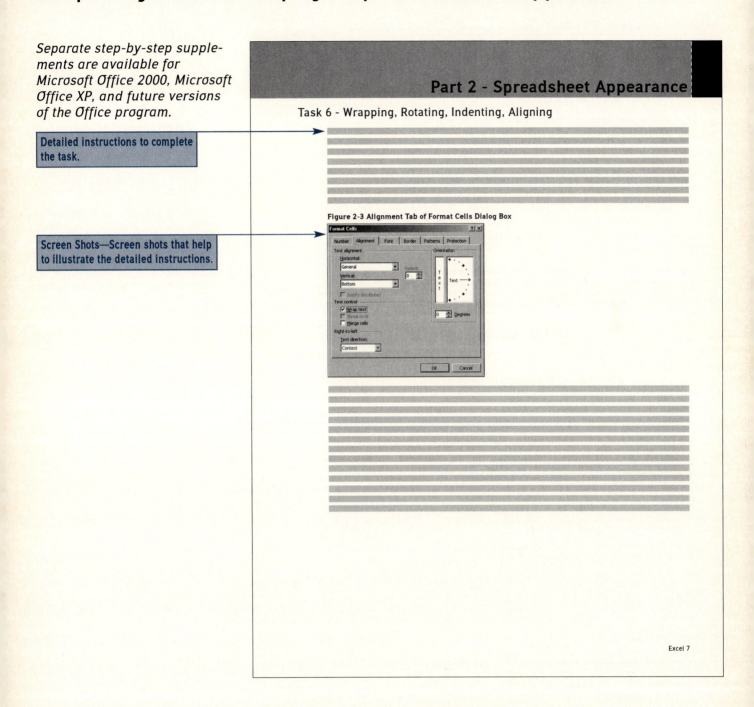

Introduction 32

Part 8 - Workgroup Collaboration and Web Pages

Application 4 - Save Document as Web Page, Hyperlinks, continued

Your Application Completed

Figure 8-8 Theater Web page

Galway Theater

The Galway Theater is beginning its fifth season of bringing quality plays to the West Side community. Thank you for your support.

The director of the Galway Theater will be choosing three plays for performance this season. One of the plays will be from an **original script** from a local playwright. If you would like to submit a script, please send us the following:

- A copy of your script
- A resume of your accomplishments
- Contact information as well as a self-addressed, stamped envelope

We will be conducting auditions soon for actors and actresses. For more information, check here often.

Schedule of Performances

Figure 8-8a Schedule Web page

Performance Schedule

We are looking forward to another successful season. We hope you will be able to attend each play.

- *Of Mice and Men*, by John Steinbeck, April 2-21
- *The Glass Menagerie*, Tennessee Williams, May 10-27
- Original Script, To Be Announced

Tickets for all performances are $8.

Back to Galway Theater Home Page

Part 3 - Getting Ready

Learning Boxes

Learning boxes in the right margin will help you complete the task or application. Read information in the boxes before using the computer. Learning boxes include:

Key Terms—definitions about the topic

Computer Concepts—broad principles about computers

Hot Tips—specific instructions about the operation of the computer

Did You Know?—interesting facts about the topic

Internet—relates Internet to the task

Extra Challenge—related activities that extend the scope of a topic

Web Site—suggestions, activities, and/or addresses for additional information and/or activities about a topic

Teamwork—group activities

Computer Security—suggestions for protecting your computer from unwanted intrusions

Ethics and Etiquette—principles for developing traits desirable for personal integrity and manners

Introduction 33

introduction unit - part 3 getting ready

Part 8 - Workgroup Collaboration and Web Pages
Application 4 - Save Document as Web Page, Hyperlinks

You work for the local community theater. Your supervisor asked you to create a Web page to advertise for the upcoming season.

What To Do

1. Open **AW App8-4** from the data files. Save the file as **Theater** followed by your initials.
2. Open **AW App8-4a** from the data files. Save the file as **Performance Schedule** followed by your initials.
3. Change the theme to Industrial or another appropriate theme.
4. Save the document as a Web page with the file name as **Schedule Web** followed by your initials. Minimize the document.
5. Switch to the Theater document. Change the theme to Industrial or another appropriate theme.
6. Save the document as a Web page with the file name **Theater Web** followed by your initials.
7. Create a hyperlink to the **Schedule Web** file using the last line of text, *Schedule of Performances*. Click the hyperlink to open the **Schedule Web** page.
8. Create a hyperlink to the Theater Web page using the last line of the text, *Back to Galway Theater Home Page*. Click the hyperlink to return to the Theater Web page.
9. Preview the Web page in the browser. Print the page.
10. Close the preview. Save, print, and close the files.

Teamwork

- Create a class Web page. Include a class calendar, schedules, homework assignments, test dates, and other activities. Include a class roster with hyperlinks to each student's Web page.

(continued on next page)

Introductory Microsoft Word Unit

Part 1 - Word Basics and Editing

Part 2 - Helpful Word Features

Part 3 - Format Text and Paragraphs

Part 4 - Working with Documents

Part 5 - Desktop Publishing

Integrated Simulation - Association for Hearing Impaired Children

Word Unit

Introductory Word 1

Part 8 – Workgroup Collaboration and Web Pages

Application 3 – Web Page Template, Hyperlink, continued

Your Application Completed

Figure 8-7 Sullivan Web page

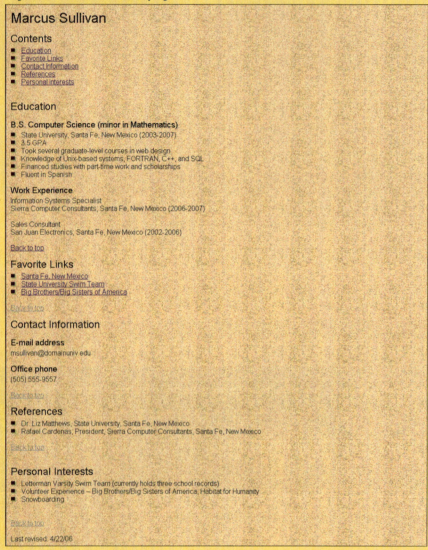

Word Unit Contents Introductory

Part 1 - Word Basics and Editing

Tasks
1 - Open Word, View Document Screen 4
2 - Key Text, Save 5
3 - Change Views 6
4 - Move the Insertion Point 7
5 - Select Text 8
6 - Backspace, Delete, Print 9
7 - Undo, Redo, Overtype 10
8 - Cut, Copy, Paste 11
9 - Drag and Drop 12
10 - Print Preview, Page Orientation 13

Applications
1 - Open, Save, Key, Orientation, Preview, Print 14
2 - Open New Document, Key, Save, Print 15
3 - Key, Drag and Drop, Copy, Paste 16
4 - Key, Overtype, Undo, Cut, Paste 18
5 - Overtype, Cut, Paste, Drag and Drop, Delete 20
6 - Edit, Proofreader's Marks, Save, Print 21

Part 2 - Helpful Word Features

Tasks
1 - Create New Folder 23
2 - AutoCorrect, AutoFormat As You Type 24
3 - Automatic Spell and Grammar Check 25
4 - AutoComplete, AutoText 26
5 - Use AutoCorrect to Insert Frequently Used Text 27
6 - Spelling and Grammar Check 29
7 - Insert Date, Thesaurus 30
8 - Find, Replace 31

Applications
1 - AutoCorrect, Thesaurus, Replace 32
2 - Spell Check, Proofreader's Marks 34
3 - Insert Date, AutoText, AutoComplete 35
4 - Thesaurus 36
5 - Spelling and Grammar Check, Insert Date, AutoComplete, Find, Replace, Thesaurus 37

Part 3 - Format Text and Paragraphs

Tasks
1 - Formatting Toolbar, Font Dialog Box, Apply New Font 40
2 - Change Font Size and Color 42
3 - Font Style, Font Effects 43
4 - Underline Style and Color, Highlights 44
5 - Change Case, Format Painter 45
6 - Margins, Adjust Line Spacing 46
7 - Align Text 47
8 - Indent Text 48
9 - Apply Styles, Vertical Alignment 51

Applications
1 - Font Size and Color, Bold, Italic, Page Orientation 52
2 - Font Size and Color, Underline Style, Style, Format Painter, Indent, Highlight 53
3 - Font, Font Size, Alignment, Vertical Alignment 54
4 - Change Font, Alignment, Line Spacing, Margins 55
5 - Spelling and Grammar Check, Replace Text, Cut and Paste, Thesaurus, Change Font, Line Spacing, Font Effect, Style 56

Part 4 - Working With Documents

Tasks
1 - Switch Between Documents, Copy and Paste Between Documents 59
2 - Insert Page Break 60
3 - Insert Header, Footer, Page Numbers 61
4 - Bulleted and Numbered Lists, Outline Numbered Lists 64
5 - Tabs, Sort 66
6 - Insert Table 67
7 - Format, Revise Table 68
8 - Modify Table, Add Borders, Shading 69

Applications
1 - Tabs, Sort 70
2 - Copy Between Documents, Footer, Insert Page Number 72
3 - Outline Numbered List 75
4 - Tabs 76
5 - Table, AutoFormat Table, Highlight 77

Part 5 - Desktop Publishing

Tasks
1 - Create Columns, Format Text 80
2 - Paragraph Borders, Shading 81
3 - Insert Clip Art 82
4 - Select, Resize Clip Art 83
5 - Page Borders 85
6 - Draw Graphics 87
7 - Edit Drawings 89
8 - Add Color, Line Styles to Objects 90
9 - Add Text to Drawings 91
10 - Add Chart 92

Applications
1 - Change Font, Alignment, Columns, Clip Art, Bullets 93
2 - Clip Art, Page Border, Change Font 95
3 - Draw Tools, Change Font 96
4 - Key Text, Text Box 97
5 - Key Text, Clip Art 98

Integrated Simulation - Association for Hearing Impaired Children

Background 99

Jobs
1 - Create Letterhead, Insert Clip Art, Key Letter 100
2 - Create Table 102
3 - Produce Report 103

Part 8 – Workgroup Collaboration and Web Pages

Application 3 – Web Page Template, Hyperlink

Marcus Sullivan has decided to post his resume to the Web using the Personal Web Page template.

What To Do

1. Open the **Personal Web Page** template on the Web Pages tab in the Templates dialog box.
2. Change the Work Information link under Contents to **Education**.
3. Change the Current Projects link under Contents to **References**.
4. Delete the Biographical Information link.
5. Change the Work Information heading to **Education**.
6. Change the Current Projects heading to **References**.
7. Delete the Biographical Information section.
8. Complete the Web page as shown in Figure 8-7. Delete information as needed.
9. Create hyperlinks for the three items under the Favorite Links heading. Search the Internet to find appropriate Web sites.
10. Insert an appropriate theme.
11. Save as **Sullivan Web Page** followed by your initials. Print and close the document.

Extra Challenge

- Create a personal Web page for yourself. Include a brief description of yourself, your family, and your interests. Insert hyperlinks to some of your favorite Web sites.

(continued on next page)

Part 1

Word Basics and Editing

Objectives

After completing this Part, you should be able to:
- Identify the parts of the Normal View screen.
- Create a new document.
- Key text.
- Save a document.
- Understand the four ways to view a document on the screen.
- Navigate through a document.
- Select and edit text.
- Print a document.
- Cut, copy and paste text.
- Use drag and drop to move or copy text.
- Preview a document.
- Change page orientation.

Part 8 - Workgroup Collaboration and Web Pages

Application 2 - Accept Changes, Delete Comments

You are the assistant to the Marketing Director of the bank. You will make the changes suggested in the comments and accept or reject all other changes.

What To Do

1. Open the **Checking Account** document from the data files. Display the Reviewing toolbar if necessary. Click the **Track Changes** button on the Reviewing toolbar to activate it.
2. Make all the changes suggested in the comments.
3. Click the down arrow beside the **Accept Change** button and choose **Accept All Changes in Document**.
4. Click the down arrow beside the **Reject Change/Delete Comment** button. Click **Delete All Comments in document**. The document should have no editing comments displayed.
5. Save, print, and close the document.

Your Application Completed

Figure 8-6 Checking Account

Extra Challenge

- Reply to your classmate who reviewed the bank reconciliation instructional guide. Add your comments to the document and return it to the reviewer. After the reviewer responds, accept or reject the proposed changes and delete the comments.

Your First Checking Account

Opening your own checking account can be exciting. You probably decided to open a checking account because you needed a safe place to keep your money safe and have access to it when you need it. Owning a checking account is a big responsibility. At Lighthouse Bank, we want to take away the fears and help you manage your account effectively.

Opening a Checking Account

To open an account, you will speak to a New Accounts Representative who will ask you to fill out a few forms, sign a signature card (which is an official record of your signature), and deposit at least $100.

Using Your Checking Account

Use neat handwriting to write the check. Write clearly the date, amount, the payee, and what the check is for. You will write the amount of your check in two places--once in figures (such as $19.25) and once in words (nineteen dollars and 25/100).

Be sure to sign your name exactly as you did on your signature card. For example, if you signed your name as Jennifer A. Davidson on the signature card, you should sign it exactly that way on your checks.

You can deposit money into your account any time by coming into the bank or using the drive-through bank. Simply fill out a deposit slip with your name, account number, and the amount you are depositing, and give it to a teller who will record the deposit and give you a receipt.

You can also deposit a check through the mail. All you need to do is enclose a deposit slip and your endorsed check in a deposit envelope available at the bank and mail to:

Lighthouse Bank
Accounting Department
Box 875409
Superior, Wisconsin 54880

If you would like to learn more about other services available, contact the Customer Service Department at 715-555-2265.

Advanced Word 47

Part 1 – Word Basics and Editing

Task 1 – Open Word, View Document Screen

What To Do

1. Open **Microsoft Word**. A blank document appears. See Figure 1-1.

Figure 1-1 Word opening screen

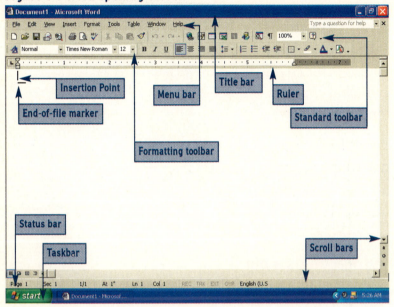

2. Locate on your computer screen the items listed in Table 1-1.

Table 1-1 Items on opening screen

Item	Function
Title bar	Displays the names of the program and the current file.
Menu bar	Contains the menu titles from which you can choose a variety of word processing commands.
Standard toolbar	Contains buttons to perform common tasks, such as printing and opening documents.
Formatting toolbar	Contains buttons for changing character and paragraph formatting, such as alignment and type styles.
Insertion Point	Shows where text will appear when you begin keying.
End-of-file marker	Horizontal line that shows the end of the document.
Ruler	Used to change indentions, tabs and margins.
Scroll bars	Allow you to move quickly to other areas of the document.
Status bar	Shows what portion of the document is on the screen and the location of the insertion point. It also displays the status of some Word features.
Taskbar	Shows the Start button, the Quick Launch toolbar and all open programs. This is part of the Windows program (not Word) and it can be located at the top, bottom, or either side of the screen.

3. Read the function for each item. Leave the blank document open for the next Task.

Hot Tips

- Open Word by clicking the **Start** button and choosing **Microsoft Word** from the **Programs** or **All Programs** menu. A new blank document will appear.
- After Word is open, you can also create a new Word document by opening the **File** menu and clicking **New** or by clicking the **New Blank Document** button on the Standard toolbar.

Introductory Word 4

Part 8 - Workgroup Collaboration and Web Pages

Application 1 - Insert Comments, Track Changes

You are the Marketing Director at a bank. You are reviewing a draft of a pamphlet for customers who are opening their first bank accounts. You are adding comments for your assistant who will make the changes.

What To Do

1. Open **AW App8-1** from the data files. Save as **Checking Account**, followed by your initials. Switch to Print Layout view, if necessary. Open the Reviewing toolbar if necessary and click the **Track Changes** button to activate it.
2. Select the title. Insert the following comment:
   Let's change the title to Your First Checking Account.
3. In the first paragraph, select the sentence beginning with *Having your own checking account....* Insert the following comment:
   Change sentence to Owning a checking account is a big responsibility. (Key the period.)
4. In the first sentence of the second paragraph, select the word **teller**. Insert the following comment:
   Should be New Accounts Representative. (Key the period.)
5. Select **$150** in the first sentence of the second paragraph. Insert the following comment:
   Should be $100. (Key the period.)
6. In the first sentence of the second paragraph, insert the word **signature** before the word *card*.
7. In the second paragraph after the heading *Using Your Checking Account* insert the word **signature** before the word *card* both times in the paragraph.
8. Delete **32 Holly Lane** in the address at the bottom of the page.
9. Insert a blank line after the address and key the following:
   If you would like to learn more about other services available, contact the Customer Service Department at 715-555-2265.
10. Save and close the document.

Extra Challenge

- Write an instructional document explaining how to reconcile a bank statement. E-mail the document to a classmate for review. Have your classmate use Track Changes to add comments and propose changes. Your teammate will e-mail the document back to you when the review is complete.

Part 1 - Word Basics and Editing

Task 2 - Key Text, Save

What To Do

1. With the blank Word document open on your screen, key the text from Figure 1-2. Watch how the words at the ends of lines wrap to the next line as they are keyed.

Figure 1-2 Text for Time Plan document

> Each day, you should take time to plan and organize your work. You can avoid wasted effort and meet your goals when you make a daily time plan.
>
> To make a daily time plan, list all the tasks you need to complete that day. Rank the tasks in order of importance. Record the tasks on a calendar and draw a line through each one as it is completed. You can also make weekly and monthly time plans following the same steps used for the daily time plan.

2. If you key a word incorrectly, just continue keying. You will learn how to correct errors later in this Part.

3. Save the document with the filename **Time Plan** followed by your initials. Leave the document open for the next Task.

Key Term

- Word Wrap — A program feature that automatically moves words to the next line when the text that is being keyed goes beyond the right margin.

Hot Tips

- As you key, the automatic spelling and grammar checker underlines errors with red and green wavy lines. Ignore these lines in this Part. They will be discussed later.
- To end a line at a specific place or to start a new paragraph, strike **Enter** once. To insert a blank line, strike **Enter** twice.

Computer Concepts

- When you save a file for the first time, choose **Save As** on the **File** menu, or click the **Save** button on the toolbar. The Save As dialog box appears in which you can name your file and choose where to save it.
- The next time you want to save changes to your document, simply choose **Save**. Word saves the document by overwriting the previous version.

Introductory Word 5

Part 8 – Workgroup Collaboration and Web Pages

Task 8 – Create Web Site Using Web Page Wizard

What To Do

1. Open the **Web Page Wizard** on the Web Page tab in the Templates dialog box. Click **Next**.
2. In the Web site title box, key **Norton Web Site** followed by your initials. In the Web site location box, key the location indicated by your teacher. Click **Next**.
3. Click **Vertical frame Structure**. Click **Next**.
4. Delete Blank Page 2, Blank Page 1, and Personal Web Page. Click **Add Template Page** button. Click **Left-aligned Column** in the Web Page Templates dialog box. Click **OK**.
5. Click **Add Existing File** button. Add **Norton History Web Page** and **Norton Jobs Web Page**. Click **Next**.
6. Select **Left-aligned Column** and click **Rename**. In the Rename dialog box, key **Norton Home Page**. Click **OK** and then **Next**.
7. Click **Browse Themes** and add the Blends theme or another appropriate theme. Click **OK**. Click **Next**. Click **Finish**.
8. Select *Main Heading Goes Here*. Key **Norton Laboratories, Inc**. Change the font to **Arial Black**, **20** point, light blue.
9. Delete the picture. Insert the laboratory clip art you have used in previous documents. Key text from Figure 8-5.
10. Click the hyperlinks to view the linked pages. Return to the home page.
11. Save and close the Web site.

Key Term

- Web site — A collection of related Web pages connected with hyperlinks.

Your Task Completed

Figure 8-5 Norton Web Site

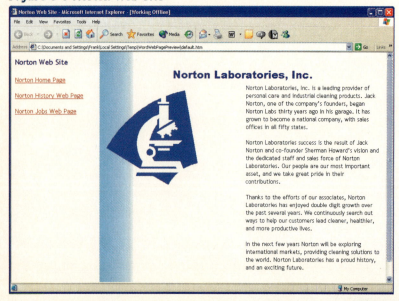

Advanced Word 45

Part 1 - Word Basics and Editing
Task 3 - Change Views

What To Do

1. With the Time Plan document open, locate each of the four view buttons on the bottom left of the screen. See Table 1-2.

Table 1-2 Document screen views

View	Description	Button
Normal	Shows a simplified layout of the page so you can quickly key, edit, and format text. Headers and footers, page boundaries, and backgrounds are not displayed.	
Web Layout	Simulates how a document will look when it is viewed as a Web page. Text and graphics appear the way they would in a Web browser. Backgrounds are visible.	
Print Layout	Shows how a document will look when it is printed. You can work with headers and footers, margins, columns, and drawing objects that are all displayed.	
Outline	Shows text in outline form so you can see the structure of your document and reorganize it easily. Headers and footers, page boundaries, graphics, and backgrounds are not displayed.	

2. Change the document to **Normal View**.
3. Change the document to **Web Layout View**.
4. Change the document to **Print Layout View**.
5. Change the document to **Outline View**.
6. Change the document back to **Normal View** and leave it open for the next Task.

Hot Tip

- To change the view of a document, click the view buttons at the bottom-left of the document window. You can also change the view from the **View** menu.

Introductory Word 6

Part 8 - Workgroup Collaboration and Web Pages

Task 7 - Create Web Page Using Template, Insert Hyperlink

What To Do

1. Open **AW Task8-7** from the data files. Save as **Norton Product List** followed by your initials. Close the document.
2. Open the **Simple Layout** template on the Web Pages tab in the dialog box that contains templates.
3. Select **Main Heading Goes Here**. Key **Norton Laboratories, Inc**. Change the font to **Arial Black**, **20** point, light blue.
4. Open **AW Task8-7a** from the data files. Save as **Norton History** followed by your initials. Copy the text and paste it under the heading *Norton Laboratories, Inc.* on the Web page. Close **Norton History**.
5. Select the phrase **List of Leading Products**. Insert a hyperlink to the Norton Product List. Click the hyperlink to open Norton Product List.
6. Select the phrase **Back to Norton History page**. Insert a hyperlink to Norton History. Click the hyperlink to return to Norton History.
7. Save the Web page as **Norton History Web Page** followed by your initials. Print and close the document.

Key Term

- Hyperlink — Underlined and colored text that links you to a different location on your document, or to an external location, such as a Web page.

Hot Tip

- To insert a hyperlink, select the text you want to make a hyperlink. Open the **Insert** menu and click **Hyperlink**. The Insert Hyperlink dialog box appears. Choose the document to be linked.

Your Task Completed

Figure 8-4 Norton History Web Page

Advanced Word 44

Part 1 - Word Basics and Editing

Task 4 - Move the Insertion Point

What To Do

1. With the Time Plan document open, study the keyboard shortcuts in Table 1-3.

Table 1-3 Keyboard shortcuts for moving the insertion point

To Move the Insertion Point	Strike
Right one character	Right arrow
Left one character	Left arrow
To the next line	Down arrow
To the previous line	Up arrow
To the end of a line	End
To the beginning of a line	Home
To the next screen	Page Down
To the previous screen	Page Up
To the next word	Ctrl+right arrow
To the previous word	Ctrl+left arrow
To the end of the document	Ctrl+End
To the beginning of the document	Ctrl+Home

2. Use the keyboard shortcuts shown in Table 1-3 to move the insertion point in the document.
3. Move the insertion point to the beginning of the document.
4. Move the insertion point to the fourth word (should) in the first line.
5. Move the insertion point to the end of the first line.
6. Move the insertion point to the second line.
7. Move the insertion point to the end of the document.
8. Move the insertion point back to the beginning of the document. Leave the document open for the next Task.

Computer Concept

- To correct errors, insert new text, or change existing text, you must know how to position the insertion point in a document. You can move the insertion point in a document using the mouse or using the keyboard commands. For short documents, it is faster to move the insertion point using the mouse. For long documents, it is faster to use the keyboard shortcuts shown in Table 1-3.

Extra Challenge

- Practice using all the keyboard shortcuts in Table 1-3 to move the insertion point in your document.

Part 8 - Workgroup Collaboration and Web Pages

Task 6 - Save Document as Web Page, Add Theme and Text Animation, Preview Document as Web Page, continued

Your Task Completed

Figure 8-3 Norton Jobs Web Page

Norton Laboratories, Inc.

Job Postings

Norton Labs has exciting career opportunities in the following areas:

Information Technology Services

Network Systems Analyst
Seeking a Lead Network Systems Analyst to provide leadership to the network and systems administration staff in the strategic design and development of the infrastructure and systems platforms, for 2300 desktops, servers, and network routers and switches over five sites. This position will be involved in a major LAN/WAN upgrade project.

Responsibilities include defining requirements, designing, cost analysis, implementing, documenting, and providing support for new and existing projects.

The position reports to the Director of Network Administration.

Requirements:
- Bachelor degree in Computer Science, Business, MIS, Engineering, and/or equivalent technical degree or experience
- 2-4 years experience in all phases of designing, engineering, and/or operating multi-site networks, servers, and projects
- Knowledge of network design, internetworking technology (frame relay, ATM, Protocols-TCP/IP, SNA, LAN switches)
- WIN2000 MCSE training/certification preferred

Network Administrator
Seeking a Network Administration Director to lead our network and systems administration department into the future. Responsible for the day-to-day operations of Norton Laboratory's network, including all system hardware and software, and enforcing all system related policies. Responsible for facilitating information flow over local area and wide area networks. Manage a Microsoft Windows NT/2000 computer network with 2300 desktops, servers, and network routers and switches over five sites.

The position reports to the Vice President of Information Technology.

Requirements:
- Bachelor degree or higher in Computer Science, Business, MIS, or Engineering
- Five years supervisory experience
- Demonstrated problem-solving skills
- Demonstrated track record of increasing responsibilities and accomplishments

Norton Laboratories offers an attractive compensation package including competitive salaries, profit sharing, matching 401(k), and a discount stock purchase plan. We provide generous health, dental and vision plans.
Norton's culture is to promote from within, and provide ongoing training and career development, including a tuition reimbursement program.

For immediate consideration, please e-mail your resume to:
lmrodriguez@norlabs.com
Please include the position you are applying for in the Subject line.

You can also mail your resume to:
Norton Laboratories, Inc.
1235 Brookhaven Avenue
Dallas, TX 75201
Attention: Luz María Rodriguez, Director of Recruiting

Part 1 - Word Basics and Editing

Task 5 - Select Text

What To Do

1. Study the keyboard shortcuts shown in Table 1-4. These shortcuts are used to select text in a document.

Table 1-4 Keyboard shortcuts to select text

To Select This	Do This
Word	Double-click the word.
One line	Move insertion point to the left of the line until it becomes an arrow and click once.
More than one line	Click one time in the left margin beside the line, and then drag the mouse downward to select the following lines. or Position the insertion point at the beginning of a line, press and hold down **Shift**, and strike the down arrow once to select one line or several times to select more lines.
Sentence	Press and hold down **Ctrl** and click in the sentence.
Paragraph	Triple-click anywhere in the paragraph. or Double-click in the left margin of the paragraph.
Multiple paragraphs	Double-click in the left margin beside the paragraph, then drag to select following paragraphs.
Entire document	Triple-click in the left margin. or Hold down **Ctrl** and click one time in the left margin. or Choose **Select All** from the **Edit** menu.

2. With the Time Plan document open, select the first line. Click one time anywhere in the document to remove the highlight.

3. Select the word **Each**. Remove the highlight.

4. Select the first paragraph. Remove the highlight.

5. Select the words **you should take time**. Remove the highlight.

6. Select the entire document. Remove the highlight and leave the document open for the next Task.

Key Term

- Selecting — Highlighting a block of text.

Computer Concepts

- Many times the text of a document needs to be selected before it can be edited. Selected text can be just one letter, a line, a paragraph or the entire text. You can select text by using the keyboard shortcuts in Table 1-4.
- You can also select text by positioning the I-beam to the left of the first character of the text you want to select. Hold down the left button on the mouse and drag the pointer to the end of the text to be selected.

Hot Tip

- You can also select items that are not next to each other. Just select the first item you want, and hold down the **Crtl** button; then select the other items you want.

Extra Challenge

- Practice selecting text using all of the commands in Table 1-4.

Introductory Word 8

Part 8 - Workgroup Collaboration and Web Pages

Task 6 - Save Document as Web Page, Add Theme and Text Animation, Preview Document as Web Page

What To Do

1. Open **AW Task 8-6** from the data files.
2. Save the document as a Web page called **Norton Jobs Web Page**, followed by your initials.
3. Add the Blends or other appropriate theme to the document.
4. Select the heading **Job Postings**. Add the Marching Red Ants or other appropriate text animation.
5. Preview the document with the Web Page Preview.
6. Save, print, and close the document. When you print the document, the theme and text animation will not show up. They are designed to be viewed only on the screen.

Key Terms

- Web page — A document created with HTML (Hypertext Markup Language) that can be viewed by a Web browser.
- Theme — A preformatted design applied to a Web page to change its appearance without changing the content.
- Text animation — Calls attention to text by creating movement within or around text.

Hot Tips

- To save a document as a Web page, open the **File** menu and click **Save as Web Page**. After keying the filename in the File name box, select **Web Page** from the drop-down list in the *Save as type* box.
- To add a theme to a Web page, open the **Format** menu and click **Theme**. The theme dialog box appears where you can make your selection.
- To add animation to text in a Web page, select the text. Open the **Format** menu and click **Font**. Click the **Text Effects** tab and choose an effect from the Animations box.
- To preview a Web page in the browser, open the **File** menu and click **Web Page Preview**.

(continued on next page)

Advanced Word 42

Part 1 - Word Basics and Editing

Task 6 - Backspace, Delete, Print

What To Do

1. With the Time Plan document open, use **Backspace** to delete the words *you should* and the blank space before it in the first sentence of the document.
2. Use **Delete** to remove the word *can* and the blank space after it in the second sentence of the first paragraph.
3. Select the words *that day* in the first sentence of the second paragraph. Strike **Delete** to remove the words from the document.
4. Use **Backspace** and **Delete** to correct any additional mistakes you may have made.
5. Print the document using the default settings.
6. Save and close the document.

Your Task Completed

Figure 1-3 Time Plan

Each day, take time to plan and organize your work. You avoid wasted effort and meet your goals when you make a daily time plan.

To make a daily time plan, list all the tasks you need to complete. Rank the tasks in order of importance. Record the tasks on a calendar and draw a line through each one as it is completed. You can also make weekly and monthly time plans following the same steps used for the daily time plan.

Hot Tips

- To delete text using the Backspace key, place the insertion point to the right of the text to be deleted. Strike **Backspace** as many times as necessary to delete the text. You can also select the text and strike the Backspace key.
- To delete text using the Delete key, place the insertion point to the left of the text to be deleted. Strike **Delete** as many times as necessary to delete the text. You can also select the text and strike the Delete key.
- To print a document, open the **File** menu and click **Print**. You can also print a document by clicking the **Print** button on the **Standard** toolbar.
- To close a document, open the **File** menu and click **Close** or click the **Close** button on the Title bar.

Part 8 – Workgroup Collaboration and Web Pages

Task 5 – Compare, Merge Documents, continued

Figure 8-2 Document with changes accepted, continued

levels and benefit package are not attracting the quality of candidates we need. We are also losing people who have acquired their training and experience here at Norton Labs. Staff turnover in the IT department averages 25% a year. This disrupts the delivery of services to the rest of the company. Moreover, the cost to recruit and train replacement staff is becoming prohibitive.

Specifically, Norton Labs is experiencing difficulty recruiting and retaining qualified computer programmers, telecommunication specialists, and systems analysts.
Harold Hastings has asked that we perform a survey of trends in the industry to determine if changes to our benefits structure are needed.

Market Environment
According to the Labor Department,

"[The area of] Computer and data processing services is projected to be the fastest growing industry in the economy, with employment expected to increase 86 percent between 2000 and 2010. Job opportunities will be excellent for most workers; professional and related workers enjoy the best prospects, reflecting continuing demand for higher level skills needed to keep up with changes in technology."[1]

As Norton Laboratories has grown, our need for higher-level skills and expertise has also increased. In the past, we were able to meet our needs through internal promotion and *ad hoc* training. In the last five years, however, we have had to recruit from the outside, principally from technical schools, colleges and universities, and even other companies. Our turnover problems began around this time.
An analysis of the turnover problem identified four critical positions responsible for most of the turnover:

Network administrators support our local area network and the corporate intranet. They install and configure our systems and make sure our computers can talk to each other. They are the ones who stay up all night if our system "goes down."

Programmers write the code for our proprietary programs, like our order entry and sales reporting system. They listen to our operations managers and our sales managers and try to make their requests a reality. It is not easy—we always want more—and we would be lost without them.

Database administrators organize all of the raw data we gather through order entry, accounting, sales reporting, and technical services systems in a logical manner so that the whole organization can get to the information it needs. They also design and maintain our security system to protect our data. For example, they installed the system *firewall*, which protects the company's system from unauthorized entry from "*hackers*". They helped write the company policy prohibiting the use of unauthorized software.

[1] Career Guide To Industries 2002-03 Edition, U.S. Bureau of Labor Statistics, January 2002, p. 172.

Recommendations
Norton Labs pays wages approximately thirty percent below the industry. In order to attract and retain IT professionals we must address this issue immediately.

Another factor affecting our retention of qualified professionals in the IT area is our lack of a continuing education program. With the rapid pace of technological change in the computer industry and our increasing reliance on information technology services, we must proved programs to ensure the professional development of our people. Many of those who have left Norton cited the lack of a professional development program as an important factor in their decision to leave.

Norton should consider implementing the following steps in order to solve our current retention problem:
1. Revise our salary tables to reflect market conditions. This would require a thirty percent across-the-board increase in the IT department.
2. Increase recruiting efforts at local community colleges, technical schools, and universities to hire entry-level specialists with the most up-to-date training.

Part 1 - Word Basics and Editing

Task 7 - Undo, Redo, Overtype

What To Do

1. Create a new Word file.
2. Key the list of commonly misspelled words shown below. Be sure to strike **Enter** after each word.

   Committee

   Installation

   Eligible

   Separate

   Received

   Personnel

   Correspondence

   Judgment

   Categories

   Accommodate

3. Insert **International** below *Installation*.
4. Click the **Undo** button. The word *International* disappears.
5. Click the **Redo** button. The word *International* appears again.
6. Use Overtype to replace the word *Separate* with the word *Adequate.*
7. Turn off Overtype.
8. Save the document with the filename **Spelling List** followed by your initials. Leave the document open for the next Task.

Key Terms

- Undo — Command that reverses recent actions.
- Redo — Command that reverses an Undo action.
- Overtype — Replaces existing text by typing over it with new text. Overtype mode is especially useful for correcting words of the same length.

Hot Tips

- Turn on **Overtype** by double-clicking **OVR** on the status bar. When overtype is on, it is shown in black. You can also turn on **Overtype** by striking the **Insert** key. Turn off Overtype by double-clicking OVR or striking the Insert key.
- To use the **Undo** command, click the **Undo** button on the Standard toolbar or choose **Undo** from the **Edit** menu.
- To use the **Redo** command, click the **Redo** button on the Standard toolbar or choose **Redo** from the **Edit** menu.

Introductory Word 10

Part 8 - Workgroup Collaboration and Web Pages

Task 5 - Compare, Merge Documents

What To Do

1. Open **AW Task8-5** from the data files. Read the document to observe the changes made by Harold Hastings. Save the file as **Hastings Comments**, followed by you initials.
2. Merge the file **IT Comments** into the Hastings Comments file. Use the **merge into new document** option.
3. Preview the document. Accept the changes and delete the comments.
4. Save the document as **IT Report Merge** followed by your initials.
5. Print and close the document.

Your Task Completed

Figure 8-2 Document with changes accepted

Hot Tip

- To compare and merge documents, open an edited version of your document. Open the **Tools** menu and choose **Compare and Merge Documents** (**Merge Documents** in Word 2000) on the submenu.

Extra Challenge

- Reread the Recruiting and Retaining IT Professionals Report. The report discusses the need for well-trained information technology professionals and the need to provide continuing education and training for these positions. Go to the U.S. Labor Department, Bureau of Labor Statistics Web page (*http://stats.bls.gov/emp/home.htm*). Research the employment opportunities in the field of computer information systems. Compare your findings with the Recruiting and Retaining IT Professionals Report. Has anything changed? What are the current trends in the industry?

(continued on next page)

Advanced Word 40

Part 1 - Word Basics and Editing

Task 8 - Cut, Copy, Paste

What To Do

1. In the Spelling List document, cut the word **Personnel**. The word is removed and placed on the Clipboard.
2. Paste **Personnel** on the line following the word *Accommodate*.
3. Copy the word **Received**. The word is copied and placed on the Clipboard.
4. Paste **Received** on the line following the word *Personnel*.
5. Click the **Paste** button again. The word *Received* is pasted again.
6. Delete the second word **Received** and delete the original word **Received**.
7. Save and leave the document open for the next Task.

Key Terms

- Clipboard — Temporary storage place in the computer's memory.
- Cut — Removes selected text from the document and places it on the Clipboard.
- Paste — Text is copied from the Clipboard to the location of the insertion point in the document.
- Copy — A copy of the selected text is placed on the Clipboard while the original text remains in the document.

Hot Tips

- To cut selected text from a document, choose **Cut** on the **Edit** menu or click the **Cut** button on the Standard toolbar.
- To copy selected text in a document, choose **Copy** on the **Edit** menu, or click the **Copy** button on the Standard toolbar.
- To paste text from the Clipboard, choose **Paste** from the **Edit** menu or click the **Paste** button on the Standard toolbar.
- You can also access the **Cut**, **Copy**, and **Paste** commands by right-clicking the mouse button on the selected text and choosing the commands from the shortcut menu.
- You can paste an item many times without copying the original each time. Click the **Paste** button or **Paste** from the **Edit** menu to copy the item multiple times.

Did You Know?

- You can use the Office Clipboard in other Office programs. For example, you could copy a chart you created in Excel to a report you are writing in Word.

Introductory Word 11

Part 8 - Workgroup Collaboration and Web Pages

Task 4 - Insert, Edit Comments

What To Do

1. The IT Comments file should be open from the previous Task. Place the insertion point at the beginning of the document. Make sure the Reviewing toolbar is showing.

2. Click the **Next** button on the Reviewing toolbar to move the insertion point to the first comment. Insert the following comment: **I have requested an updated chart from Harold.**

3. Advance to the next comment and insert a new comment. Key **See footnote 2.**

4. Advance to the next comment and insert a new comment. Key **I have requested the job descriptions from Harold.**

5. Return to the first reply comment, *I have requested an updated chart from Harold.* Delete the word **Harold** and key **Mr. Hastings**.

6. Return to the next-to-last reply comment, *I have requested the job descriptions from Harold.* Delete the word **Harold** and key **Mr. Hastings.**

7. Preview your document. Save and close the document.

Hot Tip

- To insert a comment, position the pointer in the text where you wish to comment or select the word or words. Open the **Insert** menu and choose **Comment**. You can also click the **New Comment** button on the Reviewing toolbar.

Did You Know?

- You can change the character styles inside the comments just as you can in the main document.

Advanced Word 39

Part 1 - Word Basics and Editing

Task 9 - Drag and Drop

What To Do

1. With the Spelling List document open, select the word *Accommodate*.
2. Drag it to the beginning of the list.
3. Select the word *Adequate*.
4. Copy the word *Adequate* and position it beneath *Accommodate*.
5. Delete the original word *Adequate*.
6. Use drag and drop to alphabetize the list.
7. Save, print, and close the document.

Your Task Completed

Figure 1-4 Spelling List

Accommodate
Adequate
Categories
Committee
Correspondence
Eligible
Installation
International
Judgment
Personnel
Received

Key Term

- Drag and Drop — A quick method for copying and moving text a short distance.

Hot Tips

- Use Drag and Drop to Move Text — Select the text you want to move, and then place the mouse pointer on the selected text. Click and hold down the left mouse button. A small box will appear below the pointer. Using the mouse, drag the text to the location where you want to move it. As you begin dragging, a dotted insertion point appears. Place the dotted insertion point where you want the text and release the mouse button.
- Use Drag and Drop to Copy Text — To use the drag and drop method to copy text, perform the same steps as when moving text, but hold down **Ctrl** while dragging. A box with a + (plus) sign beside it appears below the pointer. When you release the mouse button, the text is placed at the dotted insertion point location while the original selected text remains unchanged.

Part 8 - Workgroup Collaboration and Web Pages

Task 3 - Track Changes, Accept Changes

What To Do

1. The IT Comments document should be open from the previous Task. Place the insertion point at the beginning of the document.
2. Display the Reviewing toolbar, if necessary. Click the **Track Changes** button on the Reviewing toolbar to activate it.
3. Make or accept the following changes proposed by Ross Howard.
    a. Click **Next** to move to the first change, which is the addition of the words *and Retaining* in the title. Accept the change.
    b. Click **Next** twice to move to the next change, which deletes the sentence beginning *Current staffing levels*. Accept the change.
    c. Place the insertion point after the last sentence under the heading *Problem*. Key **Harold Hastings has asked that we perform a survey of trends in the industry to determine if we need to change our benefits plan.**
    d. Insert **Footnote 2** at the end of the quote under the *Market Environment* heading. Key **Career Guide to Industries 2002-03 Edition, U.S. Bureau of Labor Statistics, January 2002, p. 172.** (Key the period.)
4. Preview the document. Save the document and leave it open for the next Task.

Hot Tip

- To accept a change, click the **Accept Change** button on the Reviewing toolbar.

Computer Concept

- Word inserts revision marks directly into text to indicate where text has been added or deleted in a document. The text that has been revised is underlined and in a different color.
- You can prevent reviewers from making untracked changes to your document by clicking the **Protect Document** command on the **Tools** menu, and selecting the **Tracked changes** option under *Protect document for*.

Did You Know?

- By default, comments or tracked changes will not appear when you print the document. You can select the option to print with comments and changes in the *Print what* box in the Print dialog box.

Advanced Word 38

Part 1 - Word Basics and Editing

Task 10 - Print Preview, Page Orientation

What To Do

1. Open **IW Task1-10** from the data files.
2. Save the document with the file name **Time Management Seminar** followed by your initials.
3. Use **Print Preview** to view the document. The document is in Portrait orientation.
4. Click the **Close** button on the toolbar to return to the document.
5. Change the page orientation to **Landscape** orientation.
6. Use **Print Preview** to view the document.
7. Print from the Print Preview toolbar using the default settings.
8. Save and close the document.

Your Task Completed

Figure 1-5 Time Management Seminar

Key Terms

- Print Preview — Allows you to look at a document as it will appear when it is printed.
- Portrait Orientation — Page orientation where the document is longer than it is wide.
- Landscape Orientation — Page orientation where the document is wider than it is long.

Hot Tips

- To use Print Preview, choose **Print Preview** on the **File** menu or click the **Print Preview** button on the Standard toolbar.
- To change the page orientation, choose **Page Setup** on the **File** menu.

Part 8 - Workgroup Collaboration and Web Pages

Task 2 - Open Reviewing Toolbar, View Changes and Comments

What To Do

1. Open **AW Task8-2** from the data files. Save the document as **IT Comments** followed by your initials. Take time to read the document. This is a report prepared by Luz Maria Rodriguez with suggestions made by Ross Howard.
2. Open the Reviewing toolbar. Take time to review the buttons on the toolbar.
3. Click the **Reviewing Pane** button. (In Office 2000, open the **View** menu and click **Comments**.) The Reviewing Pane opens at the bottom of the document. The comments from Ross Howard are shown in the Reviewing Pane.
4. Scroll down the Reviewing Pane and read the comments from Ross Howard. You will answer the comments in the next Task.
5. Save the document and leave it open for the next Task.

Key Term

- Comment — A note or suggested change a reviewer makes to the author of a document.

Hot Tip

- To open the Reviewing toolbar, open the **View** menu and click **Toolbars**. Click **Reviewing** on the submenu.

Did You Know?

- The process of working together in teams, sharing comments and exchanging ideas for a common purpose is called workgroup collaboration. Tasks are often divided among team members, then the members review and suggest changes to each other's work.
- In Office XP and future versions you can view comments and other markups in comment balloons in the right margin. To view the balloons you must be in Print Layout View. In Normal View, comments are displayed in the Reviewing Pane located at the bottom of the screen.

Advanced Word 37

Part 1 - Word Basics and Editing

Application 1 - Open, Save, Key, Orientation, Preview, Print

The student council is sponsoring a series of lectures by various guest speakers. You have been asked to post flyers announcing the first lecture. Before printing flyers you need to add some text and change the orientation.

What To Do

1. Open **IW App1-1** from the data files.
2. Save the document as **Study Skills Lecture** followed by your initials.
3. Delete the letters **ing** from the word *Sharpening* in the title.
4. After the first sentence, key the following text:

    "Erase" your test jitters by learning how to manage your time, organize your work, and take good notes.

5. After the last sentence of the paragraph, key the following text:

    We will hold the lectures in the auditorium.

6. Change the orientation of the document to landscape.
7. Preview the document.
8. Save, print, and close the document.

Your Application Completed

Figure 1-6 Study Skills Lecture

Did You Know?

- Word has many useful tools to change the appearance of a document. You will learn how to use many of these tools such as adding clip art and decorative borders later in the text.

Extra Challenges

- Create a new Word document listing time management techniques you can use such as planning ahead and breaking down a large task into smaller, more manageable segments. Use the Internet to find more time management ideas.
- Microsoft Office has a powerful time management program called Outlook. Open Outlook and explore the tasks and calendar features.

Part 8 – Workgroup Collaboration and Web Pages

Task 1 – Send Documents by E-mail

What To Do

1. Start Word and open the document **AW Task8-1**. Save it as **IT Recruiting**, followed by your initials.
2. Open the **File** menu and click **Send To**. Click **Mail Recipient (as Attachment)** on the submenu.
3. In the *To* box, key the e-mail addresses for Ross Howard (**rhoward@norlabs.com**) and Harold Hastings (**hhastings@norlabs.com**). Separate the two e-mail addresses with a semicolon. Notice that the document is already attached to the e-mail.
4. In the body of the e-mail key the following: **Attached is the first draft of the IT Recruiting report. Please review the document and return it with your comments by Friday.**

   Thank you, Luz Maria Rodriguez
5. Click the **Send** button on the E-mail toolbar. The message is sent, along with the attached file. The original document appears on the screen.
6. Save and close the document.

Your Task Completed

Key Term

- E-mail — The use of a computer network to send and receive messages.

Hot Tip

- To e-mail a document directly from Word, open the document to be sent. Open the **File** menu and click **Send To**. Click **Mail Recipient** on the submenu. You can also click the **E-mail** button on the Standard toolbar.

Figure 8-1 E-Mail

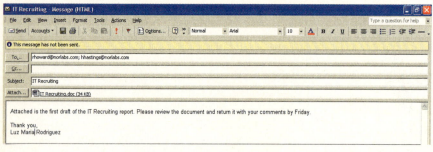

Advanced Word 36

Part 1 - Word Basics and Editing

Application 2 - Open New Document, Key, Save, Print

As secretary of the Student Council, you have been asked to write a thank you letter to Mr. Hester.

What To Do

1. Create a new Word document.
2. Key the following text:

   Dear Mr. Hester,

   Thank you for being the keynote speaker for our Student Council lecture series.

   Your talk, "Sharpen Your Study Skills" was enjoyable as well as informative. The students who attended will benefit from your outstanding ideas and suggestions.

   Because of your help, our lecture series is off to a great start.

   Sincerely,

3. Insert three blank lines after *Sincerely,* and then key your name on the fourth line.
4. Use the editing skills you have learned in this lesson to correct any mistakes.
5. Save the document as **Thank You Letter**, followed by your initials.
6. Print and close the document.

Your Application Completed

Figure 1-7 Thank You Letter

> Dear Mr. Hester,
>
> Thank you for being the keynote speaker for our Student Council lecture series.
>
> Your talk, "Sharpen Your Study Skills" was enjoyable as well as informative. The students who attended will benefit from your outstanding ideas and suggestions.
>
> Because of your help, our lecture series is off to a great start.
>
> Sincerely,
>
>
> [Student's Name]

Did You Know?

- Thank you notes are easier to write when done promptly—the day you receive a gift or attend an event.

Extra Challenge

- Write a thank you letter to someone who has done something special for you recently.

Web Sites

- You can send thank you cards as well as other greeting cards by e-mail at *http://greetings.yahoo.com* or *http://free.bluemountain.com*.

Introductory Word 15

Part 8

Workgroup Collaboration and Web Pages

Objectives

After completing this Part, you should be able to:
- Send documents by e-mail.
- Insert, view, and edit comments.
- Track changes.
- Use a wizard.
- Compare and merge documents.
- Save a document as a Web page.
- Add themes and animate text on a Web page.
- Create a Web page using a template.
- Create a Web site using the Web wizard.

Part 1 - Word Basics and Editing

Application 3 - Key, Drag and Drop, Copy, Paste

Create a checklist to send to prospects for a summer language workshop. The checklist should include the items missing from their applications.

What To Do

1. Open **IW App1-3** from the data files.
2. Save the document as **SLW Checklist** followed by your initials.
3. Insert a blank line after the first paragraph and key the following paragraph. If necessary, use the editing skills you have learned in this Part to correct any mistakes.

   The items checked below are necessary to complete your file. Please be sure these items are submitted before the May 15th deadline so we may process your application.
4. Move the items on the checklist to place them in alphabetical order.
5. Copy the entire document and place it at the bottom of the page, leaving ten blank lines between documents.
6. Preview the document. Print from the Print Preview window.
7. Save and close the document.

Extra Challenge

- Use the Internet to find the top five languages spoken in the United States. How many languages are spoken in the world?

(continued on next page)

Part 7 - Templates and Wizards

Application 4 - Create Document Using Original Template

Use the letterhead template you created for Upper Crust Catering to respond to a request from a potential client.

What To Do

1. Open the **Catering Template**.
2. Save the document as **Catering Letter** followed by your initials.
3. Insert five blank lines below the letterhead, and key the letter shown in Figure 7-9. Choose an appropriate font and size.
4. Preview the document.
5. Save, print, and close the document.
6. Delete your template from the hard drive of your computer.

Your Application Completed

Figure 7-9 Catering Letter

Teamwork

- Divide into teams. Each team is a catering business. Prepare a marketing plan to present to the class. Define the type of food you will prepare and your customer base. Think about what makes your customers unique. What advantages do you have over the competition? What are your potential problems? Create a name and logo for your company.

Upper Crust Catering
309 Third Street
White Plains, New York 10610
(914) 555-7534
www.uppercrust.com

February 20, 2006

Mrs. Kendra Elliott
4468 Marshall Street
White Plains, New York 10602

Dear Mrs. Elliott,

Thank you for your request for more information about Upper Crust Catering. I understand you are planning a reception for your son's engagement.

I have enclosed a brochure that describes our catering services and prices. If you have any questions, please give me a call.

Sincerely,

[Student Name]
Owner

Enclosure

Advanced Word 34

Part 1 - Word Basics and Editing

Application 3 - Key, Drag and Drop, Copy, Paste, continued

Your Application Completed

Figure 1-8 SLW Checklist

We are pleased that you have applied to be a part of the Summer Language Workshop at Granville University. The six-week program gives qualified high school juniors and seniors an opportunity to study a foreign language and earn college credits.

The items checked below are necessary to complete your file. Please be sure these items are submitted before the May 15th deadline so we may process your application.

Copy of SAT or ACT scores____
High school transcript____
Housing reservation form____
Letters of recommendation____
Nonrefundable $15 application fee____

We are pleased that you have applied to be a part of the Summer Language Workshop at Granville University. The six-week program gives qualified high school juniors and seniors an opportunity to study a foreign language and earn college credits.

The items checked below are necessary to complete your file. Please be sure these items are submitted before the May 15th deadline so we may process your application.

Copy of SAT or ACT scores____
High school transcript____
Housing reservation form____
Letters of recommendation____
Nonrefundable $15 application fee____

Part 7 - Templates and Wizards

Application 3 - Create Original Template

You own a catering service called Upper Crust Catering. You need to create a new letterhead that you can use as a template for all your correspondence.

Extra Challenge

- Create a letterhead template for a student organization to which you belong.

What To Do

1. Open a new Word document.
2. Create a Blank Template document.
3. Key the text for the letterhead from Figure 7-8. Choose an appropriate font and center it.
4. Insert appropriate clip art above the text. Resize if necessary.
5. Save the document as **Catering Template**. Close the document.

Your Application Completed

Figure 7-8 Catering letterhead template

Advanced Word 33

Part 1 - Word Basics and Editing

Application 4 - Key, Overtype, Undo, Cut, Paste

Your business is sponsoring a golf tournament to benefit the local food bank. Key an information flyer to post on the bulletin board.

What To Do

1. Open **IW App1-4** from the data files.
2. Save the document as **Golf Tournament**, followed by your initials.
3. Insert a blank line after the first paragraph and key the following text. Use what you have learned in this Part to correct any errors.

   Where: Forest Hills Golf Club

   When: June 22-23

   Time: Tee times begin at 8:00 a.m.

   Cost: $50 entry fee per person

   Register at the Forest Hills Pro Shop or at Shade's Auto Dealership.

4. Use Overtype to replace **When:** with **Date:**. Do not forget to turn off Overtype.
5. Select and delete the word **Where** and key **Location**.
6. Undo the change.
7. Move the last sentence of the first paragraph to the end of the last paragraph.
8. Save, print, and close the document.

(continued on next page)

Part 7 - Templates and Wizards

Application 2 - Mail Merge Wizard, continued

Your Application Completed

Figure 7-7 BSA Merge Letter

Business Students Association
Crestview High School
3804 98th Street
Dallas, Texas 75201

January 19, 2006

Mr. Michael Vincent
Vincent Marketing Inc.
1908 Cameron Road
Dallas, Texas 75207

Dear Mr. Vincent,

The Business Students Association is an organization dedicated to preparing America's youth for the challenges and responsibilities of business leadership. You can play an important part in the formation of our future leaders.

We are asking current business leaders to provide an opportunity for our students to "learn on the job" by participating in this year's Job Shadowing program. This program allows students from our high school to spend a day "shadowing" an employee at a business.

This is a wonderful chance for you to teach a young person about what is involved in running a successful company. Our members look forward to this program each year. We are careful to match students with a business that interests them.

We hope you will consider participating this year. One of our student members will be calling you next week with more information. They will also answer any additional questions you may have.

Sincerely,

[Student Name]
President, Business Students Association

Part 1 - Word Basics and Editing

Application 4 - Key, Overtype, Undo, Cut, Paste, continued

Your Application Completed

Figure 1-9 Golf Tournament

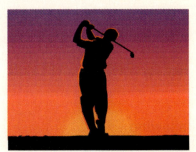

The Forest Hills Golf Tournament

Sign up this week for the Sixth Annual Forest Hills Golf Tournament! All proceeds benefit the local food bank. The first golfer to make a hole in one will win a new car from Shade's Auto Dealership.

Where: Forest Hills Golf Club
Date: June 22-23
Time: Tee times begin at 8:00 a.m.
Cost: $50 entry fee per person

Register at the Forest Hills pro shop or at Shade's Auto Dealership. For more information, call Robert Shade at 913-555-6625.

Part 7 - Templates and Wizards

Application 2 - Mail Merge Wizard

Use mail merge to send the letter about job shadowing to three businesses.

What To Do

1. Open **AW App7-2** from the data files. Save the document as **BSA Merge Letter** followed by your initials.
2. Change the top and bottom margins to 1 inch and the left and right margins to 1.75 inches.
3. Use the Mail Merge Wizard to send the letter to the following companies:

   Mr. Michael Vincent
   Vincent Marketing Inc.
   1908 Cameron Road
   Dallas, Texas 75207

   Mr. Alex Novak
   Crosswind Shipping Company
   5506 Douglas Street
   Dallas, Texas 75202

   Ms. Katherine McGuire
   Frontier Wireless
   717 Oakridge Avenue
   Dallas, Texas 75204

4. Save the list as **BSA Contacts**.
5. Print one letter. Save and close the document.

(continued on next page)

Part 1 - Word Basics and Editing

Application 5 - Overtype, Cut, Paste, Drag and Drop, Delete

The Career Placement Center is preparing informational pamphlets as a resource for people seeking employment. Edit the following page of the pamphlet.

What To Do

1. Open **IW App1-5** from the data files.
2. Save the document as **Job Interview** followed by your initials.
3. Use overtype to replace the word *candid* in the fourth sentence in the first paragraph with the word *honest*. Do not forget to turn off the overtype mode.
4. Use cut and paste to move the second paragraph and the blank line below it to the end of the document.
5. Use drag and drop to move the last sentence of the first paragraph to the end of the second paragraph.
6. Delete the word *Third* and the comma following it in the last sentence of the second paragraph and key **It is also a good idea to**.
7. Proofread the document.
8. Save, print, and close the document.

Your Application Completed

Figure 1-10 Job Interview

Preparing for a Job Interview

A job interview gives you the chance to sell yourself to a possible employer. To make a good impression, you should prepare for the interview ahead of time. First, assess your skills. Be honest with yourself when identifying your strengths and weaknesses. Second, learn as much about the employer as you can. Think about how your abilities would contribute to the organization.

Before you go into the interview, gather information you may need during the interview. This would include items such as names and addresses of former employers, names and addresses of references, a copy of your resume, school records and your social security card. Place this information in a folder and take it with you to the interview. It is also a good idea to prepare a list of questions you have about the company and the position being offered.

After the interview, be sure to write a thank you note to the person who conducted the interview. This is not only good manners, it will also remind the interviewer who you are, and will set you apart from the other candidates.

Teamwork

- With a classmate, create a new Word document listing qualities employers look for in an applicant for a job. Some examples are a person who is responsible, detail-oriented, and cooperative.

Extra Challenge

- Create a personal inventory of your strengths and weaknesses as a potential applicant for a job of your choice.

Introductory Word 20

Part 7 - Templates and Wizards

Application 1 - Use Existing Template to Prepare Business Letter, continued

Your Application Completed

Figure 7-6 Business Students Association letter

Business Students Association

Crestview High School
3804 98th Street
Dallas, Texas 75201

January 19, 2006

Mr. Ross Howard
Director of Human Resources
Norton Laboratories, Inc.
1235 Brookhaven Avenue
Dallas, Texas 75201

Dear Mr. Howard,

The Business Students Association is an organization dedicated to preparing America's youth for the challenges and responsibilities of business leadership. You can play an important part in the formation of our future leaders.

We are asking current business leaders to provide an opportunity for our students to "learn on the job" by participating in this year's Job Shadowing program. This program allows students from our high school to spend a day "shadowing" an employee at a business.

This is a wonderful chance for you to teach a young person about what is involved in running a successful company. Our members look forward to this program each year. We are careful to match students with a business that interests them.

We hope you will consider participating this year. One of our student members will be calling you next week with more information. They will also answer any additional questions you may have.

Sincerely,

[Student Name]
President, Business Students Association

Advanced Word 30

word unit - part 7 | application 1

Part 1 - Word Basics and Editing

Application 6 - Edit, Proofreader's Marks, Save, Print

You work at Springfield Pediatric Clinic. Your supervisor asks you to correct the company's telephone etiquette guide.

What To Do

1. Open **IW App1-6** from the data files.
2. Save the file as **Telephone** followed by your initials.
3. Make the corrections indicated by the proofreader's marks in Figure 1-11. See the *Appendix K Proofreader's Marks*.

Figure 1-11 Telephone etiquette guide with proofreader's marks

4. Save, print, and close the document.

Introductory Word 21

Part 7 - Templates and Wizards

Application 1 - Use Existing Template to Prepare Business Letter

You are the president of the Business Students Association at your school. Each year the association participates in a job-shadowing program which gives students the opportunity to spend a day with a professional in a local business. You need to send a letter to area businesses requesting their participation in the program.

What To Do

1. Open a new Word document.
2. Open the **Professional Letter** template.
3. Select **Company Name Here** and key **Business Students Association**. Strike **Enter** after each word.
4. In the return address section, key

   Crestview High School
   3804 98th Street
   Dallas, Texas 75201

5. Key the current date if necessary.
6. In the recipient's address section, key

   Mr. Ross Howard
   Director of Human Resources
   Norton Laboratories, Inc.
   1235 Brookhaven Avenue
   Dallas, Texas 75201

7. In the salutation key **Dear Mr. Howard,**.
8. Select the text in the body of the letter. Key the letter text shown in Figure 7-6.
9. Save the file as **BSA Letter** followed by your initials. Print and close the document.

Extra Challenge

- Compose a business letter to send to local companies requesting information explaining how they use technology to address their business needs. Some examples of questions to ask:
  - Has the company created new positions due to technology changes?
  - Does the company offer training to workers?
  - What computer skills are in demand?
  - Has the company changed operating systems or upgraded hardware?
  - How does the company deal with privacy and security issues?

(continued on next page)

Part 2

Helpful Word Features

Objectives

After completing this Part, you should be able to:
- Create a new folder.
- Use AutoCorrect, AutoFormat As You Type, AutoComplete, and AutoText.
- Make corrections using automatic spelling and grammar checking and the Spelling and Grammar Checker.
- Use AutoCorrect to insert frequently used text.
- Insert the date.
- Use the Thesaurus.
- Find specific text and replace it with other text.

Part 7 - Templates and Wizards

Task 7 - Create Labels

What To Do

1. Create a new Word document.
2. Create labels using the following address:

   Mr. Harold Hastings
   Norton Laboratories, Inc.
   1235 Brookhaven Avenue
   Dallas, Texas 75201

3. Change the product number to **5160 - Address**.
4. Print the labels on plain paper.
5. Close the document without saving.

Hot Tips

- To print labels, open the **Tools** menu and click **Letters and Mailings** (**Envelopes and Labels** in Office 2000). Click **Envelopes and Labels** on the submenu. Click the **Labels** tab.
- To change the product number of a label, click the **Options** button on the Labels tab of the Envelopes and Labels dialog box. Change the product number in the Product number box.

Part 2 – Helpful Word Features

Task 1 - Create New Folder

What To Do

1. Open **IW Task2-1** from the data files.
2. Open the Save As dialog box.
3. In the Save in box, select the drive where you want to create a new folder.
4. Create a folder named **New York City Trip**.
5. Save the document as **NYC Agenda** followed by your initials.
6. Word saves the file in the folder you created and returns to your document. Leave the document open for the next Task.

Hot Tip

- Folders can help you organize your files on your disks. To create a new folder within the current folder, click the **Create New Folder** button in the **Save As** dialog box.

Part 7 - Templates and Wizards

Task 6 - Create Envelopes

What To Do

1. Open a new Word document.
2. Create an envelope. Key the following address in the *Delivery address* box.

   Mr. Harold Hastings
   Norton Laboratories, Inc.
   1235 Brookhaven Avenue
   Dallas, Texas 75201

3. Key the following address in the *Return address* box.

   Marcus Sullivan
   8086 Tularosa Lane
   Santa Fe, New Mexico 87501

4. Change the font to **Verdana** or another appropriate font.
5. Print the envelope. (You can print the envelope on plain paper if desired.)
6. Close the document without saving.

Hot Tips

- To print envelopes, open the **Tools** menu and click **Letters and Mailings** (**Envelopes and Labels** in Office 2000). Click **Envelopes and Labels** on the sub-menu. Click the **Envelopes** tab in the Envelopes and Labels dialog box and key the addresses.
- To change the font on an envelope, click the **Options** button on the Envelope tab in the Envelope and Labels dialog box.

Did You Know?

- You can insert addresses stored in Outlook by clicking the **Insert Address** button in the Envelopes and Labels dialog box.

Part 2 - Helpful Word Features

Task 2 - AutoCorrect, AutoFormat As You Type

What To Do

1. With the NYC Agenda document open, place the insertion point on the first blank line after the list of things to do on Day 1. Key the following: **dinner at hte hotel restaurant**. (Be sure to key the misspelled word *hte*.)

2. Strike **Enter**. Notice that AutoCorrect automatically capitalized *Dinner* as the first word in a sentence immediately after you keyed it. AutoCorrect also recognized that you meant to key the word *the* and automatically changed *hte* to the correct spelling.

3. Place your insertion point on the first blank line below Day 5. Key the following text.

   1. Trip to the Empire State Building

4. Strike **Enter**. AutoFormat As You Type automatically formats the next number in the list. Key the text below next to the number shown. (Notice that AutoFormat As You Type changes 5th to 5th.)

   2. Shop on 5th Avenue

   3. First bus departs for airport at 1:00 p.m.

5. Strike **Enter** twice to stop automatic numbering.

6. Save the document and leave it open for the next Task.

Key Terms

- AutoCorrect — Corrects common spelling and grammar errors as you key text.
- AutoFormat As You Type — Automatically applies built-in formats to the text you type. For example, AutoFormat As You Type will automatically format text in a numbered or bulleted list or change 3/4 to ¾.

Part 7 - Templates and Wizards

Task 5 - Mail Merge Wizard, continued

Your Task Completed

Figure 7-5 Application Letter

Marcus Sullivan
8086 Tularosa Lane
Santa Fe, New Mexico 87501
Telephone: (505) 555-0387
E-mail: msullivan@domainuniv.edu

Mr. Harold Hastings
Norton Laboratories, Inc.
1235 Brookhaven Avenue
Dallas, Texas 75201

Dear Mr. Hastings,

Are you looking for a dynamic self-starter with a proven record of achievement in both business and academics? I am seeking an entry-level position in systems administration with your company.

I will be graduating this spring with a degree in Computer Science from State University. I have maintained a 3.5 GPA while working thirty hours a week helping clients install and implement business application systems.

In addition to financing my college education, I have had the privilege to be a Big Brother the past two years. I have learned a great deal from my "little brother" and have tried to be a good example to him.

I have also been active on campus, holding leadership positions in various service organizations. These experiences have taught me how to work with others to achieve common objectives.

Enclosed is my resume for your consideration. You can reach me at the address, telephone number, and e-mail address above. I look forward to the opportunity to discuss my qualifications and experience with you.

Sincerely,

Marcus Sullivan

Part 2 - Helpful Word Features

Task 3 - Automatic Spell and Grammar Check

What To Do

1. With the NYC Agenda open, set Word to check your spelling and your grammar as you type.

2. Place your insertion point on the second blank line after the last item on Day 5. Key the sentence that follows, taking care to key the misspelled word *contat* and the grammar error *is*.

   If you have any questions, please contat Journey Trips. Agents is available Monday - Friday from 9:00 a.m. to 7:00 p.m.

3. Strike **Enter**. Notice Automatic spell checking underlines the misspelled word *contat* with a red wavy line and the grammar error *Agents is* with a green wavy line.

4. To correct the misspelled *contat*, right-click on the misspelled word. A shortcut menu appears. See Figure 2-1.

Figure 2-1 Shortcut menu

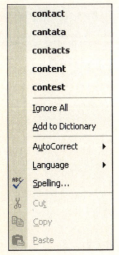

5. Left-click on the correct spelling **contact**. The correct word replaces the incorrect one and the wavy red underline disappears.

6. To correct the phrase *Agents is*, right-click on the underlined phrase. A shortcut menu appears.

7. Left-click on the correct phrase **Agents are**. The correct phrase replaces the incorrect one and the wavy green line disappears.

8. Save the document and leave it open for the next Task.

Key Terms

- **Automatic Spell Checking** — Identifies misspellings and words that are not in the dictionary by underlining them with a wavy red line immediately after you key them.
- **Automatic Grammar Checking** — Identifies grammar errors by underlining them with a wavy green line immediately after you key them.

Hot Tip

- Be sure the Automatic Spelling and Grammar checking is on by choosing **Options** on the **Tools** menu and clicking the **Spelling & Grammar** tab. Click the **Check spelling as you type** box and the **Check grammar as you type** box if they are not already checked.

Introductory Word 25

Part 7 - Templates and Wizards

Task 5 - Mail Merge Wizard

What To Do

1. Open **AW Task7-5** from the data files. Save the document as **Application Letter** followed by your initials.
2. Use Mail Merge to send the application letter and resume to the following companies:

   Mr. Harold Hastings
   Norton Laboratories, Inc.
   1235 Brookhaven Avenue
   Dallas, Texas 75201

   Mr. Rudy Gardner
   Ransom Resources, Inc.
   613 Old Mill Road
   Albuquerque, New Mexico 87120

   Ms. Vivian Osgood
   Parson/Smith Consulting
   3298 Jefferson Avenue
   Houston, Texas 77224

3. Save the list as **Resume Contacts** followed by your initials.
4. Print one letter. Save and close the document.

Key Terms

- Mail Merge — Combining a document with information that personalizes it.
- Application letter — A letter sent with a resume to introduce a person to a prospective employer and request an interview.

Hot Tip

- To start the Mail Merge Wizard, open the **Tools** menu and click **Letters and Mailings** (**Mail Merge** in Office 2000). Click **Mail Merge Wizard** on the submenu.

Extra Challenge

- Write an application letter for a job that interests you. This will be a part of your personal portfolio for employment.

Did You Know?

- Resume means summary in French.

(continued on next page)

Part 2 - Helpful Word Features

Task 4 - AutoComplete, AutoText

What To Do

1. In the upper portion of the memorandum (the **NYC Agenda** document), insert a space after *Date:*. Key **28 Febr.** Notice the screen tip appears with the word *February*.

2. Strike **Enter** to accept the AutoComplete suggestion when it appears.

3. Select **Day 1** and key **Mond**. Strike **Enter** to accept the AutoComplete suggestion *Monday* when it appears.

4. Replace each of the other *Day* headings with the consecutive days of the week. Accept each AutoComplete suggestion when it appears.

5. Place the insertion point on the first blank line after *Date:* at the top of the memo.

6. Use **AutoText** to insert the text **Subject:**. Be sure to click the insert button in the dialog box to insert the text. See Figure 2-2.

Figure 2-2 AutoText tab in the AutoCorrect dialog box

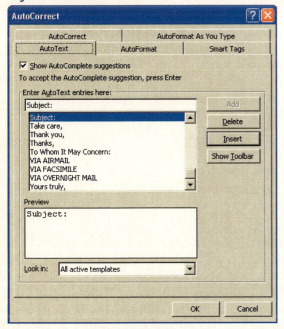

7. After *Subject:*, insert a space and key **Tentative Agenda for New York City Trip**.

8. Save the document and leave it open for the next Task.

Key Terms

- AutoComplete — After keying the first few letters, Word suggests a word in a screen tip above the insertion point. Strike **Enter** to accept the suggested word.
- AutoText — Stores frequently used text so you do not have to re-key it each time. You can use built-in entries or create your own.

Hot Tip

- To insert an entry using AutoText, open the **Insert** menu and point to **AutoText**. Click **AutoText** on the submenu to open the AutoCorrect dialog box.
- Be sure AutoComplete is on by choosing **AutoText** on the **Insert** menu, then click **AutoText**. On the AutoText tab, click the **Show AutoComplete suggestions** box.

Part 7 - Templates and Wizards

Task 4 - Resume Wizard, continued

Your Task Completed

Figure 7-4 Resume

8086 Tularosa Lane
Santa Fe, New Mexico 87501

Phone (505) 555-0387
Fax (505) 555-4775
E-mail
msullivan@domainuniv.edu

Marcus Sullivan

Objective   An entry-level position in systems administration for a growing, dynamic organization.

Education   [2003-2007]   State University   Santa Fe, New Mexico
B.S. Computer Science (minor in Mathematics)
- 3.5 GPA
- Took several graduate-level courses in web design
- Knowledge of Unix-based systems, FORTRAN, C++, and SQL
- Financed studies with part-time work and scholarships

Languages   Fluent in Spanish

Work experience   [2006-2007]   Sierra Computer Consultants   Santa Fe, NM
Information Systems Specialist (Part-time)
- Helped clients install and implement various systems, including customer billing systems, inventory control systems, and credit review systems.

Volunteer experience   Big Brothers/Big Sisters of America

Habitat for Humanity

References   Dr. Liz Matthews, State University, Santa Fe, New Mexico

Rafael Cardenas, President, Sierra Computer Consultants

Extracurricular activities   Program Chairman, Computer Service Fraternity

Letterman (2 years) Varsity Swim Team (currently hold three school records)

Summer jobs   [2002-2206]   San Juan Electronics   Santa Fe, New Mexico
Sales Consultant
- Helped customers select electronic products. Started in-store training courses for other sales consultants.

Part 2 - Helpful Word Features

Task 5 - Use AutoCorrect to Insert Frequently Used Text

What To Do

1. With the NYC Agenda document open, on the **Tools** menu, click **AutoCorrect Options** (click **AutoCorrect** in Office 2000). The AutoCorrect dialog box appears.

2. In the AutoCorrect dialog box, specify that your name will replace your initials. See Figure 2-3.

Figure 2-3 AutoCorrect tab in the AutoCorrect dialog box

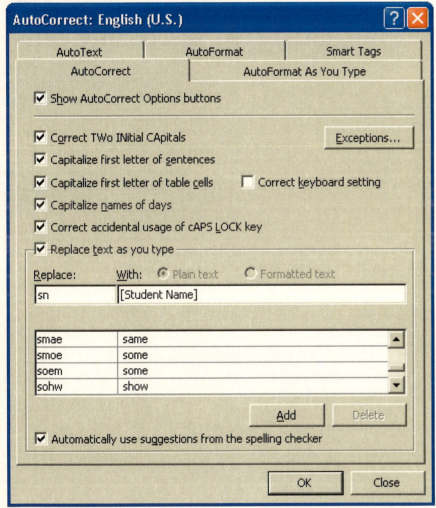

3. Click the **Add** button. Click **OK** to close the AutoCorrect dialog box.

4. In the upper portion of the memorandum, insert a space after *To:*. Key your initials and strike the space bar. AutoCorrect replaces the initials with your full name.

5. Save, print, and close the document.

(continued on next page)

Computer Concept

- You can use AutoCorrect to insert text quickly. For example, you can specify that when you key the letters *nyc*, they will always be replaced with *New York City*.

Hot Tip

- To set up the replacement text, open the **Tools** menu and click **AutoCorrect Options** (**AutoCorrect** in Office 2000). The AutoCorrect Options Dialog box appears. Key the letters to be replaced in the *Replace* box. Key the words to be inserted in the *With* box.

Part 7 - Templates and Wizards

Task 4 - Resume Wizard

What To Do

1. Open a new Word document.
2. Create a resume using the **Resume Wizard**. Use the following information to answer the questions in the wizard:

Style:	Professional
Type:	Entry-level résumé
Name:	Marcus Sullivan
Address:	8086 Tularosa Lane
	Santa Fe, New Mexico 87501
Phone:	(505) 555-0387
Fax:	(505) 555-4775
E-mail:	msullivan@domainuniv.edu
Standard Headings:	Objective
	Education
	Languages
	Work experience
	Volunteer experience
	References
	Extracurricular activities
	Summer jobs

3. After completing the wizard, use the information in Figure 7-4 to complete the resume.
4. Preview the document. Save the document as **Resume** followed by your initials.
5. Print and close the document.

Key Terms

- Wizard — A feature that allows you to create a customized document by answering questions the wizard asks you.
- Resume — Presents a person's qualifications for a job in a concise form.

Hot Tip

- To open the Resume Wizard, click the **Resume Wizard** icon on the **Other Documents** tab.

Extra Challenge

- Use the Resume Wizard to create your own resume. This will be a part of your personal portfolio for employment.

Teamwork

- With a few classmates, critique each other's resumes. Be careful to provide constructive criticism.

(continued on next page)

Advanced Word 23

Part 2 - Helpful Word Features

Task 5 - Use AutoCorrect to Insert Frequently Used Text, continued

Your Task Completed

Figure 2-4 NYC Agenda

MEMORANDUM

To: [Student Name]
From: Charles Adams, Trip Coordinator
Date: 28 February
Subject: Tentative Agenda for New York City Trip

Monday
6:30 a.m.-Leave from DFW Airport
10:57 a.m.-Arrive at LaGuardia Airport
Check into hotel
Lunch on your own
Bus tour of city
Dinner at the hotel restaurant

Tuesday
Breakfast at hotel restaurant
Tour Central Park and zoo
Lunch at Metropolitan Museum of Art
Tour Metropolitan Museum of Art
Dinner at the Premier Restaurant
Broadway Show

Wednesday
Breakfast at hotel
Take ferry to the Statue of Liberty
Lunch on ferry
Tour Ellis Island
Dinner at Elmo's Kitchen in Greenwich Village

Thursday
Breakfast at hotel
Tour Wall Street District
Lunch at Bull & Bear Restaurant
Tour United Nations Headquarters
Dinner at Rockefeller Center

Friday
1. Trip to the Empire State building
2. Shop on 5th Avenue
3. First bus departs for airport at 1:00 p.m.

If you have any questions, please contact Journey Tours. Agents are available Monday – Friday from 9:00 a.m. to 7:00 p.m.

Part 7 - Templates and Wizards

Task 3 - Create Document Using Original Template

What To Do

1. Open the **Norton Template**. If the template was saved to the default location, it should be on the General tab in the Templates dialog box.
2. Save the document as **Norton Letter** followed by your initials. This letter will be at the beginning of the Employee Handbook.
3. Insert five blank lines below the letterhead, and key the letter shown in Figure 7-3 in **Arial**, **12 point**.
4. Preview the document.
5. Save, print, and close the document.
6. Delete your template from the hard drive of your computer.

Did You Know?

- You can create a template from an existing Word document. Click **Document Template** in the Save as type box when saving the document.

Your Task Completed

Figure 7-3 Norton Letter

Part 2 - Helpful Word Features

Task 6 - Spelling and Grammar Check

What To Do

1. Open **IW Task2-6** from the data files.
2. Save the document in the **New York City Trip** folder as **NYC Letter** followed by your initials.
3. Move the insertion point to the beginning of the document and click the **Spelling and Grammar** button on the Standard toolbar. A dialog box appears which highlights spelling and grammar errors. Spelling errors are highlighted in red and grammar errors are highlighted in green.
4. Proposed grammar and spelling corrections are listed in the Suggestions box. Click on the correct word or phrase and then click **Change**. Other options for correcting or ignoring errors are listed in Table 2-1. These options will differ depending upon the version of Office used.

Table 2-1 Spelling and Grammar dialog box options

Operation	Action
Ignore Once/Ignore	Ignores only the word or grammar error displayed in red or green.
Ignore All/Ignore Rule	Ignores all instances of the same word or occurrences of the rule.
Add to Dictionary/Add	Adds the selected word to the custom dictionary.
Next Sentence	Accepts the manual changes you made to your document and continues with the spelling and grammar check.
Change	Corrects only the selected word.
Change All	Corrects all instances of the same misspelling.
Explain (Office XP only)	Provides an explanation of the grammar or style rule being applied.
AutoCorrect	Adds the word and its correction to your AutoCorrect list.
Suggestions	Displays a list of proposed spellings or grammar changes.

5. Correct the highlighted words until you get to the word *departur*.
6. When correcting the word *departur*, click **Change All**. Word replaces the error each time it occurs and continues checking.
7. When correcting the word *Kraig*, click **Ignore All**. Kraig is the correct spelling, but it is not found in the dictionary.
8. The message *The spelling and grammar check is complete.* appears. Click **OK**.
9. Save the document and leave it open for the next Task.

Key Term

- Spelling and Grammar Checker — Checks for spelling and grammar errors in a document after you finish keying.

Computer Concept

- Although the grammar checker is a helpful tool, you still need to know English grammar. The grammar checker can identify a possible problem, but you must decide if the change should be made depending on the context of the sentence.

Part 7 - Templates and Wizards

Task 2 - Create Original Template

What To Do

1. Open a new Word document.
2. Create a letterhead template for Norton Laboratories. Open the **Blank Document** template.
3. Key the text from Figure 7-2. Change the font of the company name to **Arial Black**, **14** point. Change the rest of the text to **Arial**, **Bold**, **12** point. Center the text.
4. Place your insertion point above the heading and insert clip art. Key **laboratory** in the search box. Locate and select an appropriate clip art.
5. Resize the clip art so it will be the appropriate size for use in a letterhead.
6. Save the document as **Norton Template** followed by your initials. Close the document.

Your Task Completed

Figure 7-2 Norton Template for letterhead

Hot Tips

- To create an original template, click **Blank Document** on the **General** tab. Be sure to click the **Template** option in the Create New box.
- To insert clip art, open the **Insert** menu and choose **Picture**. Choose **Clip Art** on the submenu. In the search text box, key a word or words that describe the kind of clip art you wish to insert.

Computer Concept

- Word saves regular word processing documents with the .doc extension and saves template files with the .dot extension.

Web Site

- You can access more templates on the World Wide Web. Display the New Document task pane and click **Templates on Microsoft.com**.

Advanced Word 21

Part 2 - Helpful Word Features

Task 7 - Insert Date, Thesaurus

What To Do

1. With the NYC Letter document open, place the insertion point on the second blank line above the name *Ms. Kim Phillips*.
2. Insert a date using the format similar to *June 10, 2006*.
3. Select the word **outstanding** in the second sentence of the first paragraph. Use the Thesaurus to find a synonym for the word *outstanding*.
4. Use the *exceptional (adj.)* meaning; replace the word *outstanding* with the synonym *wonderful*. See Figure 2-5. Do not forget to change the preceding *an* to *a*.

Figure 2-5 Thesaurus dialog box

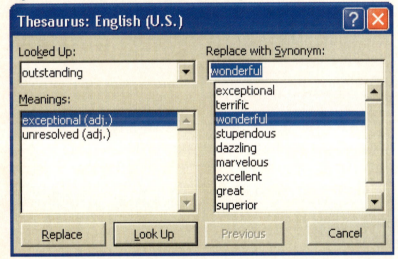

5. Select the word **advise** in the last sentence of the second paragraph.
6. Using the *counsel (v.)* meaning, replace *advise* with the synonym *recommend*.
7. Save the document and leave it open for the next Task.

Key Term

- Thesaurus — Finds a synonym, a word with a similar meaning, for a word in the document. The Thesaurus also lists antonyms, words with opposite meanings, for some words.

Hot Tips

- To insert a date or time, on the **Insert** menu, click **Date and Time** to display the Date and Time dialog box.
- To use the Thesaurus, on the **Tools** menu, point to **Language**. Click **Thesaurus** on the submenu.

Computer Concept

- Even synonyms can have different shades of meaning. Be sure a synonym makes sense in context before replacing a word with it.

Part 7 - Templates and Wizards

Task 1 - Use Existing Template

What To Do

1. Open a new Word document.
2. Open the **Professional Memo** template.
3. Select **Company Name Here** and key **Norton Laboratories**.
4. Beside *To*, key **Ross Howard, Vice President of Human Resources**.
5. Beside *From*, key **Luz Maria Rodriguez, Director of Recruiting**.
6. Beside CC, key **Harold Hastings, Vice President of IT Services**.
7. Beside *Date*, key today's date if necessary.
8. Beside *Re*, key **Compensation Analysis-IT Professionals**.
9. Select the heading and the text in the body of the memo and delete it. Key the memo text shown in Figure 7-1.
10. Save the file as **IT Memo** followed by your initials. Print and close the document.

Your Task Completed

Figure 7-1 IT Memo

Key Term

- Template — A file that contains page and paragraph formatting and text you can customize to create a new document similar to, but slightly different from, the original.

Hot Tips

- To open the Professional Memo template, choose **New** on the **File** menu. The New Document task pane opens. Click **General Templates** in the New from template section. In the Templates dialog box, click the **Memo** tab.
- To open the Professional Memo template in Office 2000, choose **New** from the **File** menu. In the New dialog box, click the **Memo** tab.

Part 2 – Helpful Word Features

Task 8 - Find, Replace

What To Do

1. With the NYC Letter document open, place the insertion point at the beginning of the document.
2. Use the Find feature to search for the word **your**. The word *your* appears five times in the document.
3. Use the Replace feature to find the word **trip** and replace it with the word **tour**. Key **trip** in the Find what box. Key **tour** in the Replace with box. See Figure 2-6.

Figure 2-6 Find and Replace dialog box

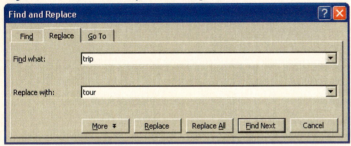

4. Click the **Replace all** button. Word made two replacements. Click **OK**.
5. Save, print, and close the document.

Your Task Completed

Figure 2-7 NYC Letter

Key Terms

- **Find** — Using the Find command, you can quickly search a document for every occurrence of a specific word or phrase you key in the Find what box. The Find command can locate either whole or partial words.
- **Replace** — Using the Replace command, you can replace a word or phrase in the Find what box with another word or phrase you key in the Replace with box. The Replace command is an extended version of the Find command.

Hot Tips

- To access the Find command, on the **Edit** menu, click **Find**.
- To access the Replace command, on the **Edit** menu, click **Replace**.

Introductory Word 31

Part 7

Templates and Wizards

Objectives

After completing this Part, you should be able to:
- Use an existing template.
- Create an original template.
- Create a document using an original template.
- Use a wizard.
- Use the Mail Merge Wizard.
- Create and print envelopes and labels.

Part 2 - Helpful Word Features

Application 1 - AutoCorrect, Thesaurus, Replace

Your company is preparing guidelines for proofreading outgoing correspondence. You need to make some additions to the document.

What To Do

1. Create a new Word document.
2. Key the proofreading guidelines shown in Figure 2-8. Use the default settings for margins.

Figure 2-8 Proofreading guidelines

> Guidelines for Proofreading Outgoing Correspondence
>
> Check Accuracy
> It is important to check the spelling and grammar usage of any document sent out by your company. Misspellings, punctuation errors, and incorrect information can embarrass and damage the credibility of an organization. If you are using a word processing program, do not rely entirely on the spell checker. It cannot determine the correct usage of words such as homonyms.
>
> Be Consistent
> Within a document, present the information logically and clearly. Use the same margins, indents, headings, hyphenation and spellings throughout the document. Consistency in a document gives the reader a sense of comfort. Inconsistencies distract the reader, causing your message to lose its impact.
>
> Check Facts
> It is important to use reliable sources to verify information such as names, addresses, telephone numbers and other facts. Do not rely on your memory.

3. Save the document as **Guidelines** followed by your initials.
4. Use the spelling and grammar checker to make any corrections in the document.
5. Use the Thesaurus to replace the word *reasonably* in the second paragraph with a word that makes sense in context.
6. Replace all occurrences of the word *paper* with the word *document*.
7. Save, print, and close the document.

Extra Challenges

- At times, it is important to know the readability statistics of a document. These statistics would include how many words are in the document and the reading level of the document. Use the Help system to find out how to display the readability statistics of the Guidelines document.
- A wildcard is a special character such as an asterisk or a question mark that represents characters when you are using the Find and Replace feature. Use wildcards when you are unsure of the spelling of a word or you are looking for words with similar spelling. Use Help to learn how to use a wildcard. Find all words that start with *in** in the Guidelines document.

(continued on next page)

Part 6 – Advanced Formatting

Application 3 - Apply Styles, Pagination, Insert Footnotes, continued

Your Application Complete

Figure 6-7 Diet

REDUCING FAT IN THE AMERICAN DIET

Introduction

Today most Americans are aware that a nutritious diet that is low in fat will lead to a longer and healthier life. To help Americans achieve this goal, the federal government develops dietary guidelines, which give advice about which foods Americans should eat to stay healthy.

Federal Dietary Guidelines

The Dietary Guidelines are released every five years by the U. S. Department of Agriculture and the U. S. Department of Health and Human Services. They are recommendations by nutrition experts who agree that enough is known about dietary effects on health to encourage certain dietary practices.

When first introduced in 1980,

> "... many groups and individuals from the health professions and the food industry questioned the scientific basis of the guidelines and even the federal government's authority to advise its citizens on what they should eat."[1]

Government officials responded by saying that the rapid pace of scientific discovery makes it impossible for average Americans to stay abreast of the most recent information. Government guidelines provide at least a starting point.

---

[1] "Dietary Guidelines for Americans: No-Nonsense Advice for Healthy Eating," *FDA Consumer*, November 1985, p.14.

Recommended Dietary Guidelines for Americans

1. Aim for a healthy weight
2. Be physically active each day
3. Let the food pyramid guide your food choices
4. Choose a variety of grains daily, especially whole grains
5. Choose a variety of fruits and vegetables daily
6. Keep food safe to eat
7. Choose a diet that is low in saturated fats and cholesterol and moderate in total fat
8. Choose beverages and food to moderate your intake of sugar
9. Choose and prepare food with less salt
10. If you drink alcoholic beverages, do so in moderation

These guidelines state that forty different nutrients are needed for good health, and no one food provides all the essential nutrients a body needs to stay healthy. Thus, the guidelines recommend that Americans eat a variety of foods from the major food groups. They also emphasize that moderate consumption is the key to good health.

Fat in the American Diet

A major emphasis of the guidelines is to encourage Americans to eat less fat. They recommend limits for total fat intake and saturated fat consumption. The guidelines stress the difference between saturated fats, which tend to raise blood cholesterol and unsaturated fats, which do not. "Aim for a total fat intake of no more that 30 percent of calories. If you need to reduce your fat intake to achieve this level, do so primarily by cutting back on saturated fats."[2] Foods high in saturated fats include high-fat dairy products such as cheese, whole milk and ice cream as well as processed meats. Everybody needs some fat in their diets, but be sure to choose unsaturated fat such as fish, nuts, olives, avocados and vegetable oils.

---

[2] U.S. Department of Agriculture and U.S. Department of Health and Human Services, *Dietary Guidelines for Americans, 2000*, 5th edition, 2000, p. 30.

Part 2 - Helpful Word Features

Application 1 - AutoCorrect, Thesaurus, Replace, continued

Your Application Completed

Figure 2-9 Guidelines

Guidelines for Proofreading Outgoing Correspondence

Check Accuracy
It is important to check the spelling and grammar usage of any document sent out by your company. Misspellings, punctuation errors, and incorrect information can embarrass and damage the credibility of an organization. If you are using a word processing program, do not rely entirely on the spell checker. It cannot determine the correct usage of words such as homonyms.

Be Consistent
Within a document, present the information logically and clearly. Use the same margins, indents, headings, hyphenation and spellings throughout the document. Consistency in a document gives the reader a sense of comfort. Inconsistencies distract the reader, causing your message to lose its impact.

Check Facts
It is important to use reliable sources to verify information such as names, addresses, telephone numbers and other facts. Do not rely on your memory.

Part 6 - Advanced Formatting

Application 3 - Apply Styles, Pagination, Insert Footnotes

You have been assigned to write a report about reducing fat in your diet for your Food and Nutrition class.

What To Do

1. Open **AW App6-3** from the data files. Save the document as **Diet** followed by your initials.
2. Apply the **Diet Title** style to the title. Apply the **Diet Heading** style to the headings.
3. Change the pagination so the *Recommended Dietary Guidelines for Americans* section is on the next page.
4. Select the quotation that begins "...*many groups and individuals*." Indent the quote .5 inch from both sides.
5. Place the insertion point after the quote. Insert the following footnote:

   "Dietary Guidelines for Americans: No-Nonsense Advice for Healthy Eating," *FDA Consumer*, **November 1985, p.14.**
6. Place the insertion point after the final quotation mark in the last paragraph. Insert the following footnote:

   U.S. Department of Agriculture and U.S. Department of Health and Human Services, *Dietary Guidelines for Americans, 2000,* **5th edition, 2000, p. 30.**
7. Number the list of recommended guidelines.
8. Highlight the first sentence in the last paragraph.
9. Preview the document. Save, print, and close the document.

Hot Tips

- To indent from both margins, use the left- and right-indent markers to set the indents at the desired points.
- To highlight text, select the text and click the arrow next to the **Highlight** button on the Formatting toolbar. Choose the color from the color palette.

(continued on next page)

Part 2 - Helpful Word Features

Application 2 - Spell Check, Proofreader's Marks

In your business communications class, you are learning about verbal and nonverbal communication. Your class assignment is to create a handout with examples of how to use body language in a job interview.

What To Do

1. Open **IW App2-2** from the data files. Print the document.
2. Use proofreader's marks to correct the ten words that contain mistakes a spelling checker would not catch.
3. Make the changes you have marked in the document.
4. Save the document as **Body Language** followed by your initials.
5. Print and close the document.

Did You Know?

- When people send e-mails, sometimes they use "emoticons" to express their feelings. Here are a few examples:
  - :-)   Smiling
  - :-o   Surprised
  - :-(Frowning

Web Sites

- Search the Web using the keyword *emoticon* to find Web sites that list other "emoticons" and "smilies."

Part 6 – Advanced Formatting

Application 2 - Clear Formatting, Create and Apply Styles, Continuous Section Breaks, Sort, continued

Your Application Completed

Figure 6-6 Bagel Menu

BAGEL MANIA
"THE BEST BAGELS IN TOWN"

All of our bagels are baked fresh daily right here at the store. We use only the freshest ingredients, and you won't find a better-tasting bagel. We serve the following types of bagels:

Blueberry	**Onion**	**Rye**
Cheese	**Plain**	**Sprout**
Chocolate Chip	**Pumpernickel**	**Walnut**
Cinnamon-Raisin	**Raspberry**	**Whole Wheat**

BREAKFAST BAGELS

Just a Bagel—A bagel with butter and our homemade jelly. $1.50
Traditional Bagel—Toasted bagel with cream cheese. $1.75
Cheesy Bagel—Bagel with three kinds of melted cheeses. $2.75
Bagelwich—Bagel with cheese, egg, and smoked salmon. $3.75

LUNCH BAGELS

PBJ Bagel—Bagel with peanut butter and our homemade jelly. $3.25
Veggie Bagel—Bagel with cheeses, sprouts, tomatoes, and onions. $4.25
Deluxe Bagel—Bagel with cream cheese, salmon and sprouts. $4.95
Club Bagel—Bagel with turkey, salmon, lettuce, and tomato. $5.50

COME AGAIN!

Part 2 - Helpful Word Features

Application 3 - Insert Date, AutoText, AutoComplete

You are a new associate with Key Financial Group. You need to make some corrections to an approach letter for a new prospect.

What To Do

1. Open **IW App2-3** from the data files.
2. Save the document as **Business Letter** followed by your initials.
3. Check the document for spelling and grammar errors.
4. Insert today's date in the second blank line above the name in the document. Use the format similar to *June 10, 2006*.
5. Insert a blank line at the end of the letter. Use AutoText to insert the words **Best Regards**.
6. Insert four blank lines. Use AutoComplete to insert your name on the fourth line.
7. Save, print, and close the document.

Your Application Completed

Figure 2-10 Business Letter

> June 10, 2006
>
> Glen H. Dickson
> 550 Cornell Street
> Indianapolis, IN 46202
>
> Dear Glen,
>
> This is to let you know that I have associated with Key Financial Group. I am happy to be working with a highly regarded group of professionals.
>
> I would like to call you to discuss the kind of service I can provide. A brief visit will not obligate you in any way, but could result in an exchange of worthwhile ideas regarding your general financial strategy.
>
> I plan to call you within the next few days to arrange an appointment at your convenience. Thank you for your consideration.
>
> Best regards,
>
>
> [Student Name]

Hot Tip

- A fragment is a sentence that lacks a verb or a subject. Right-click on the grammar error. On the shortcut menu, click **Grammar** or **About This Sentence** to learn more about fragments. In Office XP, you can also click **Explain** in the Grammar dialog box when using the Spelling and Grammar checker.

Extra Challenge

- Create a business letter to raise funds for a project of an organization to which you belong.

Part 6 - Advanced Formatting

Application 2 - Clear Formatting, Create and Apply Styles, Continuous Section Breaks, Sort

You work for a restaurant called Bagel Mania. The owner of the restaurant has asked you to format the menu to make it more readable.

What To Do C S

1. Open **AW App6-2** from the data files. Save the document as **Bagel Menu** followed by your initials.
2. Select the entire document. Clear the formatting.
3. With the document still selected, change the format to Times New Roman, 14 point, dark teal.
4. Select the title **Bagel Mania**. Create a style called **Bagel Title**. The style should be Arial, 18 point, bold, orange with shadow effect, centered and all caps. Apply the style to the title.
5. Select the heading **Breakfast Bagels**. Create a style called **Bagel Heading**. The style should be Times New Roman, 16 point, bold, dark teal, small caps, with an orange, double underline. Apply the style to the heading.
6. Select the word **Whole Wheat**. Create a style called **Bagel Names**. The style should be Arial, orange, bold. Apply the style to the word.
7. Apply the **Bagel Title** style to the subtitle "*The Best Bagels in Town*" and *Come again!*. Apply the **Bagel Heading** to *Lunch Bagels*.
8. Apply the **Bagel Names** style to the types of bagels in the list and the bagel names under breakfast bagels and lunch bagels.
9. Insert a continuous section break before and after the list of bagels. Sort the list alphabetically. Format the list into three columns. Double-space the list.
10. Change the line spacing of the first paragraph to **1.5**. Change the breakfast and lunch lists to 6-point spacing after each paragraph. Be sure to include the heading.
11. Preview the document. Save, print, and close the document.

(continued on next page)

Part 2 - Helpful Word Features

Application 4 - Thesaurus

One of your favorite attractions in New York City was the Metropolitan Museum of Art. Make the following changes to the report about the Metropolitan.

What To Do

1. Open **IW App2-4** from the data files.
2. Save the document in the **New York City Trip** Folder as **Museum** followed by your initials.
3. Use the Thesaurus to change as many words as you can without changing the meaning of the text. You should make changes to at least 15 words.
4. Save, print, and close the document.

Did You Know?

- You can also access a list of synonyms and the Thesaurus by right-clicking on the word and clicking **Synonyms** on the shortcut menu.

Web Sites

- Visit the Metropolitan Museum of Art at *www.metmuseum.org*.
- There are a large variety of museums not only in the United States, but also all over the world. View the Virtual Library of Museums at *www.icom.org/vlmp*.

Introductory Word 36

Figure 6-5 Norton Expectations, continued

Confidential Information

You are a trusted member of the Norton Laboratories team. You may have access to confidential information about the company. Remember never to share confidential information with others not authorized to have such information. Never discuss confidential company matters with outsiders unless authorized by the supervisor responsible for the information. We are confident you will respect the trust we have placed in you.

Solicitations

We encourage our associates to become involved in the community and to support worthy causes. However, these activities are properly done on your personal time, not on company time. Please do not solicit funds for any cause while at work.

Part 2 - Helpful Word Features

Application 5 - Spelling and Grammar Check, Insert Date, AutoComplete, Find, Replace, Thesaurus

You are the assistant for the Marina Bay Business Association. You need to make some changes to the minutes before submitting them at the upcoming meeting.

What To Do

1. Open **IW App2-5** from the data files.
2. Save the document as **Marina Minutes** followed by your initials.
3. Check the document's spelling and grammar and correct any errors.
4. Insert the current date on the blank line beneath *Minutes of the Business Meeting*.
5. Replace all occurrences of *club* with **association**.
6. In the *Old Business* paragraph, find a synonym for the word *objective* that makes sense in context.
7. Save, print, and close the document.

Did You Know?

- A passive sentence is one in which the subject of the sentence is acted upon. An active sentence is one in which the subject of the sentence performs the action. You should always strive to write active sentences.

Hot Tip

- To learn how to correct passive sentences, right-click on the grammar error. On the shortcut menu, click **Grammar** or **About This Sentence**. In Office XP, you can also click **Explain** in the Grammar dialog box when using the Spelling and Grammar checker.

(continued on next page)

Part 6 - Advanced Formatting

Application 1 - Verify Styles, Pagination

You work as an assistant for Norton Laboratories. Your supervisor has asked you to format the following document that will be included in the Employee Handbook.

What To Do

1. Open **AW App6-1** from the data files. Save the document as **Norton Expectations** followed by your initials. Take time to read the document because it will be included in the Employee Handbook.
2. Verify the style in the title. The style is *Expectations Title*. Change the style to **Handbook Title**.
3. Verify the style in the heading *Regular Attendance*. The style is *Expectations Heading*. Change the heading to **Handbook Heading**.
4. Change all other headings to the **Handbook Heading** style.
5. Change the pagination so the *Confidential Information* paragraph is on the next page.
6. Preview the document. Save, print, and close the document.

Your Application Completed

Figure 6-5 Norton Expectations

Teamwork

- Divide into groups. Make a list of productive work habits and attitudes each student should exhibit in the classroom. Refer to the "Your Responsibilities" document for ideas.

Extra Challenge

- You are the manager of a regional plant for Norton Laboratories. At the annual budget meeting, the possibility of closing your plant was discussed. You were told to keep this information confidential. If news of the possible closure were made public, what would be the consequences of a breach in confidentiality to the following:
  - employees of the plant and their families
  - the community where the plant is located
  - owners of the company
  - competitors of company

Your Responsibilities

Regular Attendance

You are part of a team. Our customers and sales force depend on each of us to do our jobs. Your co-workers and supervisors rely on you to accomplish our goals. Your regular attendance every day is a vital part of your contribution to the success of Norton Laboratories. We know you will take your responsibility seriously and be a reliable part of our team. If for any reason you must miss work, notify your supervisor just as soon as possible. For information about receiving pay for missed days, refer to the Sick Leave and Emergency Absences sections in this handbook. Because regular attendance is critical to the company's success, your attendance represents a major portion of your performance review.

Promptness

Just as regular attendance is important so is arriving to work on time. As with any team, everyone needs to be present in order to perform our jobs. Many people depend on you to be present and punctual. Make sure you give yourself enough time to get to work on time. Punctuality also will be an important factor in your evaluations.

Time Clock

Hourly employees must punch a time clock each day as they begin work and at quitting time. Be sure not to punch your time card before your scheduled start time or work past your quitting time unless your supervisor has approved the overtime. In addition, never, never allow someone else to punch your time card for you, and never punch someone else's time card for him or her.

(continued on next page)

Part 2 - Helpful Word Features

Application 5 - Spelling and Grammar Check, Insert Date, AutoComplete, Find, Replace, Thesaurus, continued

Your Application Completed

Figure 2-11 Marina Minutes

MARINA BAY BUSINESS AND PROFESSIONALS ASSOCIATION
Minutes of the Business Meeting
June 10, 2004

The members of the association met at 5:30 p.m. in the Green room at the Marina Bay Suites. Alex Anson opened the meeting.

ATTENDANCE	Members present were Marlene Atkins, James Baker, Aaron Campbell, Elizabeth Denton, Terry Edwards, Gary Gomez, Kim Jackson, Cecil James, Fred Jones, Chris Kelly, Martha Mason, Angela Romero, Mitch Smith, Kelly Williams, and Joan Willis.
MINUTES APPROVED	Association approved last month's minutes.
COMMITTEE REPORTS	James Baker, treasurer, reported an account balance of $1,117. Mitch Smith announced that the association has 35 members--four more than last year. He reminded members to pay their $95 dues within the next two weeks.
	Angela Romero reported on programs planned for the year. She distributed a calendar with meeting and program dates. She reminded everyone about the Communications workshop at City College on Saturday at 9:00 a.m.
OLD BUSINESS	Chris Kelly reported on the association's next fundraiser, which will be with Universal Business Products. Members will receive their catalogs next week, so they can begin selling the specialty products. The association's goal is to raise $3,000.
NEW BUSINESS	Elizabeth Denton announced a service opportunity for the association. She said the City Children's Home needs bookkeeping help. She motioned that the association provide the help. Cecil James seconded the motion. The association voted and the motion passed. Elizabeth volunteered to organize the bookkeeping schedule.
	Alex Anson recognized Terry Edwards as Member of the Month for his promotion to Production Manager at Mason Industries.
ANNOUNCEMENTS	The association adjourned the meeting at 6:35 p.m. The association scheduled the next meeting for the 27th of next month.

Part 6 - Advanced Formatting

Task 7 - Sort Lists

What To Do

1. Open **AW Task6-7** from the data files. Save the document as **Norton Directory**, followed by your initials.
2. Sort the list in alphabetical order.
3. Preview the document.
4. Save, print, and close the document.

Your Task Completed

Figure 6-4 Norton Directory

Directory of Corporate Officers

Durán, Hector—Vice President Sales, Ext. 1928
Hastings, Harold—Vice President, Information Technology Services, Ext. 1066
Hayashi, Peter—Vice President, Technical Services, Ext. 1010
Howard, Ross—Vice President, Human Resources, Ext. 1812
Howard, Sherman—President, Norton Laboratories, Inc., Ext. 1860
Jackson, Calvin—Vice President, International Operations, Ext. 1906
Norton, Jack—Chairman, Norton Laboratories, Inc., Ext. 1865
Norton, Mary—Vice President, Domestic Operations, Ext. 1836

Key Term

- **Sort** — Arranges a list of words or numbers in ascending order (A to Z; smallest to largest) or in descending order (Z to A; largest to smallest).

Hot Tip

- To sort text in a document, open the **Table** menu and choose **Sort**.

Part 3

Format Text and Paragraphs

Objectives

Upon completion of this Part, you should be able to:
- Apply different fonts, font styles, and font effects to your text.
- Change the size and color of your text.
- Use different underline styles and colors.
- Highlight text.
- Change the case of your text.
- Copy formats using the Format Painter.
- Set the margins and adjust the line spacing.
- Align text and change the vertical alignment.
- Indent text.

Part 6 - Advanced Formatting

Task 6 - Insert Footnotes, continued

Figure 6-3 Norton Benefits, continued

Retirement

Norton Laboratories provides a generous retirement and profit sharing program to help its associates prepare for retirement. All full-time associates who have attained age 18, worked 1,000 hours and six consecutive months are eligible to participate in the company's 401(k)/profit sharing plan. Participants can elect to contribute up to $15,000 a year to the plan. The contribution is deducted from your paycheck, and you don't pay income taxes on the money until you take the money out at retirement. The company, at the Board's discretion, may elect to match your contribution up to a specific percentage in any given Plan year. If you do not contribute, you will not receive any matching contribution from the company. To find out more, please refer to your Retirement Savings Plan booklet.

Holidays

Norton Laboratories provides several annual paid holidays. Each year the Human Resources department will prepare a calendar listing the dates of the holidays the company will observe. Normally the annual holidays will include the following:

- New Year's Day
- Martin Luther King Day
- Memorial Day
- Independence Day
- Labor Day
- Thanksgiving
- Christmas Eve
- Christmas Day

If the holiday falls on a Saturday, the company will close on the preceding Friday. If the holiday falls on a Sunday, the company will close on the following Monday.

Vacations

Norton Laboratories offers generous vacation benefits:

1. Employees hired between January 1 and July 31 will receive ten days' vacation after completing twelve months' service.
2. Employees hired between August 1 and December 31 will receive five days' vacation after six months' service, and five additional days after twelve months' service.
3. After five years' service an associate will receive one additional day of vacation for each year of service. For example, an associate with six years' service will have eleven days of vacation; an associate with seven years will receive twelve days, etc. Vacation days are capped at fifteen days.
4. You must take your vacation each year. Vacation can not be carried over to future periods.
5. Wages may *never* be paid in lieu of vacation time.
6. You may split your vacation, but you must take at least one week each time.
7. You will coordinate your vacation with your supervisor.

Sick Leave

All hourly employees earn one day of paid sick leave for every month in which they have no absences. You can earn up to twelve days a year. You can accumulate up to a maximum of eighteen days.[2]

---

[2] Your Company provides semi-annual seminars to review any changes in your benefits. Watch for dates and times in the newsletter.

Part 3 - Format Text and Paragraphs

Task 1 - Formatting Toolbar, Font Dialog Box, Apply a New Font

What To Do

1. Open **IW Task3-1** from the data files.
2. Save the document as **Financial Planning** followed by your initials.
3. Take time to read the document to familiarize yourself with the content and format. You will be using this document throughout this Part as well as Part 4.
4. Take time to study the Formatting toolbar (Figure 3-1) and the Font dialog box (Figure 3-2). This toolbar and dialog box will be used throughout this Part.

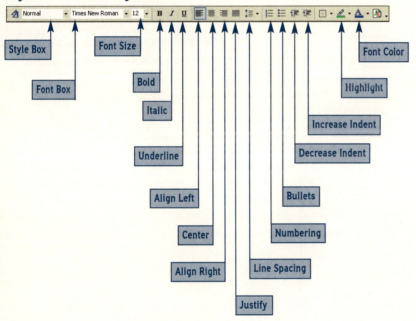

Figure 3-1 Formatting toolbar

Key Terms

- Formatting — Arranging the shape, size, type, and general make-up of a document. To format a document, use the buttons on the Formatting toolbar or the Font dialog box.
- Fonts — Designs of type. See Figure 3-3.

Hot Tips

- To apply a new font, click the arrow next to the Font box on the Formatting toolbar. Select a new font from the drop-down list. You can also change the font in the Font dialog box. You must select the text before changing the font.
- A faster way to access the Font dialog box is by right-clicking on the selected text and choosing **Font** from the shortcut menu.
- To select the entire document, on the **Edit** menu click **Select All**.
- If you only intend to make one change to selected text, using the appropriate button on the Formatting toolbar is the simpler method. If, however, you intend to make multiple changes or you want to experiment with different formats, the Font dialog box is the better method.

(continued on next page)

Introductory Word 40

Part 6 - Advanced Formatting

Task 6 - Insert Footnotes

What To Do

1. The Norton Benefits document should be open from the previous Task. Place the insertion point at the end of the Equal Opportunity paragraph.
2. Insert a footnote. Key **Norton Laboratories also complies with the Americans with Disabilities Act. A copy of the Act is available in the Human Resources department.** (Key the period.)
3. Insert a footnote after the last paragraph in the document. Key **Your company provides semi-annual seminars to review any changes in your benefits. Watch for dates and times in the newsletter.**
4. Preview the document.
5. Save, print, and close the document.

Your Task Completed

Figure 6-3 Norton Benefits

Key Term

- Footnote — Text printed at the bottom of a page, used to document quotations, figures, summaries, or other text that you do not want to include in the main body of the text.

Hot Tip

- To insert a footnote, place the insertion point in the document where you need a reference. Open the **Insert** menu and click **Reference** (or click **Footnote** in Office 2000). Choose **Footnote** on the submenu.

Computer Concept

- In Print Layout view, you can key a footnote directly at the bottom of a page without using the footnote pane.

(continued on next page)

Part 3 - Format Text and Paragraphs

Task 1 - Formatting Toolbar, Font Dialog Box, Apply a New Font, continued

Figure 3-2 Font dialog box

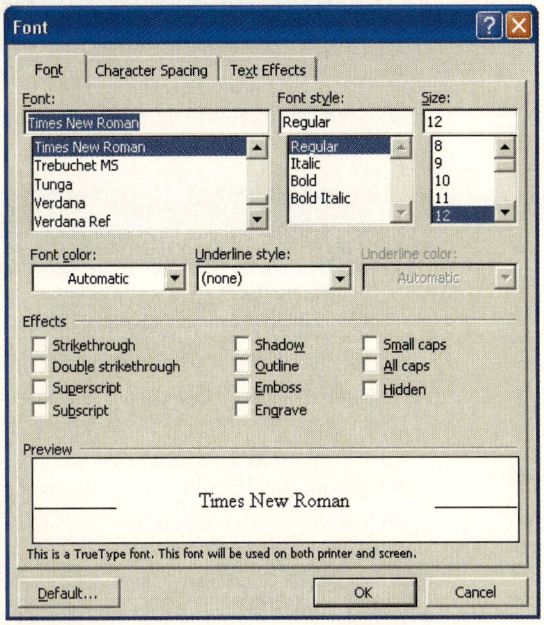

5. Note the different types of fonts. See Figure 3-3.

Figure 3-3 Different fonts

This font is called Times New Roman.

This font is called Arial.

This font is called Broadway.

This font is called Old English Text MT.

This font is called Script MT Bold.

6. Select the entire document. Change the font from Courier New to **Times New Roman**.
7. Select the title of the document, **Get a Grip on Your Money**.
8. Change the font from Times New Roman to **Arial**.
9. Save and leave the document open for the next Task.

Introductory Word 41

Part 6 - Advanced Formatting

Task 5 - Control Pagination

What To Do

1. The Norton Benefits document should be open from the previous Task. View the document in Print Preview. Notice where the current page breaks are located.
2. Select the **Retirement** heading. Use the **Page break before** option in the Paragraph dialog box to move the heading and the two lines after it to the next page.
3. Select the **Vacations** heading. Use the **Page break before** option in the Paragraph dialog box to move the heading and the three lines after it to the next page.
4. Preview the document. The heading *Retirement* should be at the top of the second page. The heading *Vacations* should be at the top of the third page.
5. Save the document and leave it open for the next Task.

Hot Tip

- To modify pagination, open the **Format** menu and click **Paragraph**. In the paragraph dialog box, click the **Line and Page Breaks** tab.

Did You Know?

- A widow is the last line of a paragraph printed at the top of a new page. An orphan is the first line of a paragraph printed at the bottom of a page. To prevent widows and orphans from occurring in the document, open the **Format** menu and click **Paragraph**. On the Line and Page Breaks tab, check the **Widows/Orphans** check box.

Computer Concepts

- Controlling pagination (that is, determining where Word inserts automatic page breaks) is an important tool to make long documents easier to read. In addition to Widow/Orphan control, which is on by default, Word provides other control options:
  - **Keep lines together** will keep lines of a paragraph together on a page. Word will move the entire paragraph to a new page if a page break occurs within the paragraph.
  - **Keep with next** will keep the selected paragraphs together on a page.
  - **Page break before** will insert a page break before the selected paragraph.

Part 3 - Format Text and Paragraphs

Task 2 - Change Font Size and Color

What To Do

1. The text of a document can be changed to different sizes. See Figure 3-4. The higher the point size the larger the print.

Figure 3-4 Font sizes

> This is Arial 10 point.
>
> This is Arial 14 point.
>
> This is Arial 18 point.

2. With the Financial Planning document open, select the entire document and change the font size to **14**.
3. Select the title and change the font size to **18**.
4. With the title still selected, change the color to **Green**.
5. Select the **Introduction** heading.
6. Change the font size to **16** and the font color to **Blue**.
7. Save and leave the document open for the next Task.

Key Term

- Font size — Determined by measuring the height of characters in units called points. A standard font size is 12 points.

Hot Tips

- To change the font size, click the arrow next to the Font Size box on the Formatting toolbar. Choose a size from the submenu. You can also change the font size in the Font dialog box.
- To change the font color, click the arrow next to the **Font Color** button on the Formatting toolbar. Choose the color from the palette. You can also change the font color in the Font dialog box.
- If you are not sure of the color on the Font color palette, hover the pointer over the color box and the name of the color will appear.

Part 6 - Advanced Formatting

Task 4 - Create Section, Apply Column Settings

What To Do

1. The Norton Benefits document should be open from the previous Task. Switch to **Normal View**.

2. Place the insertion point before *New Year's Day* in the Holidays section. Insert a continuous break.

3. Place the insertion point on the blank line after *Christmas Day*. Insert a continuous break.

4. Format the list in the Holidays section into two columns. Bullet the list.

5. Preview the document. The list should appear as shown in Figure 6-2.

Figure 6-2 Holidays list

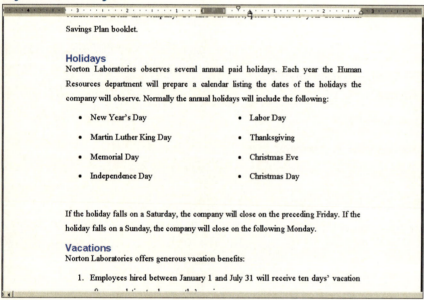

6. Save the document and leave it open for the next Task.

Key Terms

- Section — A part of a document with different formatting characteristics than other parts of the document.
- Continuous section break — A mark indicating the beginning of a new section. It does not begin a new page.

Hot Tips

- To insert a continuous section break, open the **Insert** menu and click **Break**. In the Break dialog box, click **Continuous**.
- To format a document in columns, open the **Format** menu and choose **Columns**. The Columns dialog box appears. In this dialog box, specify the number of columns you want. You can also click the **Columns** button on the Standard toolbar.
- To create a numbered or bulleted list, select the text and open the **Format** menu. Choose **Bullets and Numbering**. Select either the Bulleted tab or Numbered tab to choose a bullet or numbering format. You can also click the **Bullets** button or **Numbering** button on the Formatting toolbar.

Advanced Word 8

Part 3 - Format Text and Paragraphs

Task 3 - Font Style, Font Effects

What To Do

1. With the Financial Planning document open, select the title and bold it.
2. Select the first sentence in the first paragraph and italicize it.
3. Study the different font effects in Table 3-1.
4. Select the title again. In the Font dialog box, under Effects, choose **Shadow**.
5. Click **OK**. The words now have a shadow effect.
6. Save and leave the document open for the next Task.

Table 3-1 Font effects

Font Effect	Result
Strikethrough	~~No turning back~~
Double strikethrough	~~Caution: Hot~~
Superscript	The mountain is ^high
Subscript	The pool is ~deep
Shadow	By invitation only
Outline	Thursday
Emboss	December 18
Engrave	Jack and Claire
Small Caps	CALYPSO STREET
All Caps	GLENMERLE
Hidden	Part of this text is

Key Terms

- Font style — Formatting feature that changes the appearance of text such as bold, italic, and underline.
- Font effect — Formatting feature that enhances text. See Table 3-1.

Hot Tips

- To change the font style, select the text and click the **Bold**, **Italic**, and **Underline** buttons on the **Formatting** toolbar. You can also change the font style in the Font dialog box.
- To select a Font effect, open the **Format** menu and choose **Font**. Choose one of the options in the Effects section of the Font dialog box.

Did You Know?

- Clicking a toolbar button to turn a feature on or off is called toggling.

Introductory Word 43

Part 6 - Advanced Formatting

Task 3 - Verify Character and Paragraph Styles

What To Do

1. Open **AW Task6-3** from the data files. Save the document as **Norton Benefits** followed by your initials.
2. Take the time to read the entire document. It will be part of the employee handbook for Norton Laboratories.
3. Select the title **Norton Benefits**. Notice the style Benefits Title is in the Style box on the formatting toolbar.
4. Change the style to **Handbook Title**.
5. Select the heading **Equal Opportunity**. Notice the style Benefits Heading is in the Style box on the Formatting toolbar.
6. Change the paragraph style to **Handbook Heading**.
7. Apply the **Handbook Heading** style to the remaining headings in the document.
8. Save the document and leave it open for the next Task.

Extra Challenge

- Read about the benefits offered by Norton Laboratories. Evaluate other employment packages by studying business options including cafeteria plans, individual retirement plan (IRAs), tax sheltered annuities, retirement, commissions, benefits, and transportation.

Part 3 - Format Text and Paragraphs

Task 4 - Underline Style and Color, Highlights

What To Do

1. With the Financial Planning document open, select the **Introduction** heading.
2. Underline the heading with the double-line underline style. Change the underline color to **Blue**.
3. Select the last sentence of the document.
4. Highlight the sentence in **Turquoise**.
5. Save and leave the document open for the next Task.

Key Terms

- Underline style — Underlining options such as double lines, dotted lines, and wavy lines.
- Highlight — Emphasizes important text by shading it with color.

Hot Tips

- To change underline style, open the **Format** menu and choose **Font**. Click the down arrow next to the **Underline** style box to select a style.
- To highlight text, select the text and click the arrow next to the **Highlight** button on the Formatting toolbar. Choose the color from the color palette.

Part 6 – Advanced Formatting

Task 2 – Create, Apply Paragraph Styles, continued

Your Task Completed

Figure 6-1 Norton History

The History of Norton Laboratories

The Early Years

Norton Laboratories has enjoyed many great successes in its brief history. The company was founded by Jack Norton and Sherman Howard. Jack Norton graduated from State University with a degree in Chemistry. He began his career working for a large petroleum company and spent many years living and working overseas.

After returning to the United States, Jack developed a waterless hand soap that does not dry the hands. Borrowing money from family and friends, including his best friend and college roommate, Sherman Howard, Jack began to manufacture and sell his new invention.

The waterless hand soap was a huge success. Jack was able to quit his job at the oil company and work full time in his new venture. Soon after, his friend Sherman joined the company to manage the day-to-day operations. The company was officially founded in 1976.

Norton Laboratories Today

In the thirty years since Jack and Sherman formed Norton Laboratories, the company has grown to have $100 million in sales. With an expanded product line and a highly organized and dynamic sales force, Norton Laboratories now has over twelve thousand satisfied customers.

What's next? We continue to grow at a phenomenal rate. Our product line is expected to double in the next five years. We are looking to grow internationally. The future lacks just one thing—You!

About Our Products

Norton Laboratories is proud of the many products it makes. Our products help people and businesses lead cleaner, healthier, and safer lives. The Personal Care line includes our flagship product, the waterless hand soap, AquaFree. We also manufacture bath soaps and shampoos. These products are sold in retail stores throughout the nation. Our Industrial product line includes the industry's best-selling floor wax, CeraClear. We also

manufacture industrial cleaners and lubricants. These products are sold to businesses, industries, hospitals, schools, and municipalities. Your company is a recognized leader in the industry, and you can be proud of the contribution we all make to improve the lives of people everywhere.

Advanced Word 6

Part 3 - Format Text and Paragraphs

Task 5 - Change Case, Format Painter

What To Do

1. With the Financial Planning document open, select the title and change the case to **UPPERCASE**.
2. Select the heading, **Introduction**.
3. Use the **Format Painter** button to copy the font size and color, and apply the underline style and color to the other four headings.
4. Save and print the document. Leave it open for the next Task.

Key Term

- Format Painter — Feature that allows you to copy the format and style of a block of text rather than the text itself. You can quickly apply a complicated format and style to text.

Hot Tips

- To change the case of selected text, open the **Format** menu and choose **Change Case**.
- To use the Format Painter command, select the text with the formatting you want to copy. Click the **Format Painter** button. The pointer changes to a paintbrush and I-beam. Select the text you want to copy and the text changes to the copied format.

Introductory Word 45

Part 6 - Advanced Formatting

Task 2 - Create, Apply Paragraph Styles

What To Do

1. With the **Norton History** document open, click the **Show/Hide** button. Notice that each paragraph ends with a paragraph mark.
2. Select the first paragraph below the heading *The Early Years*.
3. Create a paragraph style called **Handbook Text**. The paragraph alignment should be justified and the line spacing should be **1.5** with **6** point paragraph spacing after the paragraph.
4. Apply the **Handbook Text** style to the first paragraph.
5. Apply the **Handbook Text** style to each paragraph in the document.
6. Preview the document.
7. Save, print, and close the document.

Key Term

- Paragraph style — Paragraph styles dictate the appearance of a paragraph. Paragraph style options such as alignment, indents, and spacing can be selected from the Font, Paragraph, Bullets and Numbering, and Tab dialog boxes.

Hot Tips

- To create a new paragraph style, open the **Format** menu and click **Styles and Formatting**. The Styles and Formatting task pane opens. Click the **New Style** button and the New Style dialog box opens. To create a new paragraph style in Office 2000, open the **Format** menu and click **Styles**. The Styles dialog box opens.
- A quick and easy way to create a new paragraph style is to format the text as you want it to appear. Click in the style box on the formatting toolbar and key the name of the style. Strike **Enter**. You can click the down arrow beside the style box to view the new style.

Did You Know?

- Word considers a paragraph any block of text that ends with a paragraph mark, even if it is just one word. To check for paragraph marks, click the **Show/Hide** button on the Standard toolbar.

(continued on next page)

Part 3 - Format Text and Paragraphs

Task 6 - Margins, Adjust Line Spacing

What To Do

1. With the Financial Planning document open, change the top margin to **1.2** inches.
2. Change the bottom margin to **.8** inch.
3. Change the left and right margins to **1** inch.
4. Note the different types of line spacing. See Figure 3-5.

Figure 3-5 Line Spacing

> The line spacing of this paragraph is single-spaced.
> This paragraph is single-spaced.
>
> The line spacing of this paragraph is 1.5 lines.
>
> This paragraph is 1.5 spaced.
>
> The line spacing of this paragraph is double-spaced.
>
> This paragraph is double-spaced.

5. Select the first paragraph of the document and double-space it.
6. Save and leave the document open for the next Task.

Key Terms

- Margins — Blank areas around the top, bottom, and sides of a page.
- Line spacing — Amount of space between lines of text. By default, Word single-spaces text. See Figure 3-5.

Hot Tips

- To change margin settings, open the **File** menu and choose **Page Setup**. Select the **Margins** tab if necessary and click on the arrows beside the margin boxes to adjust the size of the margins.
- To change line spacing, select the text. Open the **Format** menu and choose **Paragraph**. Select the **Indents and Spacing** tab and click the down arrow next to the **Line spacing** box to select a line spacing option. In Office XP, you can also click the arrow next to the **Line Spacing** button on the Formatting toolbar.

Part 6 – Advanced Formatting

Task 1 - Clear Formats, Create, Apply Character Styles

What To Do

1. With Word running, open **AW Task6-1** from the data files. Save the file as **Norton History**, followed by your initials.
2. Read the document. This document will be part of an employee handbook created for Norton Laboratories. This handbook will be used throughout this unit.
3. Select the entire document and clear the current formatting.
4. Select the title *The History of Norton Laboratories*.
5. Create a character style named **Handbook Title**. The style should be Arial Black, 16 point, teal. Underline the title with a light blue, double underline.
6. Apply the **Handbook Title** style to the title.
7. Select the heading *The Early Years*.
8. Create a new character style named **Handbook Heading**. The style should be Arial, 14 point, bold, light blue.
9. Apply the **Handbook Heading** style to the heading *The Early Years*.
10. Apply the **Handbook Heading** style to the remaining headings in the document.
11. Save the document and leave it open for the next Task.

Key Term

- Character style — Character style dictates the appearance of text. Character style options can only be selected from the Font dialog box and the Borders and Shading dialog box.

Hot Tips

- To clear formats, select the text to be cleared. Click the down arrow beside the Style box on the Formatting toolbar. On the submenu, click **Clear Formatting** or **Default Paragraph Font** (in Office 2000).
- To create a new character style in Office XP, open the **Format** menu and click **Styles and Formatting**. The Styles and Formatting task pane opens. Click the **New Style** button and the New Style dialog box opens. To create a new character style in Office 2000, open the **Format** menu and click **Style**. The Style dialog box opens.

Advanced Word 4

Part 3 - Format Text and Paragraphs

Task 7 - Align Text

What To Do

1. The text of a document can be left-aligned, centered, right-aligned, or justified. See Figure 3-6.

Figure 3-6 Text alignment

> This text is left-aligned.
>
>   This text is centered.
>
>   This text is right-aligned.
>
> This text is justified because the text is aligned at both the left and right margins. This text is justified because the text is aligned at both the left and right margins.

2. With the Financial Planning document open, select the title and center it.
3. Select the date above the title and right-align it.
4. Select the second paragraph and justify it.
5. Save and leave the document open for the next Task.

Key Term

- **Alignment** — How the text is positioned between the margins. Text can be left-aligned, centered, right-aligned, or justified. See Figure 3-6.

Hot Tip

- To align text, select the text and choose **Paragraph** on the **Format** menu. In the Paragraph dialog box, choose an alignment from the drop-down list in the Alignment box. You can also change alignment by clicking the alignment buttons on the Formatting toolbar.

Introductory Word 47

Part 6

Advanced Formatting

Objectives

After completing this Part, you should be able to:
- Clear Formats.
- Create and apply character and paragraph styles.
- Verify character and paragraph styles.
- Create a section with formatting that differs from other sections.
- Control pagination.
- Create footnotes.
- Sort paragraphs in lists.

Part 3 - Format Text and Paragraphs

Task 8 - Indent Text

What To Do

1. With the Financial Planning document open, select the first paragraph.
2. Click the **First Line Indent** marker and drag to the **.5**-inch mark. See Figure 3-7. You have created a first-line indent.

Figure 3-7 First Line Indent

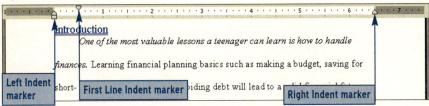

3. Select the second paragraph.
4. Click the **Left Indent** marker and drag to the **.5**-inch mark. You have created a left indent.
5. With the paragraph still selected, click the **Right Indent** marker and drag to the **6**-inch mark. You have created a right indent. The second paragraph is now indented from both margins. See Figure 3-8.

Figure 3-8 Indent from both margins

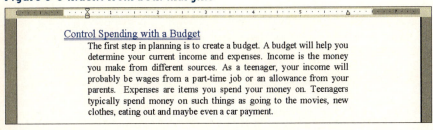

6. Save, print, and close the document.

Key Terms

- First line indent — First line is indented more than the following lines. Use the first line indent marker to set a first-line indent. See Figure 3-7
- Indent from both margins — All lines are indented on both sides of the paragraph. Use the left and right indent markers to set indents from both sides. See Figure 3-8.

(continued on next page)

Introductory Word 48

word unit - part 3   task 8

Word Unit Contents Advanced

Part 6 – Advanced Formatting

Tasks
1 - Clear Formats, Create, Apply Character Styles 4
2 - Create, Apply Paragraph Styles 5
3 - Verify Character and Paragraph Styles .7
4 - Create Section, Apply Column Settings .8
5 - Control Pagination 9
6 - Insert Footnotes 10
7 - Sort Lists 12

Applications
1 - Verify Styles, Pagination 13
2 - Clear Formatting, Create and Apply Styles, Continuous Section Breaks, Sort 15
3 - Apply Styles, Pagination, Insert Footnotes 17

Part 7 – Templates and Wizards

Tasks
1 - Use Existing Template 20
2 - Create Original Template 21
3 - Create Document Using Original Template 22
4 - Resume Wizard 23
5 - Mail Merge Wizard 25
6 - Create Envelopes 27
7 - Create Labels 28

Applications
1 - Use Existing Template to Prepare Business Letter 29
2 - Mail Merge Wizard 31
3 - Create Original Template 33
4 - Create Document Using Original Template 34

Part 8 – Workgroup Collaboration and Web Pages

Tasks
1 - Send Documents by E-mail 36
2 - Open Reviewing Toolbar, View Changes and Comments 37
3 - Track Changes, Accept Changes 38
4 - Insert, Edit Comments 39
5 - Compare, Merge Documents 40
6 - Save Document as Web Page, Add Theme and Text Animation, Preview Document as Web Page 42
7 - Create Web Page Using Template, Insert Hyperlink 44
8 - Create Web Site Using the Web Page Wizard 45

Applications
1 - Insert Comments, Track Changes 46
2 - Accept Changes, Delete Comments 47
3 - Web Page Template, Hyperlink 48
4 - Save Document as Web Page, Hyperlinks 50

Part 9 – Tables and Graphics

Tasks
1 - Create Table 53
2 - Format Table, Insert Formula 54
3 - Copy Excel Worksheet into Word, Paste Special 55
4 - Insert Clip Art, Wrap Text 57
5 - Use Drawing Tools 58
6 - Copy, Paste, Resize Objects 59
7 - Add Fill Color, Line Color 60
8 - Change Order of Layered Objects, Group Objects 61
9 - Rotate, Flip Objects 62
10 - Insert Word Art, Customize Bullets 63

Applications
1 - Create Table 64
2 - Add Clip Art, Wrap Text 65
3 - Insert Table, Paste Special, Draw, Copy, Group Objects 66
4 - Bullet Lists, Insert Clip Art, Wrap Text, Insert WordArt 68

Part 10 – Working with Long Documents

Tasks
1 - Create Outline 71
2 - Reorganize Outline 72
3 - Create Master Document 73
4 - Create Subdocument from Outline Heading 74
5 - Create Subdocument from Existing Document 75
6 - Insert Bookmarks 76
7 - Create Cross-References 77
8 - Create Table of Contents, Insert Index .78

Applications
1 - Create, Reorganize Outline 79
2 - Create Master Document, Create Subdocument 80
3 - Insert Subdocuments, Insert Bookmark, Create Table of Contents 81

Part 3 - Format Text and Paragraphs

Task 8 - Indent Text, continued

Your Task Completed

Figure 3-9 Financial Planning document

May 28, 2004

GET A GRIP ON YOUR MONEY

Introduction

One of the most valuable lessons a teenager can learn is how to handle finances. Learning financial planning basics such as making a budget, saving for short- and long-term goals, and avoiding debt will lead to a solid financial future and greater chance of achieving your dreams.

Control Spending with a Budget

The first step in planning is to create a budget. A budget will help you determine your current income and expenses. Income is the money you make from different sources. While you are a teenager, your income will probably be wages from a part-time job or an allowance from your parents. Expenses are items on which you spend your money. Teenagers typically spend money on such things as going to the movies, new clothes, eating out and maybe even a car payment.

Subtract your expenses from your income. You should have a positive balance. A positive balance means your income is more than your expenses. If you have a negative balance, you are spending more money than you earn. This means you are spending money you do not have, which could lead to debt problems. A budget will help you control your spending. Keep a record of everything you spend for a month or two. You might be surprised to learn just how much you spend on junk food!

Setting Savings Goals

You need to set goals to be sure you are spending your money on items you want. Setting goals forces you to make choices. You should have short-term goals such as saving for a stereo, sports equipment, or tickets to a concert. You should also have long-term goals like saving for a car or college.

After setting your goals, you need to develop a plan to achieve them. Look at your budget to determine what is necessary. For example, you can bring your lunch

(continued on next page)

Advanced Microsoft Word Unit

Part 6 – Advanced Formatting

Part 7 – Templates and Wizards

Part 8 – Workgroup Collaboration and Web Pages

Part 9 – Tables and Graphics

Part 10 – Working With Long Documents

Word Unit

Advanced Word 1

Part 3 - Format Text and Paragraphs

Task 8 - Indent Text, continued

Figure 3-9 Financial Planning document (continued)

> from home one day a week instead of going out to eat. This could save five dollars a week. Although this does not sound like much, five dollars a week adds up to $260 a year. This is the price of a stereo. If you invest that $5 earning 8% a year, then that five-dollar hamburger would be worth $3,683 in ten years! If you continued saving a hamburger a week for the next 50 years, you will have accumulated $158,635!
>
> ### Dangers of Credit Cards and Debt
> Too many young people get into trouble with credit cards. Instead of saving to purchase something they want, many people borrow the money. Borrowing money results in debt. Debt results in paying interest. For example, you take a trip to Europe that costs $1,500. Instead of saving the money to pay for the trip, you charge it to a credit card. If you only pay $50 a month toward the credit card bill, it would take you three years to pay off the debt. You would also pay over $400 in interest. If you made only the minimum payments, it would take you 17 _ years to pay off the debt and you would have paid over $1,800 in interest on a $1500 purchase!
>
> It is important to remember: You should not charge anything you cannot pay for that month. If you get into trouble paying your credit cards, you could damage your credit rating. Prospective employers and banks check credit ratings. Delinquent payments on credit cards show irresponsible behavior. It could prevent you from getting a job or a loan for a car.
>
> ### Conclusion
> It is important to learn good money management at a young age. The good habits you develop as a teenager will continue as an adult. Being able to stick to a budget, set and achieve savings goals, and stay out of debt demonstrates self-discipline and responsibility. Good financial planning paves the way to a sound financial future and a happier life.

Integrated Simulation - Association for Hearing Impaired Children

Job 3 - Produce Report

You are going to solicit a $1,000 contribution from the national board for the Association for Hearing Impaired Children to help fund the weeklong stay for 13 children at Camp Thunderhawk. You need to prepare a report for the board that explains why you are seeking these funds, and illustrates how you've raised money in the past.

What To Do

1. Create a new document in Word.
2. Insert a header that includes the date and a page number.
3. Write about three paragraphs (150-200 words) that explain why you need additional funds, how the money will be spent, and where money has come from in the past to support activities and programs for your chapter's members. You can use the data shown in the following table to explain how you've generated income in the past.
4. Insert a chart at the end of the report and enter the data shown in the table.
5. Format the report as desired.

	1998	2000	2002
Membership Dues	$450	$500	$650
Fund-raising	$590	$700	$1125
Donations	$125	$95	$100

6. Save the report with a name of your choice, and then print the report.

Part 3 - Format Text and Paragraphs

Task 9 - Apply Styles, Vertical Alignment

What To Do

1. Create a new Word document. This will be a cover page for the document you created in the previous Tasks.
2. Key the following text.
   [Student Name]
   Accounting 101
   Financial Planning for Teenagers
3. Select the text and apply the **Heading 1** style.
4. Center the text.
5. Vertically align the text in the center of the page.
6. Preview the document.
7. Save the document as **Financial Planning Title**, followed by your initials.
8. Print and close the document.

Your Task Completed

Figure 3-10 Financial Planning Title document

[Student Name]
Accounting 101
Financial Planning for Teenagers

Key Terms

- Style — Predefined set of formatting options that have been named and saved.
- Vertical alignment — How the text is positioned between the top and bottom margins of a document.

Hot Tips

- To apply a style, select the text and choose an existing style from the Style box on the Formatting toolbar or open the **Format** menu and choose **Styles and Formatting**. In Office XP and future versions, you can also click the **Styles and Formatting** button on the Formatting toolbar.
- To vertically align text, choose **Page Setup** on the **File** menu. Click the **Layout** tab in the Page Setup dialog box and choose **Top**, **Center**, **Justified**, or **Bottom** in the Vertical alignment box.

Integrated Simulation - Association for Hearing Impaired Children

Job 2 - Create Table

Several people have asked you for a list of the children planning to attend the camp. Create a table showing the children's names and ages.

Hot Tip

- To use a point size not listed as an option, highlight the size in the Font Size box and key the new point size.

What To Do

1. Open a new Word document.
2. Create the table shown in Figure IS-2. Use **10** point **Times New Roman**.
3. Save the document as **Camper Table** followed by your initials.
4. Print and close the document.

Your Job Completed

Figure IS-2 Camper Table

Child	Age
Macy Longfellow	9
Kerri Delaney	10
Jack Wilson	9
Lane Perkins	11
Teresa Johnson	12
Michael Rodriguez	11
Haley Gerber	11
Peyton Smith	10
Yolanda Cruz	9
Alicia Banks	12
Donna Giovannetti	12
Camille Craft	13
Van Thurber	11

Part 3 - Format Text and Paragraphs

Application 1 - Font Size and Color, Bold, Italic, Page Orientation

You have been asked to prepare a certificate for the employee of the month at the hospital where you work.

Extra Challenge

- Create a certificate honoring a person in an organization to which you belong.

What To Do

1. Open **IW App3-1** from the data files.
2. Save the document as **Certificate**, followed by your initials.
3. Change all text to **Baskerville Old Face**, **20** point, **Teal**. If the font is not available, choose another appropriate font.
4. Change the font effect of all text to **Emboss**.
5. Change the first *Employee of the Month* to **36** point, **Bold**, **Small caps**.
6. Change *Joe Harrington* to **Arial**, **28** point, **UPPERCASE**.
7. Change *June 2006* to **28** point, **Bold**, **Italic**.
8. Change page orientation to **Landscape**.
9. Save, preview, print, and close.

Your Application Completed

Figure 3-11 Certificate document

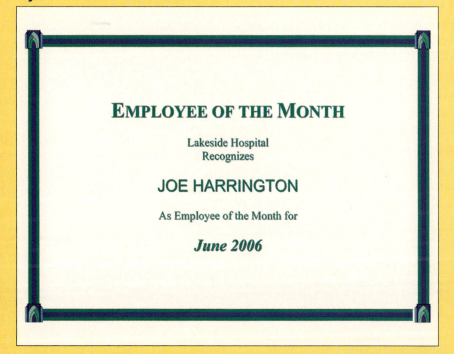

Integrated Simulation - Association for Hearing Impaired Children

Job 1 - Create Letterhead, Insert Clip Art, Key Letter, continued

Your Job Completed

Figure IS-1 Association Letter

Association for Hearing Impaired Children
Box 4590
Phoenix, AZ 85085-4800
602-555-4921

April 11, 2006

Parents of

To the Parents of

We are planning another fund-raiser to help pay the registration fees for thirteen children attending Camp Thunderhawk in Taos, New Mexico. We are holding a rummage sale at the Community Center on April 21 from 7 a.m. to 3 p.m. Our goal is to raise $1,000 to help us reach the $2,395 needed.

We would appreciate any items you could donate to the sale. Please have all items at the Community Center by 8:00 p.m., April 20. This would be a great time to get rid of unwanted items.

Thank you for all your hard work. Call me if you have any questions.

Sincerely,

[*Student Name*]

Introductory Word 101

Part 3 - Format Text and Paragraphs

Application 2 - Font Size and Color, Underline Style, Style, Format Painter, Indent, Highlight

Make changes to the guidelines for proofreading correspondence so it is more appealing to read.

What To Do

1. Open **IW App3-2** from the data files.
2. Save the document as **Guidelines**, followed by your initials.
3. Change all text to **Times New Roman**, **12** point.
4. Change title to **Tahoma**, **16** point, **Bold**, **Red**.
5. With the title still selected, add a red, double-wavy underline.
6. Apply **Heading 2** style to the heading *Check Facts*. Change the color to **Blue**.
7. Copy the format of the heading *Check Facts* to the other two headings.
8. Indent the first line of each paragraph **.5** inch.
9. Highlight the second sentence in the second paragraph **Yellow**.
10. Save, preview, print, and close.

Did You Know?

- The small lines on the tips of characters are called *serifs*. A font that has serifs, such as Times New Roman, is called a *serif font*. A font that does not have serifs, such as Arial, is called a *sans serif font*. Serif fonts are generally easier to read and are often used in the body of a document. Sans serif fonts are often used for titles, headings, and page numbers.

Your Application Completed

Figure 3-12 Guidelines document

Guidelines for Proofreading Correspondence

Check Accuracy

It is important to check the spelling and grammar usage of any document sent out by your company. Misspellings, punctuation errors, and incorrect information can embarrass and damage the credibility of an organization. If you are using a word processing program, do not rely entirely on the spell checker. It cannot determine the correct usage of words such as homonyms.

Be Consistent

Within a document, present the information logically and clearly. ==Use the same margins, indents, headings, hyphenation and spellings throughout the document.== Consistency in a document gives the reader a sense of comfort. Inconsistencies distract, causing your message to lose its impact.

Check Facts

It is important to use reliable sources to verify information such as names, addresses, telephone numbers and other facts. Do not rely on your memory.

Integrated Simulation - Association for Hearing Impaired Children

Job 1 - Create Letterhead, Insert Clip Art, Key Letter

The Association for Hearing Impaired Children is planning another fund-raiser. You need to send a letter to the parents with the details. You will integrate the document with a database file later to create form letters.

What To Do

1. Open a new Word document.
2. Change the top margin to **.5** inch.
3. Insert appropriate clip art. Center and size it as shown in Figure IS-1.
4. Key the letterhead below the clip art. See Figure IS-1. Change the font to **Franklin Gothic Heavy**. Change the font size of the first line to **14** point. If this font is not available, choose another appropriate font.
5. Key the letter as shown in Figure IS-1. Use **Times New Roman**, 11 point. You will enter the address information with a database later.
6. Save the document as **Association Letter** followed by your initials.
7. Print and close the document.

Key Terms

- Integration — Combining more than one program to complete a project.
- Source file — The file from which you are moving data.
- Destination file — The file to which you are moving data.

Computer Concept

- The easiest way to share data among applications is to cut and paste between applications. Other ways to integrate data are by linking it or embedding it.

(continued on next page)

Part 3 - Format Text and Paragraphs

Application 3 - Font, Font Size, Alignment, Vertical Alignment

A friend of yours will be married soon. She has asked you to help her design the wedding invitation.

What To Do

1. Open **IW App3-3** from the data files.
2. Save the document as **Wedding** followed by your initials.
3. Select all the text and set the font to **Edwardian Script IT**, **18** point, **Bold**. If this font is not available, choose another appropriate script font.
4. Center the text.
5. Vertically center the text.
6. Preview the document. Save, print, and close the document.

Your Application Completed

Figure 3-13 Wedding document

Did You Know?

- Click and Type is a feature used to insert text into a blank area of a document. You do not have to use spacing, alignment, or vertical alignment to position text where you want it. Just double-click in the document where you want to insert text. Use Help to learn how to turn on the Click and Type feature.

Extra Challenges

- Create invitations to the following events using font types that reflect the event.
  - Child's birthday party
  - Halloween Party
  - High School Graduation
  - Broadway play
  - Jazz concert

Integrated Simulation - Association for Hearing Impaired Children

Background

Camp Thunderhawk is a beautiful, rustic, adventure camp in the mountains of New Mexico. For the week of June 7-11, the camp will host children from ages 9 to 13, who are hearing impaired. Activities will include fishing, hiking, and horseback riding.

The Association for Hearing Impaired Children is an association dedicated to helping children with hearing disabilities. The Phoenix chapter is sponsoring thirteen children who will attend Camp Thunderhawk.

The children have already held one fund-raiser to earn money to go to the camp. In this Simulation, you will use what you have learned about Microsoft Word to create documents that will help you coordinate the group's fund-raising efforts and plans for going to camp.

In subsequent Simulations, you will use other Microsoft Office programs, integrated with one another, to assist the campers with preparations for going to camp as well as to work with Camp Thunderhawk staff members to prepare for the June camp.

Part 3 - Format Text and Paragraphs

Application 4 - Change Font, Alignment, Line Spacing, Margins

You are a summer intern at a local real estate office. The company has just launched a Web site listing of homes for sale. You have been asked to prepare the advertising copy for future postings to the company's Web site.

What To Do

1. Open **IW App3-4** from the data files.
2. Save the document as **Realtors Online** followed by your initials.
3. Format the title *Porch Light Realtors Online* to **Britannic Bold**, **20** point, and centered.
4. Format the subtitle *Advertise Your Home on the Internet* to **Britannic Bold**, **16** point, and centered.
5. Change the line spacing of the text so there is **6** pt spacing before each paragraph. Do not include the title and subtitle.
6. Change the left and right margins to **1**-inch.
7. Save, print, and close the document.

Your Application Completed

Figure 3-14 Realtors Online document

Hot Tip

- To add spaces between paragraphs, open the **Format** menu and choose **Paragraph**. You can add space before or after paragraphs by changing the values in the Before or After box of the Spacing area.

Did You Know?

- The Show/Hide command allows you to show formatting characters such as spaces, paragraph returns, and end-of-line markers. Viewing these markers will help you edit text. Click the **Show/Hide** button on the Standard toolbar to view these markers.

Extra Challenge

- Use the Help feature to learn how to save the document as a Web page.

Porch Light Realtors Online
Advertise Your Home on the Internet

One-time fee—Once you pay the initial cost of listing your house, Porch Lights will keep your ad active until your house sells.

Unlimited space—Unlike a newspaper ad, you can put as much information as you want on a Web site, including photos, detailed descriptions, and open house dates.

Reach potential buyers—Potential buyers from another city or state can do preliminary shopping over the Internet before they move.

Constantly available information—With a Web page listing, potential buyers can access information about your house at their convenience.

Low-cost advertising—A Web page listing is more cost-effective than traditional forms of advertising. For the price of a few newspaper ads, you can reach a larger audience, and never need to renew your listing.

Instant response—You can get an immediate response from an interested buyer on your Web site.

No computer required—Our Company will host your Web page on our computer. We will take care of all the technical aspects of listing your home for sale on the Internet.

Part 5 - Desktop Publishing

Application 5 - Key Text, Clip Art

You need to prepare a cover letter to accompany the Key Financial Diagram.

What To Do

1. Create a new Word document.
2. Key the cover letter shown in Figure 5-15.
3. Place your insertion point above the letterhead and insert an appropriate clip art. Key **key** in the search box.
4. Save the letter as **Key Cover Letter** followed by your initials.
5. Print and close the document.

Your Application Completed

Figure 5-15 Example Key Cover Letter

Key Financial Group
309 Third Street
Churchville, NY 14428
Telephone: (212) 555-7536

September 24, 2006

Glen H. Dickson
550 Cornell Street
Indianapolis, IN 46202

Dear Glen,

As promised, please find enclosed an analysis of your current investment portfolio. As you can see, your equity investments have performed very well. Given recent market trends, and since your daughter will be entering college in two years, I suggest we consider reallocating your assets.

I will call you to set up an appointment.

Best regards,

[Student's Name]

Enclosure

Introductory Word 98

Part 3 - Format Text and Paragraphs

Application 5 - Spelling and Grammar Check, Replace Text, Cut and Paste, Thesaurus, Change Font, Line Spacing, Font Effect, Style

As a camp counselor with word-processing experience, you have been asked to make changes to the camp's promotional brochure.

What To Do

Extra Challenge

- Experiment with different fonts, font effects, and font colors to change the appearance of the flyer.

Web Site

- Search the Internet for camps located in your area. Notice how these camps use fonts and other effects to get your attention.

1. Open **IW App3-5** from the data files.
2. Save the document as **Camp** followed by your initials.
3. Check the document for spelling and grammar errors. Make changes as needed.
4. Find the word *programs* and replace it with **activities** each time it occurs in the document.
5. Move the heading *Registration Information* and the paragraph that follows it to the end of the document.
6. Replace the word *spectacular* in the first paragraph with a synonym that makes sense in context.
7. Change the line spacing of the document to **1.5**.
8. Change the orientation to **Landscape**.
9. Change all text to **Green**.
10. Change the title *Camp Piney Ridge* to **Rockwell Extra Bold**, **28** point, **Brown**. Add the **Emboss** effect and **center**. (If the font is not available, chose another appropriate font.)
11. Change each of the headings to **Brown** with the **Heading 3** style.
12. Indent the last heading and paragraph one inch on each side and center the heading.
13. Center-align the document vertically on the page.
14. Preview and save the document.
15. Print and close the document.

(continued on next page)

Part 5 - Desktop Publishing

Application 4 - Key Text, Text Box

Prepare a diagram analyzing the investments of your client Glen Dickson.

What To Do

1. Open a new Word document.
2. Insert a pyramid diagram.
3. Key the text from Figure 5-14 in the triangle. (If you are working in Office XP, you will need to insert a level.)
4. Create the text boxes and arrows similar to those shown in Figure 5-14. Key text in text boxes.
5. Key text shown in Figure 5-14 below the diagram.
6. Save the document as **Key Financial Diagram** followed by your initials.
7. Print and close the document.

Your Application Completed

Figure 5-14 Key Financial Diagram

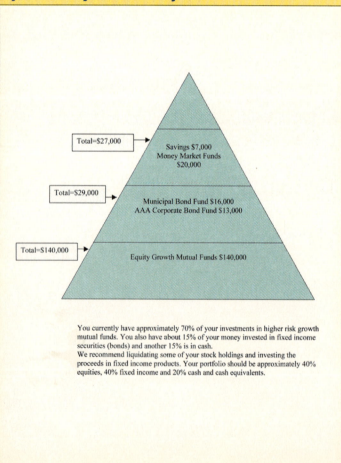

Hot Tips

- To insert a Pyramid diagram, open the **Insert** menu and choose **Diagram**. The Diagram Gallery appears. Click the **Pyramid**.
- To insert a Pyramid diagram in Office 2000, open the **Insert** menu and choose **Picture**. Click **AutoShapes** on the sub-menu. Click the **More AutoShapes** button on the AutoShapes toolbar. The More AutoShapes dialog box appears. Key **Pyramid** in the Search for clips box.

Part 3 – Format Text and Paragraphs

Application 5 - Spelling and Grammar Check, Replace Text, Cut and Paste, Thesaurus, Change Font, Line Spacing, Font Effect, Style, continued

Your Application Completed

Figure 3-15 Camp document

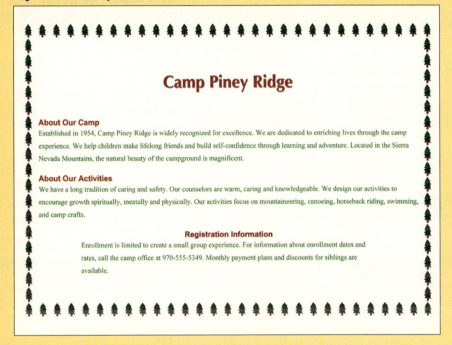

Part 5 - Desktop Publishing

Application 3 - Draw Tools, Change Font

A friend is selling his house. He asks you to create a poster to accompany information sheets listing the features of the house.

What To Do

1. Create the poster shown in Figure 5-13 using what you have learned in this Part. Follow the instructions shown in the figure.
2. Save the document as **House Sale Poster** followed by your initials.
3. Print and close the document.

Your Application Completed

Figure 5-13 House Sale Poster

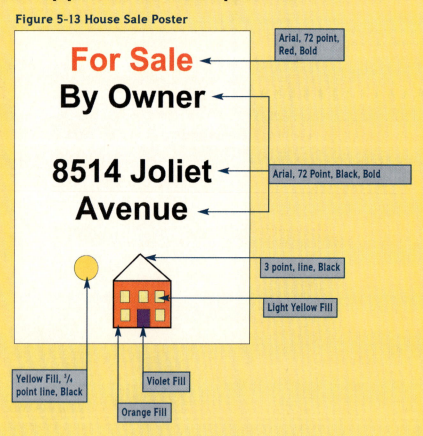

Extra Challenge

- Create a map to include with the birthday party invitation you created in the Application 2 Extra Challenge. The map should show directions from the school to your house.

Part 4

Working with Documents

Objectives

After completing this Part, you should be able to:
- Switch between two documents.
- Copy and paste between documents.
- Insert page breaks.
- Insert headers and footers.
- Apply bullet and numbering formats and create outline numbered lists.
- Set and modify tabs.
- Sort text.
- Insert and format tables.

Part 5 - Desktop Publishing

Application 2 - Clip Art, Page Border, Change Font

Your manager has asked you to create an invitation to the office holiday party.

What To Do

1. Open a new Word document.
2. Insert clip art with a holiday theme at approximately 1 ½ inches on the vertical ruler and 3 inches on the horizontal ruler. Resize and align the graphic to fit the document.
3. Key the text from Figure 5-12. Change the text to a color, font, and size of your choice.
4. Apply an appropriate page border.
5. Save the document as **Holiday Invitation** followed by your initials.
6. Print and close the document.

Your Application Completed

Figure 5-12 Example Holiday Invitation

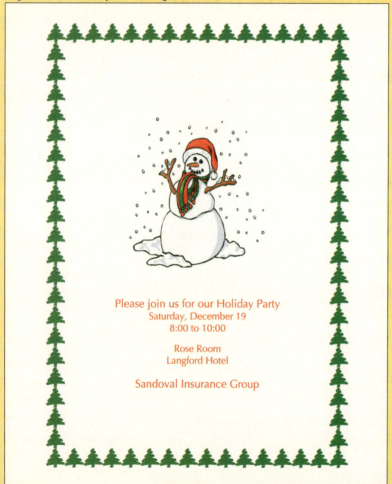

Teamwork

- As a class, make a list of the different holidays celebrated by your classmates, such as Thanksgiving, Hanukkah, Easter, Cinco de Mayo, etc. Create a greeting card celebrating one of these holidays. Be sure to use clip art and page borders.

Extra Challenge

- Create a birthday party invitation for one of your friends. The party will be at your house after school.

Part 4 - Working with Documents

Task 1 - Switch Between Documents, Copy and Paste Between Documents

What To Do

1. Open **IW Task4-1** from the data files. Save the document as **Financial Planning Final** followed by your initials.

2. Open **IW Task4-1a** from the data files. It becomes the active window. Save the document as **Financial Title 2** followed by your initials.

3. Notice that icons for both documents are displayed on the taskbar. See Figure 4-1. Change *[Student Name]* to your name.

Figure 4-1 Taskbar with buttons for open files

4. Click the **Financial Planning Final** button on the taskbar to make it the active window.

5. Select and copy the date.

6. Click **Financial Title 2** on the taskbar to display the document.

7. Move the insertion point to a new line after the existing text. Paste the copy of the date here.

8. Use the **Format Painter** to copy the format of the previous title page information to the date you just inserted.

9. Save, print, and close **Financial Title 2**. Leave the **Financial Planning Final** document open for the next Task.

Computer Concept

- When you open or create a new document, it is displayed on top of the document that is already open. The new document window becomes the active window, and an icon corresponding to the document is displayed on the taskbar. Click the taskbar icon to make the corresponding document the active window.

Hot Tip

- You can also use the Window menu to display the document you want.

Introductory Word 59

Part 5 - Desktop Publishing

Application 1 - Change Font, Alignment, Columns, Clip Art, Bullets, continued

Your Application Completed

Figure 5-11 PAWS Newsletter

Plains Animal Welfare & Shelter (P.A.W.S.)
4908 Lincoln Road
Abilene, Texas 79604
(915) 555-0200

About P.A.W.S.

Plains Animal Welfare & Shelter is a non-profit organization devoted to the shelter and care of homeless animals. We give all of our animals a thorough examination. This includes all required vaccinations, spaying and neutering. We also give cats a Feluk/FIV test. The adoption fees are $55.00 for dogs, and $40.00 for cats. Our operating hours are:

Monday-Friday—8:00 a.m. to 6:00 p.m.
Saturday—9:00 a.m. to 5:00 p.m.

We are in need of dedicated volunteers to:

- Exercise and groom the animals
- Make presentations at special events
- Help with fundraising activities
- Visit nursing homes with animals
- Maintain the web site.

To volunteer, please contact us at (915) 555-0200.

As a non-profit organization, we survive through the generous donations of organizations and individuals. In addition to financial donations, we are in need of the following items:

Leashes and collars
Pet toys
Stainless steel bowls
Cat and kitten food
Dog and puppy food
Newspapers

Thank you for your help!

Choosing a Puppy

Before you adopt a puppy, be sure to look him over carefully. Here are some specific things you should look for in choosing a healthy puppy.

Eyes - They should be clear and without discharge.

Ears - They should be clean, with no ear mites or infection. (Ear mites look like brown or black sand.)

Mouth - Tongue and gums should be pink and the bite correct.

Nose - It should not be runny. The puppy should not be sneezing.

Coat - It should be clean and glossy with no bare spots. The skin should not have any sores or dry or irritated patches.

Age - The puppy should be at least 8 weeks old and fully weaned.

Also, remember that puppies chew naturally because they are teething and they are curious. Keep forbidden items picked up and out of his reach. In addition, maintain a good supply of safe, appropriate chew toys.

Vaccination Costs
Cats and Dogs

- Rabies $10
- Distemper $15
- Leukemia $15
- FIP $12
- Parvo $15

Introductory Word 94

Part 4 - Working with Documents

Task 2 - Insert Page Break

What To Do

1. With the Financial Planning Final document open, switch to Normal View if necessary.
2. Insert a page break after the first paragraph under the *Setting Savings Goals* heading.
3. Preview the document to see the page break.
4. Close the preview window.
5. Save and leave the document open for the next Task.

Hot Tips

- To insert a page break, place the insertion point where you want the break inserted. Open the **Insert** menu and choose **Break**. The Break dialog box appears. In the Break types area, **Page break** should be selected. Click **OK**.
- To delete a page break, select the page break line and strike backspace or delete.

Computer Concept

- It is usually better to wait until you have finished keying and editing your document before inserting manual page breaks. Use Print Preview to help you determine the best place to insert a page break.

Introductory Word 60

Part 5 - Desktop Publishing

Application 1 - Change Font, Alignment, Columns, Clip Art, Bullets

You volunteer at PAWS (Plains Animal Welfare & Shelter). The director has asked you to prepare a newsletter to be distributed to the community. She has given you some information and asked you to format it into a one-page newsletter.

What To Do

1. Open **IW App5-1** from the data files.
2. Save the document as **PAWS Newsletter** followed by your initials.
3. Select the entire document and change the font to **Arial**.
4. Change the font of the name to **18** point, **Dark Blue**, **bold**. Change the font of the address and telephone number to **14** point, **Dark Blue**. Center the name, address and telephone number in the column.
5. Format the document in two columns with a line between them.
6. Format the headings *About P.A.W.S.*, *Choosing a Puppy*, and *Vaccination Costs* as **14** point, **Dark Blue**, **bold**. Center them in the columns.
7. Change the format of *Thank you for your help!* to **18** point, **Dark Blue**, centered.
8. Change the format of the operating hours and *Cats and Dogs* to **12** point, **bold**, centered.
9. Apply bullets to the volunteer jobs available, the list of needed items, and the list of vaccinations.
10. Apply the **bold**, **italic**, and **underline** styles to set off the items under *Choosing a Puppy*.
11. Place a **3** point Dark Blue border around the sentence beginning with *To volunteer*. Shade it with **Pale Blue**. Change the font size to **14**.
12. Insert appropriate clip art above the title *Choosing a Puppy*. Key **dog** in the search text box.
13. Preview the document. Adjust the spacing within the document if necessary.
14. Save, print, and close the document.

(continued on next page)

Teamwork

- With a classmate, create a newsletter about your class. Decide the name of the newsletter, what information should be included, a page design and attractive clip art. Have the class vote for their favorite.

Extra Challenge

- Use the Help feature to learn how to download and insert clip art from the Internet. Replace the clip art in the PAWS Newsletter with the clip art from the Internet.

Part 4 - Working with Documents

Task 3 - Insert Header, Footer, Page Numbers

What To Do

1. With the Financial Planning Final document open, move the insertion point to the beginning of the document.
2. Open the **View** menu and choose **Header and Footer**. The Header and Footer toolbar appears. Study the function of each button as shown in Figure 4-2.

Figure 4-2 Header and Footer toolbar

3. Key your name in the header. Your name should be left-aligned.
4. Move the insertion point to the right side of the header. Insert a page number in the header. Notice the number 2 is automatically inserted on the second page.
5. Switch to the footer. Move the insertion point to the center of the footer. Key **Get a Grip on Your Money**.
6. Close the Header and Footer toolbar.
7. Open the **File** menu and choose **Page Setup**. On the Layout tab of the Page Setup dialog box, key **.70** in the Footer box. (In Office 2000, use the Margins tab in the Page Setup dialog box.) Click **OK**.
8. Preview the document.
9. Save, print, and close the document.

(continued on next page)

Key Terms

- Header — Text printed at the top of the page.
- Footer — Text printed at the bottom of the page.

Hot Tips

- To insert headers and footers, open the **View** menu and choose **Header and Footer**. The Header and Footer toolbar appears which contains buttons to insert dates, page numbers and switch between the header and footer.
- To insert a page number, click the **Insert Page Number** button on the Header and Footer toolbar.
- To insert the current date, click the **Insert Date** button on the Header and Footer toolbar.
- To move the insertion point from header to footer or from footer to header, click the **Switch Between Header and Footer** button on the Header and Footer toolbar.

Part 5 - Desktop Publishing

Task 10 - Add Chart

What To Do

1. Open **IW Task5-10** from the data files.
2. Save the document as **Organization Chart** followed by your initials.
3. Place the insertion point centered above the letterhead.
4. Insert appropriate clip art. Key **laboratory** in the search box. Resize it to approximately 1 inch by 1 inch.
5. Insert four blank lines below the last line of text.
6. Insert an organization chart in the document comparable to that shown in Figure 5-10.
7. Key the text shown in Figure 5-10 in each box. Format the text as **10** point.
8. Preview the document.
9. Save, print, and close the document.

Your Task Completed

Figure 5-10 Organization Chart

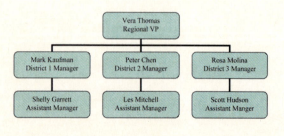

Hot Tips

- To insert an organization chart, open the **Insert** menu and choose **Diagram**. Click **Organizational Chart** in the Diagram Gallery dialog box.
- To insert an organization chart in Office 2000, open the **Insert** menu and chose **Object**, then click the **Create New** tab. In the Object type box, click **MS Organization Chart 2.0** and then click **OK**.

Introductory Word 92

Part 4 - Working with Documents

Task 3 - Insert Header, Footer, Page Numbers, continued

Your Task Completed

Figure 4-3 Financial Planning Final

[Student Name]   1

                                                        May 28, 2004

GET A GRIP ON YOUR MONEY

Introduction
   One of the most valuable lessons a teenager can learn is how to handle

finances. Learning financial planning basics such as making a budget, saving for

short- and long-term goals, and avoiding debt will lead to a solid financial future

and greater chance of achieving your dreams.

Control Spending with a Budget
   The first step in planning is to create a budget. A budget will help you determine your current income and expenses. Income is the money you make from different sources. While you are a teenager, your income will probably be wages from a part-time job or an allowance from your parents. Expenses are items on which you spend your money. Teenagers typically spend money on such things as going to the movies, new clothes, eating out and maybe even a car payment.

Subtract your expenses from your income. You should have a positive balance. A positive balance means your income is more than your expenses. If you have a negative balance, you are spending more money than you earn. This means you are spending money you do not have, which could lead to Debt problems. A budget will help you control your spending. Keep a record of everything you spend for a month or two. You might be surprised to learn just how much you spend on junk food!

Setting Savings Goals
You need to set goals to be sure you are spending your money on items you want. Setting goals forces you to make choices. You should have short-term goals such as saving for a stereo, sports equipment, or tickets to a concert. You should also have long-term goals like saving for a car or college.

Get a Grip on Your Money

(continued on next page)   **Introductory Word 62**

Part 5 - Desktop Publishing

Task 9 - Add Text to Drawings

What To Do

1. With Park Map open, select the pond.
2. Key **Shady Elms Pond** in the oval. Center the text and format as **Times New Roman**, **18** point, centered, **White**.
3. Key **City Warehouse**, **Greer Truck Stop**, and **Liberty Autos** in the three small rectangles. Center the text and format it as **Times New Roman**, **14** point, centered, **White**.
4. Key **Safari Park** in the large square. Format as **Times New Roman**, **24** point, centered, **White**.
5. Create a text box **.5** inch by **2** inches to label *Highway 27*. Place the text box in the same position shown on the map in Figure 5-9. Format the text as **Times New Roman**, **14** point, centered, **Bold**.
6. Create text boxes for *Jefferson Avenue*, *Highland Road*, and *Route 554* as shown on the map. Format text the same as *Highway 27*.
7. Preview the document. Make adjustments as needed.
8. Save, print, and close the document.

Hot Tip

- One way to add text to drawings is to right-click in the object. Choose **Add Text** on the shortcut menu. Key and format your text. Click outside the object to deselect it.
- To add a text box, click the **Text Box** button on the Drawing toolbar or open the **Insert** menu and choose **Text Box**. A crosshair pointer appears. Position the pointer where you want the text box to appear; then click and drag to create a text box.

Introductory Word 91

Part 4 - Working with Documents

Task 3 - Insert Header, Footer, Page Numbers, continued

Figure 4-3 Financial Planning Final (continued)

[Student Name]   2

After setting your goals, you need to develop a plan to achieve them. Look at your budget to determine what is necessary. For example, you can bring your lunch from home one day a week instead of going out to eat. This could save five dollars a week. Although this does not sound like much, five dollars a week adds up to $260 a year. This is the price of a stereo. If you invest that $5 earning 8% a year, then that five-dollar hamburger would be worth $3,683 in ten years! If you continued saving a hamburger a week for the next 50 years, you will have accumulated $158,635!

Dangers of Credit Cards and Debt
Too many young people get into trouble with credit cards. Instead of saving to purchase something they want, many people borrow the money. Borrowing money results in debt. Debt results in paying interest. For example, you take a trip to Europe that costs $1,500. Instead of saving the money to pay for the trip, you charge it to a credit card. If you only pay $50 a month toward the credit card bill, it would take you three years to pay off the debt. You would also pay over $400 in interest. If you made only the minimum payments, it would take you 17 _ years to pay off the debt and you would have paid over $1,800 in interest on a $1,500 purchase!

It is important to remember: You should not charge anything you cannot pay for that month. If you get into trouble paying your credit cards, you could damage your credit rating. Prospective employers and banks check credit ratings. Delinquent payments on credit cards show irresponsible behavior. It could prevent you from getting a job or a loan for a car.

Conclusion
It is important to learn good money management at a young age. The good habits you develop as a teenager will continue as an adult. Being able to stick to a budget, set and achieve savings goals, and stay out of debt demonstrates self-discipline and responsibility. Good financial planning paves the way to a sound financial future and a happier life.

Get a Grip on Your Money

Part 5 - Desktop Publishing

Task 8 - Add Color, Line Styles to Objects

What To Do

1. With Park Map open, select the oval on the map. Fill the oval with the color **Blue**.
2. Select the square on your drawing. Fill the square with the color **Lime**.
3. Select each rectangle on your drawing, and fill them with the color **Brown**.
4. Select the line labeled *Highway 27* on your map. Change the width to **4 ½**-point thick line and the color **Red**.
5. Select the square. Change the line around the square to **6**-point thick line and the color **Green**.
6. Save and leave the document open for the next Task.

Hot Tips

- To change the color of an object, select the object you want to fill. Click the **Fill Color** button on the Drawing toolbar. Choose a color from the color box.
- To change the color of a line, select the line you want to change. Click the **Line Color** button and choose a color from the color box.
- To change the line style, select the line you want to change. Click the **Line Style** button on the Drawing toolbar and choose a line style from the Line Style menu.

Introductory Word 90

Part 4 - Working with Documents

Task 4 - Bulleted and Numbered Lists, Outline Numbered Lists

What To Do

1. Open **IW Task4-4** from the data files.
2. Save the document as **Outline** followed by your initials.
3. Bullet the four items under *Income Sources*.
4. Number the four items under *Payroll Deductions*.
5. Place the insertion point on the blank line below the heading *Employment Benefits*.
6. Key the outline numbered list that follows. Use the **Increase Indent** button and the **Decrease Indent** button to create a multilevel list. Use the Bullets and Numbering dialog box to select the format that matches what is shown.

1) **Insurance**
   a) **Medical**
   b) **Life**
   c) **Dental**
   d) **Disability**
2) **Vacation**
   a) **Holidays**
   b) **Personal Days**
3) **Leave**
   a) **Sick**
   b) **Emergency**
   c) **Family**

7. Save, print, and close the document.

Key Terms

- Bullet — A character or symbol placed before text, usually in a list, to add emphasis.
- Outline Numbered List — A list with two or more levels of bullets or numbering.

Hot Tips

- To create a numbered or bulleted list, select the text and open the **Format** menu. Choose **Bullets and Numbering**. Select either the Bulleted tab or Numbered tab to choose a bullet or numbering format. You can also click the **Bullets** button or **Numbering** button on the Formatting toolbar.
- To create an outline numbered list, open the **Format** menu and choose **Bullets and Numbering**. Click the Outline Numbered tab and select an outline format. Click the **Increase Indent** and **Decrease Indent** buttons on the Formatting toolbar to build the multilevel list.

(continued on next page)

Part 5 - Desktop Publishing

Task 7 - Edit Drawings

What To Do

1. With Park Map open, draw a rectangle similar to *City Warehouse* on the map shown in Figure 5-9.
2. With the rectangle still selected, make three copies of the rectangle.
3. With the last rectangle still selected, drag the rectangle to the right so it is in the same position as *Liberty Autos*.
4. Select the next rectangle and drag it to the same position as *Greer Truck Stop* on the map.
5. Select the last rectangle and drag it to the same position as *Safari Park* on the map. Use the handles to create a square 2 inches by 2 inches.
6. Save and leave the document open for the next Task.

Hot Tips

- To edit a drawing object, click on the object to select it. Sizing handles appear around the object. Drag one of the handles inward or outward to make the object smaller or larger. Select and press Delete or Backspace to delete an object.
- Cut, copy, and paste objects the same way you do text. The Cut and Copy commands place a copy of the selected image on the Clipboard. Pasting an object from the Clipboard places the object in your drawing. To paste more than one object, click the Paste button.
- To move an object, click on the object to select it. Press and hold the mouse button while you drag the object to its new location.

Part 4 - Working with Documents

Task 4 - Bulleted and Numbered Lists, Outline Numbered Lists, continued

Your Task Completed

Figure 4-4 Outline

Income Sources
    Salary
    Interest Income
    Contract Work
    Dividends

Payroll Deductions
    1. Social Security
    2. FICA
    3. Insurance
    4. Retirement

Employment Benefits
1) Insurance
    a) Medical
    b) Life
    c) Dental
    d) Disability
2) Vacation
    a) Holidays
    b) Personal Days
3) Leave
    a) Sick
    b) Emergency
    c) Family

Part 5 - Desktop Publishing

Task 6 - Draw Graphics, continued

Figure 5-9 Park Map

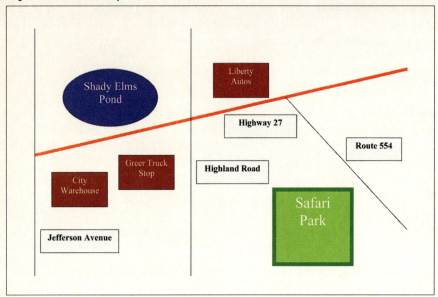

5. Draw an oval about 1 ½ inches tall and 2 ½ inches wide. Place the oval in the upper-left side of the document positioned similar to Shady Elms Pond.

6. Draw a line from the upper-left corner to the lower-left corner positioned similar to Jefferson Avenue.

7. Create the other roads on the map. Be sure to click the Line button each time you draw a line.

8. Preview your document.

9. Save the document as **Park Map** followed by your initials. Leave the document open for the next Task.

Part 4 - Working with Documents

Task 5 - Tabs, Sort

What To Do

1. Open **IW Task4-5** from the data files.
2. Save the document as **Equipment** followed by your initials.
3. Explore the tab stops available by either clicking on the tab button at the left side of the ruler bar or by opening the Tabs dialog box. Tabs can be left-aligned, right-aligned, centered, or aligned at the decimal point. See Table 4-1.

Table 4-1 Common tab stops

Tab	Tab Name	Function
L	Left Tab stop	Left-aligns selected text at the point indicated on the horizontal ruler. This is the default tab.
┘	Right Tab stop	Right-aligns selected text at the point indicated on the horizontal ruler. This is useful for aligning page numbers in a table of contents.
┴	Center Tab stop	Centers selected text at the point indicated on the horizontal ruler. This is used with titles or announcements.
⊥	Decimal Tab stop	Aligns selected text on the decimal point at the point indicated on the horizontal ruler. This is helpful when preparing price lists, invoices, or menus.

4. Select all the data except the title.
5. Set a left tab marker at the 1.5-inch mark. Be sure to clear all previous markers.
6. Set a decimal tab marker at the 5.75-inch mark with a dotted leader.
7. Sort the list in ascending alphabetic order.
8. Save, print, and close the document.

Your Task Completed

Figure 4-5 Equipment

```
                    COMPUTER EQUIPMENT

         CPU 2 GHz..........................................350.00
         DVD-RW/CD-RW Drive...........................240.00
         Graphics Card 128 MB...........................185.00
         Hard Drive 100 GB................................200.00
         Keyboard...............................................55.00
         Mouse.................................................. 45.00
         RAM 512 MB........................................ 125.00
         Sound Card..........................................175.00
         Speakers..............................................165.00
         Super VGA Color Monitor 21"..................415.00
         Telephone Modem 56K............................75.00
```

Key Terms

- **Tabs** — Mark the place where the insertion point will stop when the Tab key is struck.
- **Sort** — Arranges a list of words or numbers in ascending order (A to Z; smallest to largest) or in descending order (Z to A; largest to smallest).

Hot Tips

- To set tabs, open the **Format** menu and choose **Tabs**. The Tabs dialog box appears. Key the tab stop positions and the tab alignment. Click **Set** to set the tabs. You can also set a tab by clicking the tab button at the far left of the ruler. Select the tab you want and click on the ruler where you want to set the tab.
- To remove a tab, drag it off the ruler.
- To sort text in a document, open the **Tables** menu and choose **Sort**.

Part 5 - Desktop Publishing

Task 6 - Draw Graphics

What To Do

1. Open a new Word document. Change the orientation to landscape.
2. Display the Drawing toolbar if necessary. See Figure 5-8.

Figure 5-8 Drawing toolbar

3. Review the buttons available on the Drawing toolbar. Table 5-1 describes the functions of a number of these buttons.

Table 5-1 Drawing tools

Button	Name	Function
□	Rectangle	Draws rectangles and squares. To use, click and hold the mouse button; then drag to draw. To create a perfect square, hold down the Shift key as you drag.
╲	Line	Draws straight lines. To use, position the pointer where you want the line to begin; then click and hold the mouse button, and drag to where you want the line to end.
○	Oval	Draws ovals and circles. To use, click and hold the mouse button; then drag to draw the oval or circle. To create a perfect circle, hold down the Shift key as you drag.
▶	Select Objects	Lets you select and manipulate objects. To use, click on the arrow. The insertion point assumes the pointer shape.

4. Study the map in Figure 5-9. You will be drawing a map similar to this one.

Hot Tip

- To access the drawing toolbar, open the **View** menu and click **Toolbars**. Click **Drawing** on the submenu. Or you can click the **Drawing** button on the Standard toolbar to display the Drawing toolbar.

(continued on next page)

Introductory Word 87

Part 4 - Working with Documents

Task 6 - Insert Table

What To Do

1. Open **IW Task4-6** from the data files.
2. Save the document as **Voting Memo** followed by your initials.
3. Position the insertion point on the second blank line below the second paragraph.
4. Insert a table with **3** columns and **5** rows.
5. Key the data into the table as shown in Figure 4-6.

Figure 4-6 Data for the table

Precinct	Place	Address
1	G. W. Carver Elementary	4590 Pagosa Avenue
2	Jefferson Junior High	3501 Sullivan Boulevard
3	Lancaster High	1200 Belknap Road
4	Creston High	1780 Ogallala Road

6. Save and leave the document open for the next Task.

Key Term

- Table — An arrangement of data in rows and columns, similar to a spreadsheet.

Hot Tip

- To create a table, open the **Table** menu and point to **Insert**. Click **Table** on the submenu. The Insert Table dialog box appears. You can also click the **Insert Table** button on the Standard toolbar.

Part 5 - Desktop Publishing

Task 5 - Page Borders, continued

Your Task Completed

Figure 5-7 Example *Wedding2* **invitation**

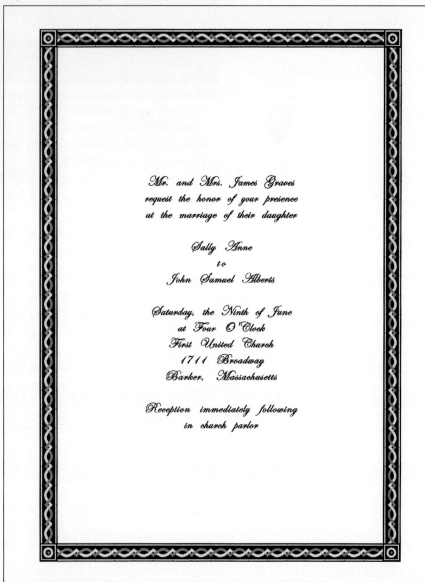

Part 4 - Working with Documents

Task 7 - Format, Revise Table

What To Do

1. With the Voting Memo document open, select the first row and center the text.
2. With the first row still selected, change the font size to **14** point, **Bold**.
3. Select the first column and center the text.
4. Drag the left border of the *Precinct* column to the right to reduce the column width. The column should be only slightly wider than the column heading.
5. Insert a new row below *Precinct 4*.
6. In the new row, key the following data:

    5   Lincoln Elementary   900 Holly Avenue
7. Center the table.
8. Save and leave the document open for the next Task.

Hot Tips

- To select a row, position the pointer to the left of the row (outside the table) and click.
- To select a column, position the pointer above the column until the pointer changes to a downward-pointing arrow and click.
- To insert a row, select a row and choose **Insert** on the **Table** menu. Choose *Rows Above* or *Rows Below* depending on where you want the row to appear.
- To insert a column, select a column and choose **Insert** on the **Table** menu. Choose *Columns to the Left* or *Columns to the Right* depending on where you want the column to appear.
- To center a table, select the table. Open the **Table** menu and choose **Table Properties**. Click on the Tables tab and choose **Center**.

Introductory Word 68

Part 5 - Desktop Publishing

Task 5 - Page Borders

What To Do

1. Open **IW Task5-5** from the data files.
2. Save the file as **Wedding2** followed by your initials.
3. Use the Page Border tab of the Borders and Shading dialog box to choose a predefined art border appropriate for a wedding invitation. See Figure 5-6.

Figure 5-6 Page Border tab in Borders and Shading dialog box

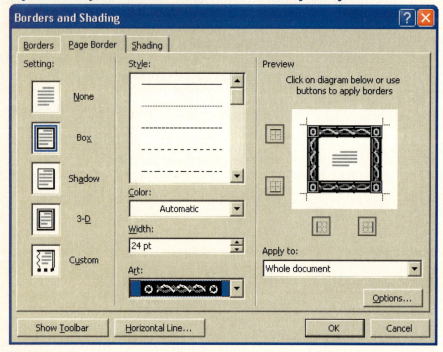

4. Specify that the border should be measured from the text.
5. Preview the document and then close the preview.
6. Save, print, and close the document.

Hot Tips

- To add borders to pages, open the **Format** menu and choose **Borders and Shading**. On the Page Border tab, you can choose the setting, line style, width, and color of border you want. In the Art box, you can choose predefined art borders.
- To specify where the border should be measured from, click the **Options** button on the Page Border tab. In the Measure from box specify **Text** or **Edge of page**.

(continued on next page)

Introductory Word 85

Part 4 - Working with Documents

Task 8 - Modify a Table, Add Borders, Shading

What To Do

1. With the Voting Memo document open, insert a row above the first row.
2. In the new row, key **Cast Your Vote!** and merge the cells. Center the text if necessary. The new text should be centered across the entire table.
3. Change the height of each row to **.30**.
4. Vertically align the data in the center of the cells.
5. Change the color of the borders to Red. Shade the table Pale Blue.
6. Save, print, and close the document.

Your Task Completed

Figure 4-7 Voting Memo

MEMORANDUM

To: All members, Lancaster Chamber of Commerce
From: Dinah Elliot-Young, Chairman
Date: January 17, 2006
Subject: Voting on January 31

Saturday, January 31, is the scheduled run-off election for the mayor of Lancaster. The Chamber of Commerce is encouraging each registered voter to go to the polls and participate in one of our most valuable rights—the right to vote.

Please make your plans now to vote between 7 a.m. and 7 p.m. on January 31. I also urge you to use your influence to encourage your friends, neighbors, and fellow workers to vote. Following are the precinct voting places:

Cast Your Vote!		
Precinct	**Place**	**Address**
1	G. W. Carver Elementary	4590 Pagosa Avenue
2	Jefferson Junior High	3501 Sullivan Boulevard
3	Lancaster High	1200 Belknap Road
4	Creston High	1780 Ogallala Road
5	Lincoln Elementary	900 Holly Avenue

Your individual involvement in this election can affect your future as well as the future of Lancaster. Thanks for your participation.

Hot Tips

- To merge cells, open the **Table** menu and choose **Merge Cells.**
- To change the width or height of a row or column using the Table Properties dialog box, select the row or column you want to change. Open the **Table** menu and choose **Table Properties**. Click the **Row** tab to change the height or the **Column** tab to change the width.
- To vertically align text in a cell, click the **Cell** tab in the Table Properties dialog box. Choose the alignment in the Vertical alignment section.
- To change the color of the borders and add shading, select the table. Open the **Table** menu and choose **Table Properties**. Click the **Table** tab and then click the **Borders and Shading** button. The Borders and Shading dialog box opens. Click the **Borders** tab to change the borders. Click the **Shading** tab to change the shading.

Part 5 - Desktop Publishing

Task 4 - Select, Resize Clip Art, continued

Your Task Completed

Figure 5-5 Example PTA Newsletter

STRATFORD HIGH
PTA Newsletter
September, 2006

From Our Principal:

The opening of school always brings excitement and enthusiasm to the teachers and staff at Stratford High School. We are eager to get to know your children. As you know, we at Stratford High are committed to educational excellence and the preparation of your child for the future. One way you can help as a parent is to stay involved with your child's education. Please feel free to visit the school at anytime and do not hesitate to call me if you have any questions. Please plan to attend the Parent Orientation and Open House on September 12th. I am looking forward to a great school year. John English

From the PTA President:

Welcome Back! We all know the importance of being involved with our children's education. One way to do this is by joining the PTA. The Stratford PTA has a great tradition of hard work and great accomplishments. With your ideas and involvement, we will continue to provide the greatest advantages possible for our children. For questions and membership information, please call me at 452-0094. Sandy Long

Fall Festival – October 25th

Plans are underway for the Annual Fall Festival. This year's festival promises to be better than ever with more booths, a bigger food court and tons of fun - the only thing that is missing is your help. Please call Renée Allen at 452- 7839 for more information and to volunteer to help.

New Faculty

We are pleased to welcome the following new faculty and staff to Stratford:
- Danielle Collins – Sophomore English
- Ross Woodall – Science
- Cassandra Arnold – Senior Math
- Benjamin Owen – Art
- Brad Mackey - Counselor

Stratford T-shirts for Sale

Show your Stratford spirit by wearing a Stratford Spirit shirt. T-shirts are available in a variety of colors and sizes for only $9.00. Contact the PTA for information.

College Entrance Exams

High School counselors will be sending you information about college entrance exams. Testing sessions will begin the Saturday October 19th. Your child can register either by mail or online. After school tutorials will begin on Monday, September 16th.

Dates to Remember
September 12th   Open House 6:30 p.m.
September 20th   Football Game – Westbrook High 7:00 p.m.
September 23rd   Volunteer Orientation – 2:00 p.m.
September 27th   Football Game – Monroe High – 7:00 p.m.
September 29th   PTA Meeting – 6:30 p.m.
October 11th   Homecoming - Fullerton High 7:00 p.m.
October 18th   Football Game - Brown High 7:00 p.m.

The editors of the Stratford PTA Newsletter invite parents and students to submit articles for publication in the newsletter. The stories should be about Stratford students, teachers or happenings at school. Put your news story in the PTA box in the office. Remember to include your name, grade and phone number.

Part 4 - Working with Documents

Application 1 - Tabs, Sort

Your supervisor has asked you to create a chart of overnight shipping rates to post in the mailroom.

What To Do

1. Open **IW App4-1** from the data files.
2. Save the document as **Shipping Rates** followed by your initials.
3. Place the insertion point two lines below the paragraph.
4. Set left tabs at **1.75** inches, **3** inches, and **4.75** inches.
5. Key the headings **Company**, **Cost**, **Weight Limit**, and **Delivery Time** in bold using the tabs. Strike **Enter**.
6. Clear all tabs. Set a decimal tab with dot style leaders at **1.94** inches.
7. Set a center tab with dot style leaders at **3.5** inches.
8. Set a right tab with dot style leaders at **5.63** inches.
9. Using the tabs just set, key the following information:

    | **Zippy** | $14.50 | 2 lbs. | 10:00 a.m. |
    | **Pronto** | $9.99 | 10 oz. | 12:30 p.m. |
    | **Lightning** | $11.75 | 1 lb. 4 oz. | 1:00 p.m. |
    | **Speed Air** | $12.95 | 3 lbs. | 3:00 p.m. |

10. Sort the list in ascending order.
11. Indent the first line of the first paragraph **.5** inch.
12. Change the line spacing in the shipping rates table to **1.5** lines.
13. Save, print, and close the document.

Extra Challenges

- Create the shipping rate table using the buttons in the tab box at the far left of the ruler instead of the Tabs dialog box.
- Sort the chart by price in descending order. Use the Help feature if necessary.

(continued on next page)

Part 5 - Desktop Publishing

Task 4 - Select, Resize Clip Art

What To Do

1. With PTA Newsletter open select and center the Fall clipart.
2. With the clip art still selected, use the handles to resize it to approximately 1 ½ inches tall by 2 inches wide. Figure 5-4 illustrates the location of the sizing handles.

Figure 5-4 Selection rectangle with sizing handles

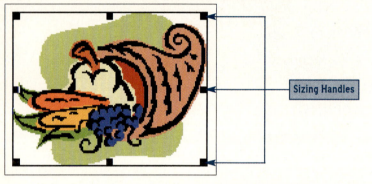

3. Select and center the school clip art.
4. With the clip art still selected, use the handles to resize it to approximately 2 inches tall by 3 inches wide.
5. Preview the document. The heading *New Faculty* should be at the top of the second column. Adjust the line spacing or the size of the clip art if necessary.
6. Save, print, and close the document. Leave Word open for the next Task.

Key Terms

- Selection rectangle — The box that appears around a graphic when you select it.
- Sizing handle — The small squares that appear on the selection rectangle that allow you to resize a graphic.

Hot Tips

- To edit clip art, click on the clip art to select it. A selection rectangle with sizing handles appears around the clip art. To resize the clip art, drag the handle inward or outward to make the object smaller or larger.
- To center clip art, click on the clip art to select it. Click the **Center** button on the Formatting toolbar.

(continued on next page)

Part 4 - Working with Documents

Application 1 - Tabs, Sort, continued

Your Application Completed

Figure 4-8 Shipping Rates

Overnight Shipping

Please consult this table to determine which overnight shipping company would be most cost effective when you mail a document. Consider the weight of your package and necessary delivery time when making a decision. Packing labels and envelopes are located on the shelf next to the copier.

Company	Cost	Weight Limit	Delivery Time
Lightning	$11.75	1 lb. 4 oz.	1:00 p.m.
Pronto	$9.99	10 oz.	12:30 p.m.
Speed Air	$12.95	3 lbs.	3:00 p.m.
Zippy	$14.50	2 lbs.	10:00 a.m.

Part 5 - Desktop Publishing

Task 3 - Insert Clip Art

What To Do

1. With PTA Newsletter open, place the insertion point above the heading *Fall Festival—October 25th*.
2. Insert appropriate clip art. Key **Fall** in the search box.
3. Place the insertion point above the heading *College Entrance Exams*.
4. Insert appropriate clip art. Key **School** in the search box.
5. Save and leave the document open for the next Task.

Key Term

- Clip art — Graphics that are already drawn and are available for use in documents.

Hot Tip

- To insert clip art, open the **Insert** menu and choose **Picture**. Choose **Clip Art** on the submenu. In the search text box, key a word or words that describe the kind of clip art you wish to insert.

Computer Concept

- Clip art actually includes other media types besides clip art, such as photographs, movies, and sounds. You can also connect to the Web to access more images.

Part 4 - Working with Documents

Application 2 - Copy Between Documents, Footer, Insert Page Number

Continue to revise the Guidelines for Proofreading Documents.

What To Do

1. Open **IW App4-2** from the data files. Save the document as **Guidelines Final** followed by your initials.
2. Open **IW App4-2a** from the data files.
3. Select all the text and copy it.
4. Switch to the Guidelines Final document and paste the text below the paragraph under the *Be Consistent* heading.
5. Bullet and sort the list of spelling words in ascending order.
6. Insert a page break after the spelling list.
7. Insert the company name, **Key Financial Group,** left-aligned in the header. Insert the date right-aligned in the header.
8. Insert the page number right-aligned in the footer.
9. On the Layout tab of the Page Setup dialog box, key **.70** in the Footer box. (In Office 2000, use the Margins tab in the Page Setup dialog box.)
10. Save, print, and close the document. Close the IW App4-2a document.

Did You Know?

- When Word automatically inserts a page break it is called a soft break or automatic page break. When you manually insert a page break it is called a hard or manual page break.
- You can change the bullet character to a different graphic or picture by clicking the Customize button on the Bulleted tab in the Bullets and Numbering dialog box.

Extra Challenge

- Make a list of your three favorite songs, three favorite books, and three favorite movies. Choose a different bullet to symbolize each list. (*Hint:* The Webdings font and the Wingdings fonts have many fun characters you can use.)

(continued on next page)

Part 5 - Desktop Publishing

Task 2 - Paragraph Borders, Shading

What To Do

1. With PTA Newsletter open, select the heading **Dates to Remember** and the dates below it.
2. Open the Borders and Shading dialog box and select the Borders tab if necessary. See Figure 5-2.

Figure 5-2 Borders tab in Borders and Shading dialog box

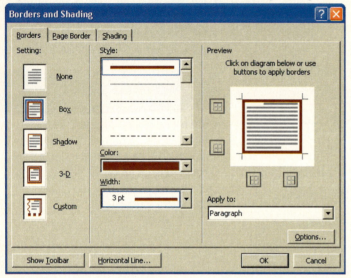

3. Insert a Dark Red border with a **3**-point width around the paragraph.
4. Select the **Shading** tab. Shade the paragraph with Gold. See Figure 5-3.

Figure 5-3 Shading tab in Borders and Shading dialog box

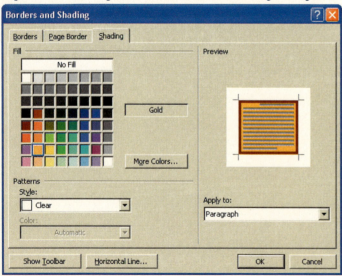

5. Save and leave the document open for the next Task.

Key Terms

- Borders — Lines placed around text for emphasis or decoration.
- Shading — Adding colors or grays to emphasize text.

Hot Tips

- To add borders to a paragraph, select the text you want to border. Open the **Format** menu and choose **Borders and Shading**. In the Borders tab of the Borders and Shading dialog box, specify the border setting, style, color, and width of line.
- To add shading to a paragraph, select the text you want to shade. Open the **Format** menu and choose **Borders and Shading**. In the Shading tab, specify the shading, pattern, and color you want.

Introductory Word 81

Part 4 – Working with Documents

Application 2 - Copy Between Documents, Footer, Insert Page Number, continued

Your Application Completed

Figure 4-9 Guidelines Final

Key Financial Group   7/5/04

Guidelines for Proofreading Correspondence

Check Accuracy

It is important to check the spelling and grammar usage of any document sent out by your company. Misspellings, punctuation errors, and incorrect information can embarrass and damage the credibility of an organization. If you are using a word processing program, do not rely entirely on the spell checker. It cannot determine the correct usage of words such as homonyms. Use resources to help you correct grammar and punctuation errors. When in doubt, look it up. Attending seminars or classes on editing can sharpen your skills and make you a more valuable employee.

Check Spelling

The following words are commonly misspelled:

- Address
- Business
- Calendar
- Environment
- February
- Grammar
- Manual
- Noticeable
- Receive

1

(continued on next page)

Part 5 - Desktop Publishing

Task 1 - Create Columns, Format Text

What To Do

1. Open **IW Task5-1** from the data files.
2. Save the document as **PTA Newsletter** followed by your initials.
3. Place the insertion point at the beginning of the document if necessary
4. Format the text into two columns using the Columns dialog box. See Figure 5-1. Set the spacing between the columns to **0.6** inch and insert a line between the two columns.

Figure 5-1 Columns dialog box

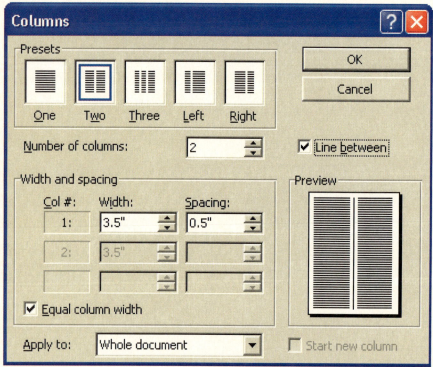

5. Justify the text in the columns. (Be sure to select all the text first.)
6. Change the title *Stratford High* to **36** point, centered.
7. Change the subtitle *PTA Newsletter* to **20** point, centered.
8. Change the date to **16** point, centered.
9. Preview the document to view the columns.
10. Save and leave the document open for the next Task.

Key Term

- Desktop publishing — The process of combining text to create attractive documents.

Hot Tips

- To format a document in columns, open the **Format** menu and chose **Columns**. The Columns dialog box appears. In this dialog box, specify the number of columns you want. You can also click the **Columns** button on the Standard toolbar.
- To insert a line between the columns, click the **Line between** box in the Columns dialog box.

Computer Concept

- Unless you specify otherwise, all columns will be equal width.

Introductory Word 80

Part 4 - Working with Documents

Application 2 - Copy Between Documents, Footer, Insert Page Number, continued

Figure 4-9 Guidelines Final, continued

> Key Financial Group   7/5/04
>
> **Be Consistent**
> Within a document, present the information logically and clearly. Use the same margins, indents, headings, hyphenation and spellings throughout the document. Consistency in a document gives the reader a sense of comfort. Inconsistencies distract, causing your message to lose its impact.
>
> If possible, have another person proofread the document. A person who is not familiar with the document can identify inconsistencies and words or sentences with unclear meanings.
>
> **Check Facts**
> It is important to use reliable sources to verify information such as names, addresses, telephone numbers and other facts. Do not rely on your memory.
>
> 2

Part 5

Desktop Publishing

Objectives

After completing this Part, you should be able to:
- Format text into columns.
- Add borders and shading.
- Insert and scale clip art.
- Draw objects.
- Select and resize objects.
- Change the appearance of objects.
- Add text to drawings.
- Create and modify charts and diagrams.

Part 4 – Working with Documents

Application 3 - Outline Numbered List

As the student assistant to the superintendent of the Lancaster School District, you have been asked to key the agenda for the next Board of Trustees meeting.

What To Do

1. Create a new word document.
2. Set the top margin at **1.5** inches and the bottom, left, and right margins at **1** inch.
3. Key the agenda in Figure 4-10 as an outline numbered list using the format shown.

Figure 4-10 Agenda

```
                LANCASTER INDEPENDENT SCHOOL DISTRICT

                    Agenda for Board of Trustees Meeting

                      4:00 p.m., Monday, March 14, 2006


    I.   Verify quorum.
    II.  Approve minutes for February 21, 2006 meeting
    III. Approve the Tax Report for January, 2006
    IV.  Committee Reports
            A. Curriculum
            B. Textbooks
            C. Construction
            D. Building Maintenance
    V.   Old Business
            A. Maintenance Contracts
            B. Cafeteria
    VI.  New Business
            A. Recognition of students participating in School Clean-up Week
            B. Short-term Borrowing
    VII. Next Meeting, Thursday, April 19, 2006
```

4. Save the document as **Agenda** followed by your initials.
5. Print and close the document.

Hot Tip

- You can also strike the **Tab** key to indent (demote) an item and **Shift+Tab** keys to decrease the indent (promote) an item in an outline numbered list.

Extra Challenge

- Create an agenda of your own. Experiment with the different outlined numbered list formats on the Outline Numbered tab in the Bullets and Numbering dialog box.

Introductory Word 75

Part 4 - Working with Documents

Application 5 - Table, AutoFormat Table, Highlight, continued

Your Application Completed

Figure 4-13 Baseball Schedule

Webster Grove Baseball
2304 50th Street
Webster Grove, MO 63134

We are excited to kick off our Spring Season Baseball League. All games will be played at the John Newsom Baseball Complex (north field). The schedule for this season is as follows:

Reese Medical Center Mustangs		
Team	Date	Time
A & B Muffler Eagles	April 10	3:00
Champion Sport Comets	April 17	12:00
Butler Plumbing Bulldogs	April 24	10:00
Harding Insurance Stars	May 1	12:00
Bruin Carpet Raiders	May 8	3:00
Rapid Pager Cougars	May 22	10:30

Your coaches will distribute your jerseys at the first game. Please be at the field at least 15 minutes prior to the game so the coaches can complete their lineups.

If you have any questions, please contact the Webster Grove Baseball League office at 555-580-4932.

Good Luck and Have Fun!

Part 4 - Working with Documents

Application 4 - Tabs

You recently graduated from high school and enrolled in a local junior college. You want a better paying part-time job while attending school. Before beginning your job search, you need to write your resume.

What To Do

1. Create a new word document.
2. Set all margins at **.75** inch.
3. Set a left tab **1** inch from the left margin.
4. Key and format the resume in Figure 4-11. Use underline, bold, and all caps where shown.

Figure 4-11 Resume

SUSAN L. MARTIN
5524 Grandview Road
Clearwater, FL 33759-9047
727-555-9613

GOAL	An entry level administrative assistant position with an opportunity for advancement.

WORK EXPERIENCE

<u>Assistant to the Receptionist</u>, Business Department
Prescott Junior College, Clearwater, Florida
September 2006 to present
Duties: Use computer to enter data, greet visitors, and answer telephone.

<u>Recreation Assistant</u>, Clearwater Summer Sports Camp
Summer, 2006
Duties: Taught soccer to third and fourth graders.

<u>Cashier (Part-time)</u>, Classics Video, Clearwater, Florida
October 2005 to May 2006
Duties: Assisted customers and operated cash register.

EDUCATION

Prescott Junior College, Clearwater, Florida
September 2006 to present

West High School, Clearwater, Florida
Graduated May 31, 2006
Grade Point Average: 3.5
Business Subjects: Accounting, Office Administration, Keyboarding

EXTRACURRICULAR ACTIVITIES

Secretary, Future Business Leaders of America
National Honor Society
Varsity Soccer team
Quill and Scroll, Journalism Honor Society

Habitat for Humanity
Friends of the Library

REFERENCES

Furnished upon request.

5. Save the document as **Resume** followed by your initials.
6. Print and close the document.

Extra Challenges

- You would like to apply for an administrative assistant position with Reeves and Lloyd Inc. Use the format of the resume in this application to create your own resume.
- Create a cover letter to accompany the resume. The contact person is Mary Lopez, personnel director for Reeves and Lloyd, Inc. Use the personal-business letter format found in Models for Formatted Documents appendix (*Appendix F*).

Teamwork

- Trade your resume and cover letter with a classmate. Edit each other's work using the proofreader's marks. A chart of proofreader's marks is found in *Appendix K*.

Introductory Word 76

Part 4 - Working with Documents
Application 5 - Table, AutoFormat Table, Highlight

Your company, Reese Medical Center, has decided to enter a team in the city baseball league. Prepare a table with the team's schedule to distribute to the team members.

What To Do

1. Open **IW App4-5** from the data files.
2. Save the document as **Baseball Schedule** followed by your initials.
3. Insert a table on the second blank line after the first paragraph. Format the table with three columns and six rows.
4. Key the data in the table as shown in Figure 4-12.

Figure 4-12 Baseball table data

Team	Date	Time
A & B Muffler Eagles	April 10	3:00
Champion Sports Comets	April 17	12:00
Butler Plumbing Bulldogs	April 24	10:00
Harding Insurance Stars	May 1	12:00
Bruin Carpet Raiders	May 8	3:00

5. Center the three headings, and change the font size to 14 point, bold.
6. Center the date and time columns.
7. Add a new row after *Bruin Carpet Raiders* and key the following data:

   Rapid Pager Cougars May 22 10:30

8. Add a new row above the first row, and key **Reese Medical Center Mustangs**. Merge the cells.
9. Apply AutoFormat Table **Colorful 1** to the table.
10. Save, print, and close the file.

Hot Tips

- Table AutoFormats are predesigned formats you can apply to your tables. To use Table AutoFormat, open the **Table** menu and choose **Table AutoFormat**.
- You can access table-formatting commands quickly by right-clicking in the table.

Extra Challenge

- Use the Help feature to learn how to change the position of a table on a page using the table move handle and resize a table using the table resize handle.

Introductory Word 77

Appendices

Appendix A -	Windows Basics
Appendix B -	Computer Concepts
Appendix C -	Concepts for Microsoft Office Programs
Appendix D -	Keyboarding Touch System Improvement
Appendix E -	Ten-Key Numeric Touch System Improvement
Appendix F -	Models for Formatted Documents
Appendix G -	Task Filenames and Descriptions
Appendix H -	Application Filenames and Descriptions
Appendix I -	E-Mail Writing Guides
Appendix J -	Letter Writing Guides
Appendix K -	Proofreader's Marks
Appendix L -	Microsoft Office Specialist Program
Appendix M -	Start-Up Checklist

Appendices

Appendix A - Windows Basics

This appendix will familiarize you with the Windows 98, Windows 2000, and Windows XP operating systems. It contains the basic information you need to move around your desktop and manage the files, folders, and other resources you work with every day. It also covers the Windows Help system.

Starting Windows

If Windows is already installed, it should start automatically when you turn on the computer. If your computer is on a network, you may need some help from your teacher.

TASK A-1

1. Turn on the computer.
2. After a few moments, Microsoft 98, Windows 2000, or Windows XP appears.
3. Leave your computer on for the next Task.

The Mouse

A **mouse** is a device that rolls on a flat surface and has one or more buttons on it. The mouse allows you to communicate with the computer by pointing to and manipulating graphics and text on the screen. The **pointer**, which appears as an arrow on the screen, indicates the position of the mouse. The four most common mouse operations are point, click, double-click, and drag:

Point—Moving the mouse pointer to a specific item on the screen.

Click—Pressing the mouse button and quickly releasing it while pointing to an item on the screen. (The term *click* comes from the noise you hear when you press and release the button.)

Double-click—Clicking the mouse button twice quickly while keeping the mouse still.

Drag—Pointing to an object on the screen, pressing and holding the left mouse button, and moving the pointer while the button is pressed. Releasing the button ends the drag operation.

The Desktop

When Windows starts up, the desktop displays on the screen. The **desktop** is the space where you access and work with programs and files. Figure A-1 illustrates a typical desktop screen. Your screen may vary slightly from those shown in the figures. For example, your screen may display icons that were installed with Windows or shortcut icons you've created. You can customize and organize your desktop by creating files, folders, and shortcuts.

Appendix A 2

Appendix A - Windows Basics

Figure A-1 Typical desktop screen

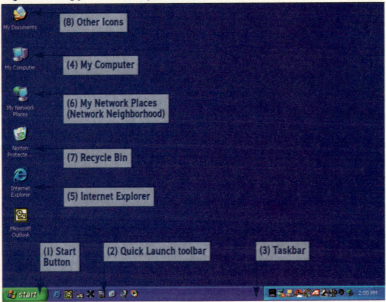

The main features of the desktop screen are labeled and numbered on the figure and discussed below:

1. The **Start** button brings up menus that give you a variety of options, such as starting a program, opening a document, finding help, or shutting down the computer.
2. The **Quick Launch** toolbar to the right of the Start button contains icons so you can display the desktop or quickly start frequently used programs.
3. The **Taskbar**, located at the bottom of the screen, tells you the names of all open programs.
4. **My Computer** is a program that allows you to see what files and folders are located on your computer.
5. **Internet Explorer** is a Web browser that allows you to surf the Internet, read e-mail, create a Web page, or download your favorite Web sites right to your desktop.
6. **Network Neighborhood** (Windows 98), **My Network Places** (Windows XP and Windows 2000) shows all the folders and printers that are available to you through the network connection, if you have one.
7. The **Recycle Bin** is a place to get rid of files or folders that are no longer needed.
8. Other *icons*, or small pictures, represent programs waiting to be opened.

Windows makes it easy to connect to the Internet. Just click the Launch Internet Explorer Browser button on the Quick Launch toolbar. The Quick Launch toolbar also has buttons so you can launch Outlook Express, view channels, and show the desktop.

Appendix A - Windows Basics

With Windows you can incorporate Web content into your work by using the Active Desktop, an interface that lets you put "active items" from the Internet on your desktop. You can use channels to customize the information delivered from the Internet to your computer. By displaying the Channel bar on your desktop you can add, subscribe to, or view channels.

TASK A-2

1. Click the button to Launch Internet Explorer on the Quick Launch toolbar.
2. Click the **Show Desktop** button on the Quick Launch toolbar to display the Windows desktop.
3. Click the **Internet Explorer** button on the taskbar to return to the browser window.
4. Choose **Close** on the **File** menu to close Internet Explorer.
5. Point to the **Start** button.
6. Click the left mouse button. A menu of choices appears above the Start button, similar to that shown in Figure A-2.
7. If you are using Windows 98 or 2000, Point to **Settings**, and then click **Control Panel** on the submenu. If you are using Windows XP, click **Control Panel** on the menu. A new window appears. The title bar at the top tells you that Control Panel is the name of the open window. Leave this window open for the next Task.

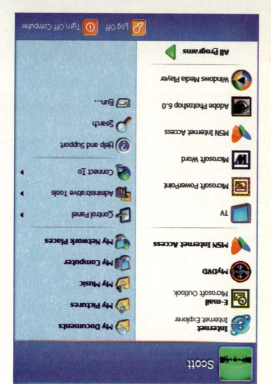

Figure A-2 Start menu in Windows XP

Appendix A - Windows Basics

Using Windows

Many of the windows you will work with have similar features. You can work more efficiently by familiarizing yourself with some of the common elements as shown in Figure A-3, and explained below.

1. A *Title bar* is at the top of every window and contains the name of the open program, window, document, or folder.
2. The *Menu bar* lists available menus from which you can choose a variety of commands.
3. The *Standard toolbar*, located directly below the menu bar, contains commands you can use by simply clicking the correct button.
4. The *Address bar* tells you which folder's contents are being displayed. You can also key a Web address in the Address bar without first opening your browser.
5. At the bottom of the window is the *Status bar* that gives you directions on how to access menus and summarizes the actions of the commands that you choose.

Figure A-3 Window elements

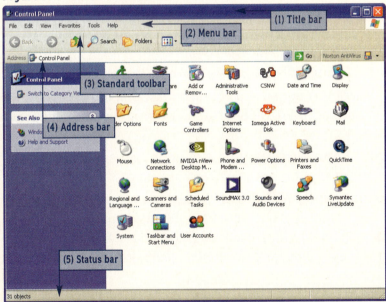

Moving and Resizing Windows

Sometimes you will have several windows open on the screen at the same time. To work more effectively, you may need to move or change the size of a window. To move a window, click the title bar and drag the window to another location. You can resize a window by dragging the window borders. When you position the pointer on a horizontal border, it changes to a vertical two-headed arrow. When you position the pointer on a vertical border, it changes to a horizontal two-headed arrow.

Appendix A - Windows Basics

You can then click and drag the border to change the width or height of the window. It is also possible to resize two sides of a window at the same time. When you move the pointer to a corner of the window's border, it becomes a two-headed arrow pointing diagonally. You can then click and drag to resize the window's height and width at the same time.

TASK A-3

1. Move the Control Panel window by clicking on the title bar and holding the left mouse button down. Continue to hold the left mouse button down and drag the Control Panel until it appears to be centered on the screen. Release the mouse button.
2. Point anywhere on the border at the bottom of the Control Panel window. The pointer turns into a vertical two-headed arrow.
3. While the pointer is a two-headed arrow, drag the bottom border of the window down to enlarge the window.
4. Point to the border on the right side of the Control Panel window. The pointer turns into a horizontal two-headed arrow.
5. While the pointer is a two-headed arrow, drag the border of the window to the right to enlarge the window.
6. Point to the lower-right corner of the window border. The pointer becomes a two-headed arrow pointing diagonally.
7. Drag the border upward and to the left to resize both sides at the same time until the window is about the same size as the one shown in Figure A-4. Leave the window on the screen for the next Task.

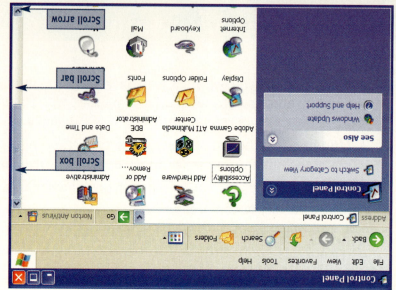

Figure A-4 Scroll bars, arrows, and boxes

Appendix A - Windows Basics

Scroll Bars

A **Scroll bar** appears on the edges of windows any time there is more to be displayed than a window can show at its current size (see Figure A-4). A scroll bar can appear along the bottom edge (horizontal) and/or along the right side (vertical) of a window. Scroll bars appeared in the last step of the preceding Task because the window was too small to show all the icons at once.

Scroll bars are a convenient way to bring another part of the window's contents into view. On the scroll bar is a sliding box called the **Scroll box**. The scroll box indicates your position within the window. When the scroll box reaches the bottom of the scroll bar, you have reached the end of the window's contents. **Scroll arrows** are located at the ends of the scroll bar. Clicking on a scroll arrow moves the window in that direction one line at a time.

TASK A-4

1. On the horizontal scroll bar, click the scroll arrow that points to the right. The contents of the window shift to the left.
2. Press and hold the mouse button on the same scroll arrow. The contents of the window scroll quickly across the window. Notice that the scroll box moves to the right end of the scroll bar.
3. You can also scroll by dragging the scroll box. Drag the scroll box on the horizontal scroll bar to the left.
4. Drag the scroll box on the vertical scroll bar to the middle of the scroll bar.
5. The final way to scroll is to click on the scroll bar. Click the horizontal scroll bar to the right of the scroll box. The contents scroll left.
6. Click the horizontal scroll bar to the left of the scroll box. The contents scroll right.

    Resize the Control Panel until the scroll bars disappear. Leave the window open for the next Task.

Other Window Controls

Three other important window controls, located on the right side of the title bar, are the **Maximize button**, the **Minimize button**, and the **Close button** (see Figure A-5). The Maximize button enlarges a window to the full size of the screen. The Minimize button shrinks a window to a button on the taskbar. The button on the taskbar is labeled and you can click it any time to redisplay the window. The Close button is used to close a window.

Appendix A - Windows Basics

When a window is maximized, the Maximize button is replaced by the **Restore button** (see Figure A-6). The Restore button returns the window to the size it was before the Maximize button was clicked.

Figure A-5 Maximize, Minimize, and Close buttons

Figure A-6 Restore button

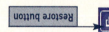

TASK A-5

1. Click the **Maximize** button. The window enlarges to fill the screen.
2. Click the **Restore** button on the Control Panel window (see Figure A-6).
3. Click the **Minimize** button on the Control Panel window. The window is reduced to a button on the taskbar.
4. Click the **Control Panel** button on the taskbar to open the window again.
5. Click the **Close** button to close the window.

Menus and Dialog Boxes

To find out what a restaurant has to offer, you look at the menu. You can also look at a menu on the computer's screen to find out what a computer program has to offer. **Menus** in computer programs contain options for executing certain actions or tasks.

When you click the Start button, as you did earlier in this appendix, a menu is displayed with a list of options. If you choose a menu option with an arrow beside it, a submenu opens that lists additional options. A menu item followed by an ellipsis (...) indicates that a dialog box will appear when chosen. A **dialog box**, similar to the Turn off computer dialog box shown in Figure A-7, appears when more information is required before the command can be performed. You may have to key information, choose from a list of options, or simply confirm that you want the command to be performed. To back out of a dialog box without performing an action, press Esc, click the Close button, or choose Cancel (or No).

Appendix A 8

Appendix A - Windows Basics

Figure A-7 Turn off computer/Shut Down Windows dialog box

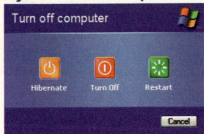

TASK A-6

1. Click the **Start** button. A menu appears.
2. Click **Shut Down** (or **Turn Off Computer**). The Shut Down Windows dialog box (or a similar window) appears. See Figure A-7.
3. Click **Cancel** to back out of the dialog box without shutting down.

In a Windows application, menus are accessed from a menu bar (see Figure A-8). A menu bar appears beneath the title bar in each Windows program and consists of a row of menu names such as File and Edit. Each name in the menu bar represents a separate *drop-down menu*, containing related options. Drop-down menus are convenient to use because the commands are in front of you on the screen, as shown in Figure A-8. Like a menu in a restaurant, you can view a list of choices and pick the one you want.

Figure A-8 Drop-down menu

You can give commands from drop-down menus using either the keyboard or the mouse. Each menu on the menu bar and each option on a menu is characterized by an underlined letter called a *mnemonic*. To open a menu on the menu bar using the keyboard, press Alt plus the mnemonic letter shown on the menu name. To display a menu using the mouse, simply place the pointer on the menu name and click the left button.

Appendix A - Windows Basics

Just as with the Start menu, drop-down menus also have items with right-pointing arrows that open submenus, and ellipsis that open dialog boxes. Choosing an item without an ellipsis or a right-pointing arrow executes the command. To close a menu without choosing a command, press Esc.

TASK A-7

1. Open the Notepad accessory application by clicking **Start, Programs, Accessories,** and then **Notepad.** If using Windows XP, open the Notepad accessory application by clicking **Start, All Programs, Accessories,** and then **Notepad.** (See Figure A-9.)
2. Click **Edit** on the menu bar. The Edit menu appears.
3. Click **Time/Date** to display the current time and date.
4. Click **File** on the menu bar. The File menu appears (see Figure A-10).
5. Click **Exit**. A save prompt box appears.
6. Click **No**. The Notepad window disappears and you return to the desktop.

Figure A-9 Opening menus in an application

Figure A-10 Selecting the Exit command

Hot Tip

- In Windows XP system applications, the mnemonics are displayed only when you strike the Alt key. They are displayed on the Start menu only if you access the menu by striking Ctrl + Esc.

Appendix A - Windows Basics

Windows Help

This appendix has covered only a few of the many features of Windows. For additional information, Windows has an easy-to-use Help system. Use Help as a quick reference when you are unsure about a function. Windows Help is accessed through the Help (or Help and Support) option on the Start menu. Then, from the Windows Help dialog box, you can choose to see a table of contents displaying general topics and subtopics, or to search the Help system using the Index or Search options. If you are working in a Windows program, you can get more specific help about topics relating to that program by accessing help from the Help menu on the menu bar.

Many topics in the Help program are linked. A *link* is represented by colored and/or underlined text. (In Windows XP the underline appears when you move the cursor over the link.) You can also tell you are pointing to a link when the mouse icon changes to a pointing hand. By clicking a link, the user "jumps" to a linked document that contains additional information.

In Windows versions prior to Windows XP, using the buttons on the toolbar controls the display of information. The Hide button removes the left frame of the Help window from view. The Show button will restore it. The Contents tab is useful if you want to browse through the topics by category. Click a book icon to see additional Help topics. Click a question mark to display detailed Help information in the right frame of the Help window.

In all versions of Windows, the Back and Forward buttons allow you to move back and forth between previously displayed Help entries. The Options button offers navigational choices, as well as options to customize, refresh, and print Help topics.

TASK A-8

1. Open the Windows Help program by clicking the **Start** button, and then **Help**. If you are using *Windows XP*, click **Start** and then **Help and Support**.
2. If you're using *Windows 98* or *Windows 2000*, click the **Hide** button on the toolbar to remove the left frame, if necessary. If you are using *Windows XP*, skip to step 5.
3. Click the **Show** button to display the left frame again, if necessary.
4. Click the **Contents** tab if it is not already selected.
5. *Windows 2000* users: Click **Introducing Windows 2000 Professional** and then click **How to Use Help**. Your screen should appear similar to Figure A-11A.

   Windows 98 users: Click **Introducing Windows 98** and then click **How to Use Help**. Your screen should appear similar to Figure A-11B.

   Windows XP users: Click **What's new in Windows XP**. Your screen should appear similar to Figure A-11C.

Appendix A - Windows Basics

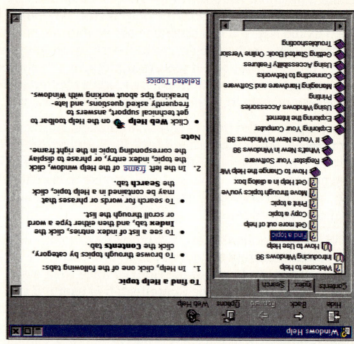

Figure A-11B Windows 2000 Help program

Figure A-11A Windows 98 Help program

Appendix A - Windows Basics

Figure A-11C Windows XP Help program

6. *Windows 2000* users: Click **Find a Help Topic**.

   Windows 98 users: Click **Find a topic**.

   Windows XP users: Click **What's new topics** and then **What's new for Help and Support**.

7. Read the Help window and leave it open for the next Task.

When you want to search for help on a particular topic, use the Index tab and key in a word. Windows will search alphabetically through the list of Help topics to try to find an appropriate match. Double-click a topic to see it explained in the right frame of the help window. Sometimes a Topics Found dialog box will appear that displays subtopics related to the item. Find a subtopic that you'd like to learn more about and double-click it.

TASK A-9

1. Click the **Index** tab (or the **Index** button on the toolbar).
2. *Windows 2000* users: Begin keying **printing** until *printing* is highlighted in the list of index entries.

   Windows 98 users: Begin keying **printing** until *printing* is highlighted in the list of index entries.

   Windows XP users: Begin keying **help** until *help and support for Windows XP* is highlighted in the list of index entries.
3. *Windows 2000* users: Click **printing Help topics** and then **from a Server** to display information in the right frame.

   Windows 98 users: Double-click the **Help topics** subtopic to display information in the right frame.
   Windows XP users: Double-click the **copying and printing Help Topics**, then double-click **To print a Help topic or page**.

Appendix A - Windows Basics

4. *Windows 2000* users: Read the Help window, and then print the information by following the instructions you read.
   Windows 98 users: Read the Help window, and then print the information by following the instructions you read.
   Windows XP users: Read the Help window, and then print the information by clicking the **Print** button on the toolbar.

5. *Windows 2000* users: Click **Back** to return to the previous Help entry.
   Windows 98 users: Click **Back** to return to the previous Help entry.
   Windows XP users: Click the back arrow to return to the previous Help entry.

6. *Windows 2000* users: Click **Forward** to advance to the next help entry.
   Windows 98 users: Click **Forward** to advance to the next help entry.
   Windows XP users: Double-click **Copying and printing Help topics** again and then double-click To copy a Help topic or page to see another Help entry.

7. Close the Help program by clicking the **Close** button.

The Search tab (Search box in Windows XP) is similar to the Index tab, but will perform a more thorough search of the words or phrases that you key. By using the Search option, you can display every occurrence of a particular word or phrase throughout the Windows Help system. Double-click on the topic most similar to what you are looking for and information is displayed in the Help window.

If you need assistance using the Windows Help program, choose *Introducing Windows*, *How to Use Help* from the Contents tab, or *What's new in Windows XP* from the Home tab and then *What's New Topics* if you are using Windows XP.

If you are using an Office application, you can also get help by using the Office Assistant feature.

Other Features

One of Windows' primary features is its file management capabilities. Windows comes with two file management utilities: My Computer and Windows Explorer. The Recycle Bin utility also helps you manage files. When open, these utilities display a standard toolbar like the one shown in Figure A-12. Your toolbar may look different from Figure A-12 depending on the customization. To customize your toolbar, choose Toolbars on the View menu, and Customize on the submenu.

Appendix A 14

Appendix A - Windows Basics

Figure A-12 Standard toolbar

The Back and Forward buttons let you move back and forth between folder contents previously displayed in the window. The Up button moves you up one level in the hierarchy of folders. You can use the Cut, Copy, and Paste buttons to cut or copy an object and then paste it in another location. The Undo button allows you to reverse your most recent action. The Delete button sends the selected object to the Recycle Bin. The Properties button displays a Properties dialog box with information about the selected object. The View button lists options for displaying the contents of the window.

My Computer

As you learned earlier, there is an icon on your desktop labeled My Computer. Double-clicking this icon opens the My Computer window, which looks similar to the one shown in Figure A-13. The My Computer program is helpful because it allows you to see what is on your computer. First double-click the icon for the drive you want to view. That drive's name appears in the title bar and the window displays all the folders and files on that drive.

Figure A-13 Windows XP My Computer window

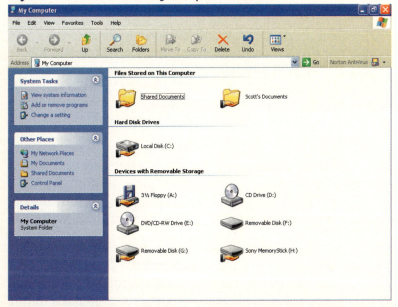

Hot Tip

- You can change how folders and files are displayed by choosing **Web Page** (except in Windows XP), **Large Icons**, **Small Icons**, **List**, or **Details** on the **View** menu.

Because computer disks have such a large capacity, it is not unusual for a floppy disk to contain dozens of files, or for a hard disk to contain hundreds or thousands of files. To organize files, a disk can be divided into folders. A *folder* is a place where files and other folders are stored. They help keep documents organized on

Appendix A - Windows Basics

a disk just the way folders would in a file cabinet. Folders group files that have something in common. You can also have folders within a folder. For example, you could create a folder to group all of the files you are working on in computer class. Within that folder, you could have several other folders that group files for each tool or each chapter.

When you double-click a folder in My Computer, the contents of that folder are displayed—including program files and data files. Double-clicking a program file icon will open that program. Double-clicking a data file icon opens that document and the program that created it.

To create a new folder, double-click a drive or folder in the My Computer window. Choose New on the File menu and then choose Folder on the submenu. A folder titled *New Folder* appears, as shown in Figure A-14. You can rename the folder by keying the name you want. Once you have created a folder, you can save or move files into it.

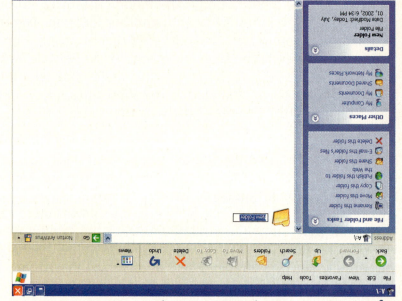

Figure A-14 New folder (Thumbnail view)

TASK A-10

1. Double-click the **My Computer** icon on your desktop.
2. Double-click the drive where you want to create a new folder.
3. Choose **New** on the **File** menu and then choose **Folder** on the submenu. A folder titled New Folder appears.
4. Name the folder **Time Records**. Press **Enter**.
5. Choose **Close** on the **File** menu to close the window.

Appendix A 16

Appendix A - Windows Basics

Windows Explorer

Another way to view the folders and files on a disk is to use the Windows Explorer program. To open it, click Start, Programs, and then Windows Explorer for Windows 98 and Start, Program, Accessories, and then Windows Explorer for Windows XP and Windows 2000. The Explorer window is split into two panes. The left pane shows a hierarchical, or "tree" view of how the folders are organized on a disk; the right side, or Contents pane, shows the files and folders located in the folder that is currently selected in the tree pane. Explorer is a useful tool for organizing and managing the contents of a disk because you can create folders, rename them, and easily delete, move, and copy files.

TASK A-11

1. *Windows 2000* users: Open Windows Explorer by clicking **Start**, **Programs**, **Accessories**, and then **Windows Explorer**.

   Windows 98 users: Open Windows Explorer by clicking **Start**, **Programs**, and then **Windows Explorer**.

   Windows XP users: Open Windows Explorer by clicking **Start**, **Programs**, **Accessories**, and then **Windows Explorer**.

2. In the tree pane, double-click (single-click in Windows XP) the drive where the *Time Records* folder you just created is located.

3. Select the **Time Records** folder in the Contents pane of the Explorer window.

4. Choose **Rename** on the **File** menu.

5. Key **Finance**. Press **Enter**.

6. Leave Windows Explorer open for the next Task.

Recycle Bin

Another icon on the desktop that you learned about earlier is the Recycle Bin. It looks like a wastebasket and is a place to get rid of files and folders that you no longer need. Items that have been "thrown away" will remain in the Recycle Bin from which they can be retrieved until you empty the Recycle Bin.

TASK A-12

1. Windows Explorer should still be open from the previous Task.

2. Right-click the **Finance** folder.

Appendix A - Windows Basics

3. Choose **Delete** on the shortcut menu. The Confirm Folder Delete dialog box appears.
4. Click **Yes**. The folder is removed.
5. Choose **Close** on the **File** menu to close Windows Explorer.

Summary

In this appendix, you learned:

- The desktop organizes your work. Clicking the Start button displays options for opening programs and documents, and shutting down the computer. You can connect to the Internet using the Explorer browser and you can use the Active Desktop and channels to incorporate Web content into your work.
- Windows can be moved, resized, opened, and closed. If all the contents of a window cannot be displayed in the window as it is currently sized, scroll bars appear to allow you to move to the part of the window that you want to view. Windows can be maximized to fill the screen or minimized to a button on the taskbar.
- Menus allow you to choose commands to perform different actions. Menus are accessed from the Start button or from a program's menu bar near the top of the window. When you choose a menu command with an ellipsis (...), a dialog box appears that requires more information before performing the command. Choosing a menu option with an arrow opens a submenu.
- The Windows Help program provides additional information about the many features of Windows. You can access the Help program from the Start button and use the Contents, Index, or Search features to get information. You can also get help from the Help menu within Windows programs.
- Folders group files that have something in common. To organize a disk, it can be divided into folders where files and other folders are stored. Other useful features of Windows include My Computer, which lets you see what is on your computer; Windows Explorer, which helps organize and manage your files; and the Recycle Bin for deleting unneeded files or folders.

Appendix B - Computer Concepts

What Is a Computer?

A computer is a mechanical device that is used to store, retrieve, and manipulate information (called data) electronically. You enter the data into the computer through a variety of input devices, such as a keyboard, mouse or joystick; process it, and output it in a number of ways: such as a monitor, projector, or printer. Computer software programs run the computer and let you manipulate the data.

Hardware

The physical components, or parts, of the computer are called hardware. The main parts are the central processing unit (CPU), the monitor, the keyboard, and the mouse. Peripherals are additional components, such as printers and scanners.

Input Devices. You enter information into a computer by keying on a keyboard or by using a mouse—a hand-held device—to move a pointer on the computer screen. A controller is an input device often used with computer games that moves a pointer, or character, on the screen. A modem is another input device; it receives information via a telephone line. Other input devices include scanners, trackballs, and digital tracking devices. You can use scanners to "read" text or graphics into a computer from a printed page, or to read bar codes (coded labels) to keep track of merchandise in a store or other inventory. Similar to a mouse, a trackball has a roller ball you turn to control a pointer on the screen. Digital tracking devices are an alternative to the trackball or mouse; situated on the keyboard of a laptop, they allow you to simply press a finger on a small electronic pad to control the pointer on the screen. See Figure B-1.

Figure B-1 Keyboard, mouse, and controller

Appendix B - Computer Concepts

Processing Devices. The central processing unit (CPU) is a silicon chip that processes data and carries out instructions given to the computer. The data bus includes the wiring and pathways by which the CPU communicates with the peripherals and components of the computer. See Figure B-2.

Figure B-2 Central processing unit

Storage Devices. The hard drive is a device that reads and writes data to and from a round magnetic platter, or disk. The data is encoded on the disk much the same as sounds are encoded on magnetic tape. The hard drive is called hard because the disk is rigid, unlike a floppy disk drive, which reads and writes data to and from a removable non-rigid disk, similar to a round disk of magnetic tape. The floppy disk is encased in a plastic sleeve to protect its data. The floppy disk's main advantage is portability. You can store data on a floppy disk and transport it for use on another computer.

At one time, the largest hard drive was 10 MB, or 10,000,000 bytes, of data. A byte stands for a single character of data. At the current time, typical hard drives range from 40 gigabytes to 120 gigabytes.

Another storage device is the CD, or compact disk, which is a form of optical storage. Information is encoded on the disk by a laser and read by a CD-ROM drive in the computer. These disks have a great advantage over floppies because they can hold vast quantities of information—the entire contents of a small library, for instance. However, most computers cannot write (or save) information to these disks; CD-ROMs are Read-Only Memory (ROM) devices. Drives are now available that write to CDs. Although these drives used to be very expensive and therefore were not used widely, they are becoming more affordable. The great advantage of CDs is their ability to hold graphic information—including moving pictures with the highest quality stereo sound.

Appendix B - Computer Concepts

Similar to a CD, the digital video drive can read high-quality cinema-type disks. A digital video disk (DVD) is a 5-inch optical disk, and it looks like an audio CD or a compact disk. It is a high-capacity storage device that contains 4.7 GB of data, which is a seven-fold increase over the current CD-ROMs. There are two variations of DVDs that offer even more storage—a 2-layer version with 9.4 GB capacity, and double-sided disks with 17 GB.

These highest-capacity disks are designed to eventually replace the CD-ROM to store large databases. A DVD disk holds 133 minutes of data on each side, which means that two two-hour movies could be held on one disk.

Another storage medium is magnetic tape. This medium is most commonly used for backing up a system, which means making a copy of files from a hard drive. Although it is relatively rare for a hard drive to crash (that is, to have the data or pointers to the data be partially or totally destroyed), it can and does happen. Therefore, most businesses and some individuals routinely back up files on tape. If you have a small hard drive, you can use floppy disks or CD-ROMs to back up your system. See Figure B-3.

Figure B-3 Storage disk

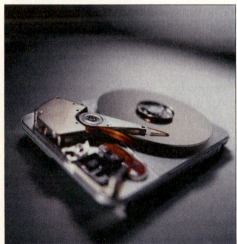

Output Devices. The monitor on which you view your work is an output device. It provides a visual representation of the information stored in, or produced by, your computer. The monitor for today's typical system is the SVGA (super video graphics array). It provides a very sharp picture because of the large number of tiny dots, called pixels, which make up the display as well as its ability to present the full spectrum of colors. Most laptop computers use a liquid crystal display (LCD) screen that is not as clear a display because it depends on the arrangement of tiny bits of crystal to

Appendix B - Computer Concepts

present an image. However, the latest laptops use new technology that gives quality near or equal to that of a standard monitor.

Printers are another type of output device. They let you produce a paper printout of information contained in the computer. Today, most printers are of the laser type, using a technology similar to a photocopier to produce a high-quality print. Like a copy machine, the laser printer uses heat to fuse a powdery substance called toner to the page. Ink-jet printers use a spray of ink to print. Laser printers give the sharpest image. Ink-jet printers provide nearly as sharp an image, but the wet printouts can smear when they first are printed. However, most color printers are ink jet; these printers let you print information in its full array of colors as you see it on your SVGA monitor. Laser color printers are available, but are more costly. See Figure B-4.

Figure B-4 Printer

Modems are another output device, as well as an input device. They allow computers to communicate with each other by telephone lines. Modems convert information in bytes to sound media to send data and then convert it back to bytes after receiving data. Modems operate at various rates or speeds; typically today, a computer will have a modem that operates at 33.6 Kbps to 56 Kbps baud (a variable unit of data transmission) per second or better.

Local telephone companies currently offer residential ISDN services that provide connection speeds up to 128 Kbps and digital subscriber line technologies (DSL), which can provide speeds beyond 1.5 Mbps. Other alternatives include fast downstream data connections from direct broadcast satellite (DBS), fixed wireless providers, and of course, high-speed cable modems.

Appendix B 4

Appendix B - Computer Concepts

Laptops and Docking Stations. A laptop computer is a small folding computer that literally fits in a person's lap. Within the fold-up case is the CPU, data bus, monitor (built into the lid), hard drive (sometimes removable), a 3.5-inch floppy drive, a CD-ROM drive, and a trackball or digital tracking device. The advantage of the laptop is that it is portable—you can work anywhere because you can use power either from an outlet or from the computer's internal, rechargeable batteries. The drawbacks are the smaller keyboard, liquid crystal monitor, smaller capacity, and higher price. The newer laptops offer full-sized keyboards and higher quality monitors. As technology allows, storage capacity on smaller devices is making it possible to offer laptops with as much power and storage as a full-sized computer. The docking station is a device into which you slide a closed laptop that becomes the desktop computer. Then you can plug in a full-sized monitor, keyboard, mouse, printer, and so on. Such a setup lets you use the laptop like a desktop computer while at your home or office.

Personal Digital Assistants (PDA). A personal digital assistant is a pocket-sized electronic organizer that helps you to manage addresses, appointments, expenses, tasks, and memos. This information can be shared with a Windows-based or Macintosh computer through a process called synchronization. By placing your PDA in a cradle that is attached to your computer you can transfer the data from your PDA's calendar, address, or memo program into your computer's information manager program, such as Outlook. The information is updated on both sides, making your PDA a portable extension of your computer. See Figure B-5.

Figure B-5 Personal digital assistant

Functioning
All of the input, processing, storage, and output devices function together to make the manipulation, storage, and distribution of data and information possible.

Appendix B - Computer Concepts

Data and Information Management. Data is information entered into and manipulated in a computer. Manipulation includes computation, such as adding, subtracting, and dividing; analysis planning, such as sorting data; and reporting, such as presenting data for others in a chart. Data and information management runs software on computer hardware.

Memory. There are two kinds of memory in a computer—RAM and ROM. RAM, or Random Access Memory, is a number of silicon chips inside a computer that hold information as long as the computer is turned on. RAM is what keeps the software programs up and running and keeps the visuals on your screen. RAM is where you work with data until you save it to a hard or floppy disk. Early computers had simple programs and did little with data, so they had very little RAM—possibly 4 or fewer megabytes. Today's computers run very complicated programs that stay resident (remain available to the user at the same time as other programs) and run graphics. Both of these tasks take a lot of memory; therefore, today's computers have at least 64 or more megabytes of RAM. ROM, or read-only memory, is the small bit of memory that stays in the computer when it is turned off. It is ROM that lets the computer boot up, or get started. ROM holds the instructions that tell the computer how to begin to load its operating system software programs. Figure B-6 shows random access memory.

Figure B-6 Random access memory

Speed. The speed of a computer is measured by how fast the drives turn to reach information to be retrieved or to save data. The measurement is in megahertz (MHz). Early personal

Appendix B 6

Appendix B - Computer Concepts

computers worked at 4.77 to 10 megahertz; today, machines run at 1000 MHz (or 1GHz) or more. Another factor that affects the speed of a computer is how much RAM is available. Since RAM makes up the work area for all programs and holds all the information that you input until you save, the more RAM available, the quicker the machine will be able to operate.

One other area of speed must be considered, and that is how quickly the modem can send and receive information. As mentioned earlier, modem speed is measured in baud. The usual modem runs at 33,600 or 56,000 baud per second or more.

Communications. Computers have opened up the world of communications, first within offices via LANs (local area networks that link computers within a facility via wires) and, later, via the Internet. Using the Internet, people can communicate across the world instantly with e-mail and attach files that were once sent by mailing a floppy disk. Also, anyone with a modem and an access service can download information from or post information to thousands of bulletin boards.

Software

A program is a set of mathematical instructions for the computer. Software is the collection of programs and other data input that tells the computer how to operate its machinery, how to manipulate, store, and output information, and how to accept the input you give it. Software fits into two basic categories: systems software and applications software. A third category, network software, is really a type of application.

Systems Software. Systems software refers to the operating system (OS) of the computer. The OS is a group of programs that is automatically copied in RAM every couple of seconds from the time the computer is turned on until the computer is turned off. Operating systems serve two functions: they control data flow among computer parts, and they provide the platform on which application and network software work—in effect, they allow the space for software and translate its commands to the computer. The most popular operating systems in use today are the Macintosh operating system, and a version of Microsoft Windows, such as Windows 98, Windows XP, Windows 2000, or Windows NT.

Macintosh has its own operating system that has evolved over the years since its introduction. From the beginning, Macintosh has used a graphical user interface (GUI) operating system since its introduction in the mid-1970s. The OS is designed so users click with a mouse on pictures, called icons, or on text to give commands to the system. Data is available to you in WYSIWYG

Appendix B - Computer Concepts

(what-you-see-what-you-get) form; that is, you can see on-screen what a document will look like when it is printed. Graphics and other kinds of data, such as spreadsheets, can be placed into text documents. However, GUIs take a great deal of RAM to keep all of the graphics and programs operating.

The OS for IBM and IBM-compatible computers (machines made by other companies that operate similarly) originally was DOS (disk operating system). It did not have a graphical interface. The GUI system, Windows™, was developed to make using the IBM/IBM-compatible computer more friendly. Users no longer had to memorize written commands to make the computer carry out actions, but could use a mouse to point and click icons or words. Windows 3.1, however, was a translating system that operated on top of DOS—not on its own.

Windows 3.1 was a GUI system that operated on top of DOS; Windows 3.1 was not an operating system by itself. It allowed you to point and click on graphics and words that then translated to DOS commands for the computer. Data was available to you in WYSIWYG (what-you-see-is-what-you-get) form. Graphics and other kinds of data, such as spreadsheets, could be placed into text documents by Object Linking and Embedding (OLE). However, Windows 3.1, because it was still using DOS as its base, was not really a stay-resident program. In other words, it did not keep more than one operation going at a time; it merely switched between operations quickly. Using several high-level programs at the same time, however, could cause problems, such as memory failure. Therefore, improvements were inevitable.

Windows 98 and Windows ME are their own operating systems, unlike the original Windows 3.1. Windows has DOS built-in, but does not operate on top of it—if you go to a DOS prompt from Windows, you will still be operating inside a Windows system, not in traditional DOS. Windows is the logical evolution of GUI for IBM and IBM-compatible (now more commonly known as Windows-based) machines. It is a stay-resident, point-and-click system that automatically configures hardware to work together. With all of its ability comes the need for more RAM or this system will operate slowly. Newer versions of Windows continue to be released.

Applications Software. When you use a computer program to perform a data manipulation or processing task, you are using applications software. Word processors, databases, spreadsheets, desktop publishers, fax systems, and online access systems are all applications software.

Appendix B - Computer Concepts

Network Software. Novell™ and Windows NT are two kinds of network software. A network is a group of computers that are hardwired (hooked together with cables) to communicate and operate together. Some computer networks use RF (radio frequency) technology to communicate with each other. This is called a wireless network, because you do not need to hook the network together with cables. In a typical network one computer acts as the server, which controls the flow of data among the other computers, called nodes, on the network. Network software manages this flow of information. Networks have certain advantages over stand-alone computers. They allow communication among the computers; they allow smaller capacity nodes to access the larger capacity of the server; and they allow several computers to share peripherals, such as one printer, and they can make it possible for all computers on the network to have access to the Internet.

History of the Computer

Though various types of calculating machines were developed in the nineteenth century, the history of the modern computer begins about the middle of the last century. The strides made in developing today's personal computer have been truly astounding.

Early Development

ENIAC, designed for military use in calculating ballistic trajectories, was the first electronic, digital computer to be developed in the United States. For its day, 1946, it was quite a marvel because it was able to accomplish a task in 20 seconds that took a human three days to do. However, it was an enormous machine that weighed more than 20 tons and contained thousands of vacuum tubes, which often failed. The tasks that it could accomplish were limited, as well. See Figure B-7.

From this awkward beginning, however, the seeds of an information revolution grew. Significant dates in the history of computer development are the first electronic stored program in 1948, the first junction transistor in 1951, the replacement of tubes with magnetic cores in 1953, the first high-level computer language in 1957, the first integrated circuit in 1961, the first minicomputer in 1965, the invention of the microprocessor (the silicon chip) and floppy disk in 1971, and the first personal computer in 1974 (made possible by the microprocessor). These last two inventions launched the fast-paced information revolution in which we now all live and participate.

Appendix B - Computer Concepts

Figure B-7 Computing's early beginnings

The Personal Computer

The PC, or personal computer, was mass marketed by Apple beginning in 1977, and by IBM in 1981. It is this desktop device with which people are so familiar and which, today, contains much more power and ability than did the original computer that took up an entire room. See Figure B-8. The PC is a small computer (desktop size or less) that uses a microprocessor to manipulate data. PCs may stand alone, be linked together in a network, or be attached to a large mainframe computer.

Figure B-8 The personal computer

Computer Utilities and System Maintenance

Computer operating systems let you run certain utilities and perform system maintenance. When you add hardware or software, you might need to make changes in the way the system operates.

Appendix B 10

Appendix B - Computer Concepts

Beginning with the Windows 95 version, most configuration changes are done automatically; however, other operating systems might not, or you might want to customize the way the new software or hardware will interface (coordinate) with your system. Additionally, you can make alterations such as the speed at which your mouse clicks, how fast or slow keys repeat on the keyboard, and what color or pattern appears on the desktop or in GUI programs.

You need to perform certain maintenance regularly on computers. You should scan all new disks and any incoming information from online sources for viruses. Some systems do this automatically; others require you to install software to do it. From time to time, you should scan or check the hard drive to see that there are no bad sectors or tracks and to look for corrupted files. Optimizing or defragmenting the hard disk is another way to keep your computer running at its best. You can also check a floppy disk if it is not working properly. Programs for scanning a large hard drive could take up to half an hour to run; checking programs run on a small hard drive or disk might take only seconds or minutes. Scanning and checking programs often offer the option of "fixing" the bad areas or problems, although you should be aware that this could result in data loss.

Society and Computers
The electronic information era has probably impacted society as much or more than the agricultural and industrial eras affected the lives of our ancestors.

Ethics Using Computers
When you access information—whether online, in the workplace, or via purchased software—you have a responsibility to respect the rights of the creator of that information. Treat electronic information in a copyrighted form—the intellectual property of the author—the same way as you would a book, article, or patented invention. For instance, you must give credit when you access information from a CD-ROM encyclopedia or a download from an online database. Also, information you transmit must be accurate and fair.

When you use equipment that belongs to your school, a company for which you work, or others, you must not:
1. Damage computer hardware and must not add or remove equipment without permission.
2. Use an access code or equipment without permission.
3. Read others' electronic mail.
4. Alter data belonging to someone else without permission.
5. Use the computer for play during work hours or use it for personal profit.
6. Access the Internet for nonbusiness use during work hours.

7. Add to or take away from the software programs.
8. Make unauthorized copies of data or software.
9. Copy software programs to use at home or at another site in the company without multisite permission.
10. Copy company files or procedures for personal use.
11. Borrow computer hardware for personal use without asking permission.

Internet Access and Children

Many online services allow parents or guardians to control what areas of the service users can access. Because there are some discussion topics and adult information that are inappropriate for youth, take advantage of this access-limiting capability. Families using direct Internet access can purchase software for this purpose. If this software is not available, the solution must be very careful monitoring of a child's computer use.

Security, Safety, and Privacy

The September 11, 2001, terrorist attack on the World Trade Center and the Pentagon has raised the entire country's awareness of the security of our citizens and our country. President Bush established the Department of Homeland Security soon after this date.

Electronic communications is the fastest way terrorists communicate. We must all raise our level of security awareness while communicating with computers.

Just as you would not open someone else's mail, you must respect the privacy of e-mail sent to others. When interacting with others online, you must keep confidential information confidential—such as the address of a new friend made online. Do not endanger your privacy, safety, or financial security by giving out personal information to someone you do not know. A common scam (trick) on some online services is for someone to pretend to work for the service and ask for your access code or password, which controls your service account. Never give this out to anyone online because the person can use it and charge a great deal of costly time to your account. Also, just as you would not give a stranger your home address, telephone number, or credit card number if you were talking on the street, take those same precautions online.

Career Opportunities

In one way or another, all of our careers involve the computer. Whether you are a grocery checker using a scanner to read the prices, a busy executive writing a report on a laptop on an airplane, or a programmer creating new software—almost everyone uses computers in their jobs. And, everyone in a business processes information in some way. There are also specific careers available if you want to work primarily with computers.

Appendix B 12

Appendix B - Computer Concepts

Appendix B - Computer Concepts

Schools offer computer programming, repair, and design degrees. The most popular jobs are systems analysts, computer operators, and programmers. Analysts figure out ways to make computers work (or work better) for a particular business or type of business. Computer operators use the programs and devices to conduct business with computers. Programmers write the software for applications or new systems.

There are courses of study in using CAD (computer-aided design) and CAM (computer-aided manufacturing). Computer engineering and architectural design degrees are now available. Scientific research is done on computers today, and specialties are available in that area. There are positions available to instruct others in computer software use within companies and schools. Also, technical writers and editors must be available to write manuals on using computers and software. Computer-assisted instruction (CAI) is designing a system of teaching any given subject on the computer. The learner is provided with resources, such as an encyclopedia on CD-ROM, in addition to the specific learning program with which he or she interacts on the computer. Designing video games is another exciting and ever-growing field of computer work.

Figure B-9 Career opportunities in computing

What Does the Future Hold?

The possibilities for computer development and application are endless. Things that were dreams or science fiction only 10 or 20 years ago are a reality today. New technologies are emerging. Some are replacing old ways of doing things; others are merging with those older devices. We are learning new ways to work and play because of the computer. It is definitely a device that has become part of our offices and our homes.

Appendix B - Computer Concepts

Emerging Technologies

The various technologies and systems are coming together to operate more efficiently. For instance, since their beginnings, Macintosh and Windows-based systems could not exchange information well. Today, you can install compatibility cards in the Power Macintosh and run Windows, DOS, and Mac OS on the same computer and switch between them. Macs (except for early models) can read from and write to MS-DOS and Windows disks. And you can easily network Macintosh computers with other types of computers running other operating systems. In addition, you can buy software for a PC to run the Mac OS and to read Macintosh disks. New technology in the works will allow you to incorporate both systems and exchange information even more easily.

Telephone communication is also being combined with computer e-mail so users can set a time to meet online and, with the addition of voice technology, actually speak to each other. The present drawbacks are that users must e-mail and make an appointment to meet online rather than having a way just to call up each other, and speaking is delayed rather than in real-time. Although not perfected, this form of communication will certainly evolve into an often-used device that will broaden the use of both the spoken and written word.

Another emerging technology is a visual system that allows computer users to use a small camera and microphone wired into the computer so, when they communicate via modem, the receiver can see and hear them.

This technology is in its infancy—the pictures tend to be a bit fuzzy and blur with movement; however, improvements are being made so sharp pictures will result. For the hearing impaired, this form of communication can be more effective than writing alone since sign language and facial expression can be added to the interaction. CUCME is a logical next step from the image transfer files now so commonly used to transfer a static (nonmoving) picture.

A great deal of research and planning has gone into combining television and computers. The combined device has a CPU, television-as-monitor, keyboard, joystick, mouse, modem, and camera. Something like the multiple communications device that science fiction used to envision, this combined medium allows banking, work, entertainment, and communication to happen all through one piece of machinery—and all in the comfort of your home. There are already printers that function as a copier, fax machine, and scanner.

Trends

One trend is for larger and faster hard drives. Forty- and 80-gigabyte hard drives have virtually replaced the 540-megabyte

Appendix B - Computer Concepts

drives, and 200-gigabyte drives are appearing on the scene. RAM today is increasing exponentially. The trend is to sell RAM in units of 32 or 64 megabytes to accommodate the greater purchases of 128, 256, and larger blocks of RAM. All of these size increases are due to the expanding memory requirements of GUIs and new peripherals, such as CUCME devices and interfaces with other devices. Although the capacities are increasing, the actual size of the machines is decreasing. Technology is allowing more powerful components to fit into smaller devices—just as the 3½-inch floppy disk is smaller and holds more data than the obsolete 5½-inch floppy.

Another trend is the increased use of computers for personal use in homes. This trend is likely to continue in the future.

Home Offices. More and more frequently, people are working out of their homes—whether they are employees who are linked to a place of business, or individuals running their own businesses. Many companies allow workers to have a computer at home that is linked by modem to the office. Work is done at home and transferred to the office. Communication is by e-mail and telephone. Such an arrangement saves companies workspace and, thus, money. Other employees use laptop computers to work both at home and on the road as they travel. These computers, in combination with a modem, allow an employee to work from virtually anywhere and still keep in constant contact with her or his employer and customers.

With downsizing (the reduction of the workforce by companies), many individuals have found themselves unemployed or underemployed (working less or for less money). These people have, in increasing numbers, begun their own businesses out of their homes. With a computer, modem, fax software, printer, and other peripherals, they can contract with many businesses or sell their own products or services. Many make use of the Internet and World Wide Web to advertise their services.

Home Use. As the economy has tightened, many people are trying to make their lives more time- and cost-efficient. The computer is one help in that search. Having banking records, managing household accounts, and using electronic banking on a computer saves time. The games and other computer interactions also offer a more reasonable way of spending leisure dollars than some outside entertainment. For instance, it might not be feasible to travel to Paris to see paintings in the Louvre Museum; however, it might be affordable to buy a CD-ROM that lets you take a tour of that famous facility from the comfort of your chair in front of your computer. This can be quite an educational experience for children and a more restful one for those who might tire on the trip but can easily turn off the computer and come back to it later. Young people can benefit enormously from

Appendix B - Computer Concepts

this kind of education as well as using the computer to complete homework, do word processing, create art and graphics, and, of course, play games that sharpen their hand-to-eye coordination and thinking skills.

Purchasing a Computer

After you decide to take the plunge and purchase a computer, the selection of a new computer system should be done carefully to be sure that your needs are fulfilled. This section will help you evaluate what computer is best suited for you and help you purchase a new computer.

Choosing a Computer System

This is perhaps the most critical step. It is important to consider what kinds of tasks you wish to perform on your computer. Windows-based machines have more available software and are more common in businesses, whereas Macintosh computers excel at desktop publishing and graphics. After you decide which type of computer you will buy, you must decide whether to buy a desktop or laptop. Your funds will probably decide this for you. Laptops generally cost more than desktop computers. If you need the portability a laptop has to offer and can afford the additional cost, then it might be the choice for you. Otherwise, desktops are very suitable for use in business, home, and school.

Outlining Your Needs

After you decide what kind of computer you will buy, it is time to confirm the details. When purchasing a computer, you should consider several specific components. The recommended minimum of a few of these are noted in Table B-I.

Table B-1 Computer components

	Windows-based	Macintosh
Processor	Pentium/Celeron	PowerPC G3
Speed	> 800MHz	> 800MHz
Memory (RAM)	> 256	> 256
Hard Drive Size	> 40	> 40
CD Speed[1]	40X	40X
Modem/Fax[2]	56Kbps	56Kbps
Expansion Slots	5	2 to 6
Operating System	Windows XP	Mac OS X
Video Card	64	64
Sound Card	64	64
Zip Drive	100	100

[1]Other choices include CDRW, DVD or DVDRW
[2]Other choices include ISDN, DSL, and Cable

Appendix B 16

Appendix B - Computer Concepts

Depending on what you plan to do with your computer, you might need different components. For instance, if you plan to do a large amount of video and graphical analysis and manipulation, you probably want at least 256 megabytes of RAM, rather than 128 megabytes. High-powered gaming requires a faster video card with more RAM, as would any emerging technologies such as MPEG and virtual reality. If your office plans to do a large amount of online publishing and commerce via the Internet, a faster modem connection is necessary.

Comparative Shopping

Next comes the most challenging task: finding your computer system. Perhaps the most effective way of doing this is to make a spreadsheet similar to the one in Table B-2. This lets you directly compare systems from different companies. Using what you have learned in this book about spreadsheets, you could create charts to show how the different computer systems relate to each other graphically.

Table B-2 Computer system spreadsheet

Features	Preferred Features	System 1	System 2	System 3
Manufacturer				
Model				
Processor	Pentium 4			
Speed	1.5 GHz			
Memory (RAM)	256			
Price				
Hard Drive Size	80 GB			
Price				
CD/DVD	DVD			
Price				
Modem/Fax	56 Kbps			
Price				
Expansion Slots	5			
Price				
Video Card	64MB			
Price				
Sound Card	32MB			
Price				

Making the Final Decision

After you complete the charts, it is time to purchase your computer. Resist the temptation to buy the cheapest or most powerful system. The cheapest computer might be of lesser quality and might not have the features you desire. It is important to get a system powerful enough to last you at least three years but still be within your budget. The most powerful system might contain more features than you need, and could be too expensive. The most expensive computer does not guarantee superior quality. Sometimes the most expensive system contains free software or other extras that you do not need. Consider the manufacturer's reputation when deciding where to purchase your system. Some unbiased sources for this information include the Internet, where customers who have purchased computers often voice their opinions, and consumer magazines. Other points to consider include financing, warranty, available training, and technical support and service.

Before you begin to comparison shop, be aware of hidden costs. For instance, many large chain stores offer computer packages that might not include a monitor. If a system does not include a monitor, you must add this cost. In addition to your system, you might need a printer or extra software. If your system will be mailed to you, then you must also consider shipping, handling, and sales tax costs.

Table B-2 Computer system spreadsheet, continued

Features	Preferred Features	System 1	System 2	System 3
Zip Drive	250MB			
Price				
Printer				
Price				
Software				
Price				
Subtotal				
Sales tax				
Shipping				
Total Price				

Appendix C - Concepts for Microsoft Office Programs

Introduction

Microsoft Office is an integrated software package. An ***integrated software package*** combines several computer programs. Office consists of a word-processing program (Word), a spreadsheet program (Excel), a presentation program (PowerPoint), a database program (Access), a schedule/organization program (Outlook), a desktop-publishing program (Publisher), and a Web page program (FrontPage).

The word-processing program (Word) enables you to create documents such as letters and reports. The spreadsheet program (Excel) lets you work with numbers to prepare items such as budgets or to determine loan payments. The presentation program (PowerPoint) can be used to create slides, outlines, speaker's notes, and audience handouts. The database program (Access) helps you organize information such as addresses or inventory items. The schedule/organization program (Outlook) increases your efficiency by keeping track of e-mail, appointments, tasks, contacts, events, and to-do lists. The desktop-publishing program (Publisher) helps you design professional looking documents. The Web page program (FrontPage) enables you to create and maintain your own Web site.

Because Office is an integrated package, the programs can be used together. For example, numbers from a spreadsheet can be included in a letter created in the word processor or in a presentation.

Word

Word is the word-processing application of the Office programs. In today's busy world, it is necessary to prepare and send many types of documents. Word processing is the use of a computer and software to produce professional-looking documents, such as memos and letters (see Figure C-1). You can also create documents that are more complex, such as newsletters with graphics, and documents that can be published as Web pages.

Figure C-1 Business letter in Word

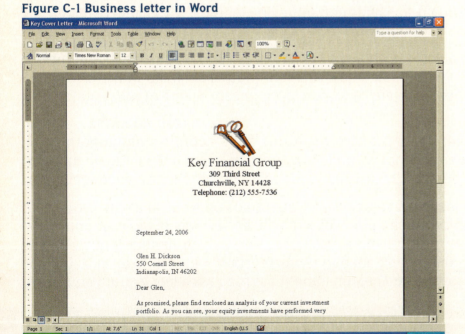

Appendix C - Concepts for Microsoft Office Programs

Keying text in Word is easy because it automatically moves, or wraps, text to the next line. After you key your text, you may want to edit it. Use the Spelling and Grammar checker to identify spelling and grammar errors. Correct the errors using the Backspace and Delete keys to delete text, and Overtype to key over text. Cut, Copy, and Paste commands allow you to move and copy data. Word also has an Undo command that reverses your last command.

Word has many automated features that help you create and edit documents. AutoCorrect corrects errors as you enter text; AutoFormat As You Type applies built-in formats as you key; AutoComplete suggests the entire word after keying the first few letters; and AutoText inserts frequently used text.

Word allows you to easily format a document to make it readable and attractive. Formatting includes making decisions about margins, tabs, headings, indents, text alignment, fonts, colors, styles, headers and footers. Word encourages you to be creative because you can try new formats and change formats in seconds.

You can also enhance documents by adding graphics or pictures that help illustrate the meaning of the text and make the page more attractive. Word provides pictures called clip art, as well as predefined shapes, diagrams, and charts. Drawing tools permit you to create your own graphics.

Excel

Excel is the spreadsheet application of the Office programs. A **spreadsheet** is a grid of rows and columns containing numbers, text, and formulas. The purpose of a spreadsheet is to solve problems that involve numbers. Without a computer, you might try to solve these types of problems by creating rows and columns on ruled paper and using a calculator to determine results. Computer spreadsheets also contain rows and columns (see Figure C-2), but they perform calculations much faster and more accurately than spreadsheets created with pencil, paper, and calculator.

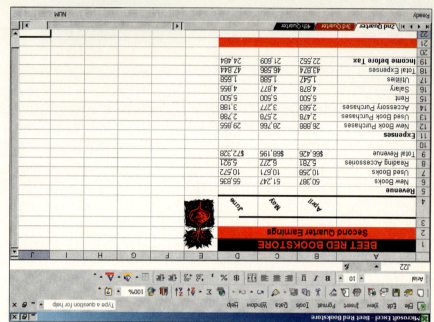

Figure C-2 Excel spreadsheet

Appendix C 2

Appendix C - Concepts for Microsoft Office Programs

Spreadsheets are used in many ways. For example, a spreadsheet can be used to calculate a grade in a class, to prepare a budget for the next few months, or to determine payments to be made on a loan. The primary advantage of spreadsheets is the ability to complete complex and repetitious calculations accurately, quickly, and easily. For example, you might use a spreadsheet to calculate your monthly income and expenses.

Besides calculating rapidly and accurately, spreadsheets are flexible. Making changes to an existing spreadsheet is usually as easy as pointing and clicking with the mouse. Suppose, for example, you have prepared a budget on a spreadsheet and have overestimated the amount of money you will need to spend on gas and electric and other utilities. You may change a single entry in your spreadsheet and watch the entire spreadsheet recalculate the new budgeted amount. You can imagine the work this change would require if you were calculating the budget with pencil and paper.

Excel uses the term *worksheet* to refer to computerized spreadsheets. Sometimes you may want to use several worksheets that relate to each other. A collection of related worksheets is a *workbook*.

PowerPoint

PowerPoint is a program that is helpful in creating presentations in a variety of ways. Presentations can be created using slides, outlines, speaker's notes, and handouts. See Figure C-3. A PowerPoint presentation can include text, clip art, pictures, video, sound, tables, and charts. PowerPoint allows you to apply design templates, custom animations and insert hyperlinks into a presentation. Slide transitions can be added to further customize a presentation. Other Office programs can be used in conjunction with PowerPoint. Word outlines, charts, and tables can all be incorporated into PowerPoint presentations. Excel charts can be imported into a presentation, and presentations can be saved as Web pages and published on the Web. After you complete a presentation, you can rehearse your timing and delivery using the rehearsal functions. PowerPoint presentations are usually viewed using a projector on a screen, but you can also use a television monitor or an additional monitor connected to your computer.

Appendix C - Concepts for Microsoft Office Programs

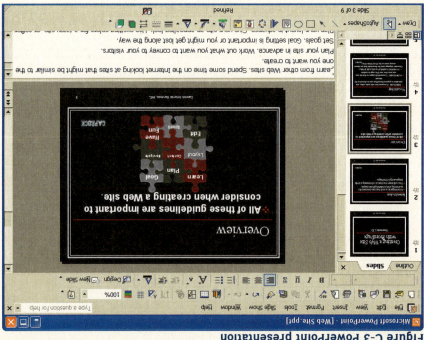

Figure C-3 PowerPoint presentation

Access

Access is a *database management system* program. A computerized database management system allows you to store, retrieve, analyze, and print information. You do not, however, need a computer to have a database management system. A set of file folders can be a database management system. There are distinct advantages, however, to using a computerized database management system.

A computerized database management system (DBMS) is much faster, more flexible, and more accurate than using file folders. A computerized DBMS is also more efficient and cost-effective. A program such as Access can store thousand of pieces of data in a computer or on a disk. The data can be quickly searched and sorted to save time otherwise spent digging through file folders. For example, a database created in Access could find all the people with a certain zip code faster and more accurately than you could by searching through a large list or through folders.

A database is made up of many small sets of data called *records*. For example, in an Employee database, all the information about an employee is a record. See Figure C-4. Information in a record can include the employee's phone number, name, address, social security number, department, and title. In a database, these categories of information are called *fields*. In Access, data is organized into a *table*. Tables store data in a format similar to a spreadsheet. In a table, records appear as rows of data and fields appear as columns.

Appendix C 4

Appendix C - Concepts for Microsoft Office Programs

Figure C-4 Employee database in Access

Emp Number	Last Name	First Name	SS Number	Address	Zip Code	Department	Title	Birthdate	Salary
1	Alexander	Audrey	564-43-2209	5611 Red River	79835-1290	Sales	Manager	2/28/1955	3300
2	Spiegel	Brad	452-89-5411	1290 11th St	79833-2323	Advertising	Account Executive	1/12/1970	2790
3	Broach	Trent	366-23-5287	2020 Canyon Drive	79833-5611	Sales	Manager	12/8/1966	3000
4	Stanford	Shawna	433-62-8944	9853 98th St	79835-9853	Public Relations	Manager	10/22/1960	3150
6	Soliz	Christina	355-23-8712	8241 Toledo	79832-4660	Sales	Sales Representative	5/28/1956	2820
7	Mendoza	Mark	521-87-2319	4582 104th St	79833-2324	Advertising	Graphic Artist	7/18/1968	2575
8	Lovelace	Dave	355-45-9392	2246 Hillcrest Dr	79835-2300	Sales	Sales Representative	10/9/1962	2820
9	Shapiro	Beth	533-83-2336	8010 Salisbury Ave	79832-4678	Marketing	Secretary	3/23/1976	1700
10	Lyle	Sandra	455-31-5662	4552 Canyon Dr	79833-5662	Marketing	Coordinator	4/23/1968	1980
11	Lutrick	Colin	567-22-9845	3441 Glenroe Blvd	79832-3578	Advertising	Creative Director	12/14/1961	3400
12	Davis	Hillary	356-27-5398	4276 Mesa Ave	79833-8700	Marketing	Manager	11/12/1960	3170
13	Wang	Scott	262-78-2929	8770 Geneva Ave	79835-3286	Advertising	Account Executive	8/30/1972	2800
14	Pharr	Alex	488-43-7591	3819 Simmons St	79832-9823	Sales	Sales Representative	7/22/1963	2650

Outlook

Outlook is a desktop information manager that helps organize information, communicate with several people, and manage time. It is easy to use and can quickly summarize your day's activities from Calendar, Tasks, and the Inbox. See Figure C-5. Various features of Outlook allow you to send and receive e-mail messages, schedule events and meetings, record information about business and personal contacts, make to-do lists, record your work, and create reminders. Outlook organizes all this information into categories for viewing and printing. For example, you might group all the information on your important customers into the *Key Customer* category. You can also create a new category for specific groups, such as a *Texas Customers* category, for information on your customers located in Texas.

Figure C-5 Outlook Today screen

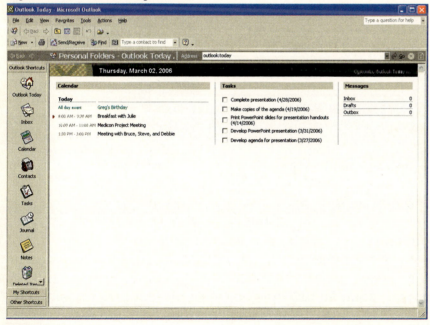

Because Outlook is integrated, you can use it easily with all other Office programs. For example, you can send and receive e-mail messages in Outlook and you can move a name and address from a Word document into your Outlook Contacts List. Outlook has a wide variety of features.

Appendix C - Concepts for Microsoft Office Programs

Publisher

Publisher is a desktop-publishing program that you can use to create a wide assortment of documents, such as business cards, calendars, personalized stationery, and menus. See Figure C-6. Publisher contains hundreds of pre-designed templates you can use as the basis for projects. Personal information sets can be used to store information about your business, organization, or family. Customizations such as logos can be added to an entire series of documents by using the By Design Set option included in the program. All you have to do is add your own custom touches to create your own professional-looking publications.

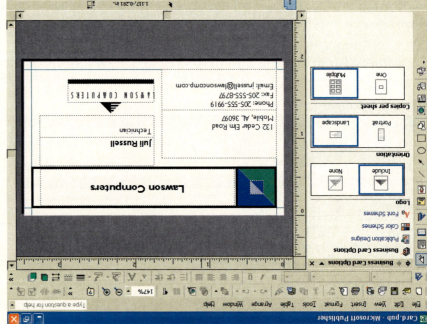

Figure C-6 Business card created in Publisher

FrontPage

FrontPage is a Web page design program that can help you create professional-looking Web pages. See Figure C-7. You do not have to learn HTML formatting codes in order to create a Web page using FrontPage. FrontPage contains preset themes that allow you to apply designs and color schemes either to a single page or to your entire Web site. The theme feature also allows you to change colors, graphics, and text to give your Web pages a consistent and professional appearance. Banners, navigation bars, borders, photo galleries, tables, hyperlinks, and an image map can also be easily added to a Web page using FrontPage.

Appendix C - Concepts for Microsoft Office Programs

Figure C-7 Web Page created in FrontPage

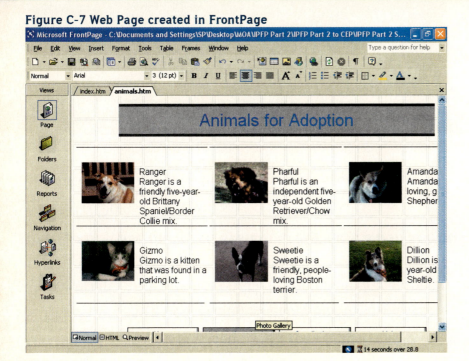

Appendix D - Keyboarding Touch System Improvement

INTRODUCTION

***Your Goal** – Improve your keyboarding skill using the touch system.*

Why Improve Your Keyboarding Skills?

- To key faster and more accurately every time you use the computer for the rest of your life.
- To increase your enjoyment while using the computer.

Getting Ready to Build Skills

Get ready by:

1. a. Clearing your desk of everything except your book and a pencil or pen.
   b. Positioning your keyboard and book so that you are comfortable and able to move your hands and fingers freely.
   c. Keeping your feet flat on the floor, sitting with your back erect.
2. Taking a two-minute timed writing, page D-10, now according to your teacher's directions.
3. Calculating your Words A Minute (WAM) and Errors A Minute (EAM) using the instructions on the timed writing progress chart, page D-11. This will be your base score to compare to future timed writings.
4. On the Base Score line (page D-11), recording the Date, WAM, and EAM.
5. Repeating the timed writing as many times as you can.
6. Recording each attempt on the Introduction line of the chart.

SKILL BUILDER 1

***Your Goal** – Use the touch system to key j u y h n m spacebar.*

What To Do

1. Place your fingers on the home row as shown in Figure D-1.

Computer Concepts
- Letters are struck in a counterclockwise direction from the j key to the u y h n m keys.
- Remember to say the letter softly as you strike it.
- Return your j finger to the home row after striking keys with a quick, sharp stroke.
- You never use your left thumb to key.

Hot Tip
- You will key faster and more accurately when using the touch system instead of looking from the copy and then to the keyboard and striking keys with one or two fingers—the "hunt and peck" system.

Appendix D - Keyboarding Touch System Improvement

Figure D-1 Place your fingers on the home row

2. Look at Figure D-2. Notice how later (in step 3) you will strike the letters j u y h n m in a counterclockwise () direction. You will strike the spacebar with your right thumb.

Figure D-2 Strike all of these keys with your right index finger—the home finger j

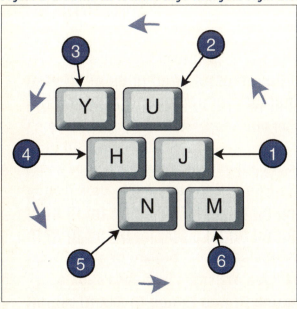

Hot Tips

- Ignore errors. You will always key text that is bold and is not italicized.
- If you have difficulty reaching for any key, for example the y key, practice by looking at the reach your fingers make from the j key to the y key until the reach is visualized in your mind. The reach will become natural with very little practice.
- You may want to start on a clean line by striking the Enter key.

3. Look at your keyboard. Softly say the letters as you strike each key three times (3X), counterclockwise from 1 to 6 with a blank space in between. After striking each letter in the circle, strike j, called the home key, 3X as shown. Don't worry about errors. Start keying:

jjj uuu jjj yyy jjj hhh jjj nnn jjj mmm

jjj uuu jjj yyy jjj hhh jjj nnn jjj mmm jjj

Appendix D - Keyboarding Touch System Improvement

4. Repeat the same drill as many times as it takes to reach your comfort level.

   jjj uuu jjj yyy jjj hhh jjj nnn jjj mmm
   jjj mmm jjj nnn jjj hhh jjj yyy jjj uuu jjj

5. Close your eyes and visualize each key under each finger as you repeat the drill in step 4.
6. Look at the following two lines and key:

   jjj jjj jjj juj juj juj jyj jyj jyj jhj jhj jhj jnj jnj jnj jmj jmj jmj
   jjj jjj jjj juj juj juj jyj jyj jyj jhj jhj jhj jnj jnj jnj jmj jmj jmj

7. Repeat step 4, this time concentrating on a rhythmic, bouncy stroking of the keys.
8. Close your eyes and visualize the keys under your fingers as you key the drill in step 4 from memory.
9. Look at the following two lines and key these groups of letters:

   j ju juj j jy jyj j jh jhj j jn jnj j jm jmj j ju juj j jy jyj j jh jhj j jn jnj j jm jmj
   jjj ju jhj jn ju jm jh jy ju jm jy ju j jh ju jy jh jy jn ju j jy jn ju jy jh jn jy jm jy

10. You may want to repeat Skill Builder 1, striving to improve keying letters that are most difficult for you.

SKILL BUILDER 2

Your Goal – Use the touch system to key f r t g b v.

What To Do

1. Place your fingers on the home row as you did in Skill Builder 1, Figure D-1.
2. Look at Figure D-3. Notice how (later in step 3) you will strike the letters f r t g b v in a clockwise (↻) direction. Strike the spacebar with your right thumb.

Figure D-3 Strike all of these keys with your left index finger—the home finger f

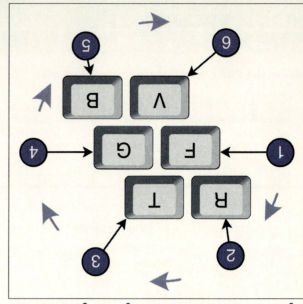

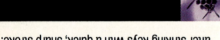
Computer Concept

- Always return your f finger to the home row after striking keys with a quick, sharp stroke.

Teamwork

- If possible, ask a student next to you to call out the letters, so low that only you can hear, as you key them with your eyes closed (for example, f g t b v r). You can then call out the letters to your partner. Make suggestions for each other on how to improve using the Keyboarding Technique Checklist on page D-12.

Appendix D 3

Appendix D - Keyboarding Touch System Improvement

3. Look at your keyboard. Softly say the letters as you strike the keys 3X each, clockwise from 1 to 6, with a blank space in between. After striking each letter in the circle, strike the home key f 3X as shown. Don't worry about errors. Ignore them.

   fff rrr fff ttt fff ggg fff bbb fff vvv

   fff rrr fff ttt fff ggg fff bbb fff vvv fff

4. Repeat the same drill two more times using a quicker, sharper stroke.

   fff rrr fff ttt fff ggg fff bbb fff vvv

   fff rrr fff ttt fff ggg fff bbb fff vvv fff

5. Close your eyes and visualize each key under each finger as you repeat the drill in step 4.

6. Look at the following two lines and key these groups of letters:

   fff fff fff frf frf frf ftf ftf ftf fgf fgf fgf fbf fbf fbf fvf fvf fvf

   fff fff fff frf frf frf ftf ftf ftf fgf fgf fgf fbf fbf fbf fvf fvf fvf

7. Repeat step 6, this time concentrating on a rhythmic, "bouncy" stroking of the keys.

8. Close your eyes and visualize the keys under your fingers as you key the drill in step 4 from memory.

9. Look at the following two lines and key these groups of letters:

   fr frf ft ftf fg fgf fb fbf fv fvf

   ft fgf fv frf ft fbf fv frf ft fgf

10. You are about to key your first words. Look at the following lines and key these groups of letters:

    jjj juj jug jug jug rrr rur rug rug rug

    ttt tut tug tug tug rrr rur rub rub rub

    ggg gug gum gum gum mmm mum

    mug mug mug hhh huh hum hum hum

11. Complete the Keyboarding Technique Checklist, page D-12.

SKILL BUILDER 3
Your Goal – Use the touch system to key k i , d e c.

Keys k i ,

What To Do

1. Place your fingers on the home row, as shown in Figure D-4

Teamwork

- Ask your classmate to call out the letters in random order as you key them with your eyes closed. For example: k i , d e c. Do the same for your classmate.
- Ask your classmate or your teacher to complete the Keyboarding Technique Checklist.

Appendix D - Keyboarding Touch System Improvement

Figure D-4 Striking keys k i , d e c

2. Look at your keyboard and locate these keys: k i ,
3. Look at your keyboard as much as you need to. Softly say the letters as you strike each key 3X as shown, with a space between each set of letters.

   kkk iii kkk ,,, kkk iii kkk ,,, kkk iii kkk ,,, kkk iii kkk ,,, kkk

4. Look at the line in step 3 and repeat the drill two more times using a quicker, sharper stroke.
5. Close your eyes and repeat the drill in step 3 as you visualize each key under each finger.
6. Repeat step 5, concentrating on a rhythmic, bouncy stroking of the keys.

Keys d e c

1. Place your fingers on the home row.
2. Look at your keyboard and locate these keys: d e c .
3. Look at your keyboard. Softly say the letters as you strike each key 3X as shown, with a space between each set of letters.

   ddd eee ddd ccc ddd eee ddd ccc ddd eee ddd ccc ddd

4. Look at the line in step 3 and repeat the drill two more times using a quicker, sharper stroke.
5. Close your eyes and repeat the drill in step 3 as you visualize each key under each finger.
6. Repeat step 5, concentrating on a rhythmic, bouncy stroking of the keys.
7. Look at the following lines and key these groups of letters and words:

   **fff fuf fun fun ddd ded den den
   ccc cuc cub cub vvv vev vet
   fff fuf fun fun ddd ded den den
   ccc cuc cub cub vvv vev vet**

8. Complete the Keyboarding Technique Checklist, page D-12.

Appendix D 5

Appendix D - Keyboarding Touch System Improvement

SKILL BUILDER 4
Your Goal – Use the touch system to key l o . s w x and the left Shift key.

Keys l o .

What To Do

1. Place your fingers on the home row as shown in Figure D-5.

Figure D-5 Striking keys l o . s w x

2. Look at your keyboard and locate the following keys: l o . (period key)
3. Look at your keyboard. Softly say the letters as you strike each key 3X with a space between each set of letters.

   lll ooo lll ... lll ooo lll ... lll ooo lll ... lll ooo lll ... lll ooo lll ... lll ooo lll ... lll

4. Look at the line in step 3 and repeat the drill two more times using a quicker, sharper stroke.
5. Close your eyes and repeat the drill in step 3 as you visualize each key under each finger.
6. Repeat step 5, concentrating on a rhythmic, bouncy stroking of the keys.

Keys s w x

1. Place your fingers on the home row.
2. Look at your keyboard and locate the following keys: s w x
3. Look at your keyboard. Softly say the letters as you strike each key 3X with a space between each set of letters.

   sss www sss xxx sss www sss xxx sss www sss xxx sss www sss xxx sss

4. Look at the line in step 3 and repeat the same drill two more times using a quicker, sharper stroke.
5. Close your eyes and repeat the drill in step 3 as you visualize each key under each finger.
6. Repeat step 5, concentrating on a rhythmic, bouncy stroking of the keys.

Appendix D - Keyboarding Touch System Improvement

Left Shift Key

1. Look at the following two lines and key the line, and then the sentence. Hold down the left Shift key with the little finger of your left hand to make capitals of letters struck by your right hand.

   jjj JJJ jjj yyy YYY yyy YYY nnn NNN nnn NNN mmm MMM

   Just look in the book. You can key well.

2. Complete the keyboarding Technique Checklist, page D-12.

SKILL BUILDER 5

Your Goal – Use the touch system to key ; p / a q z and the right Shift key.

Keys ; p /

What To Do

1. Place your fingers on the home row as shown in Figure D-6.

Figure D-6 Striking keys ; p / a q z

2. Look at your keyboard and locate the following keys: ; p /

3. Look at your keyboard. Softly say the following letters as you strike each key 3X with a space in between:

   ;;; ppp ;;; /// ;;; ppp ;;; /// ;;; ppp ;;; ///

   ;;; ppp ;;; /// ;;; ppp ;;; /// ;;; ppp ;;; ///

4. Look at the lines in step 3 and repeat the drill two more times using a quicker, sharper stroke.

5. Close your eyes and repeat the drill in step 3 as you visualize each key under each finger.

6. Repeat step 5, concentrating on a rhythmic, bouncy stroking of the keys.

Keys a q z

1. Place your fingers on the home row.

2. Look at your keyboard and locate the following keys: a q z

Appendix D 7

Appendix D - Keyboarding Touch System Improvement

3. Look at your keyboard. Softly say the following letters as you strike each key 3X with a space in between:

   aaa qqq aaa zzz aaa qqq aaa zzz aaa qqq aaa zzz aaa qqq aaa zzz aaa

4. Look at the line in step 3 and repeat the same drill two more times using a quicker, sharper stroke.
5. Close your eyes and repeat the drill in step 3 as you visualize each key under each finger.
6. Repeat step 5, concentrating on a rhythmic, bouncy stroking of the keys.

Right Shift Key

1. Look at the following lines and key them. Hold down the right Shift key with the little finger of your right hand to make capitals of letters struck by your left hand.

   sss SSS rrr RRR

   Strike the key quickly. Relax when you key.

2. Complete the Keyboarding Technique Checklist, page D-12.

SKILL BUILDER 6
Your Goal – Use the touch system to key all letters of the alphabet.

Hot Tip
- You will probably have to key slowly. Strive for accuracy, not speed.

What To Do

1. Close your eyes. Do not look at the keyboard and key all letters of the alphabet as shown:

   aaa bbb ccc ddd eee fff ggg hhh iii jjj

   kkk lll mmm nnn ooo ppp qqq rrr sss

   ttt uuu vvv www xxx yyy zzz

2. Repeat step 1, striking keys with a rhythmic, bouncy touch.
3. Repeat step 1, but faster than you did for step 2.
4. Key the following:

   aa bb cc dd ee ff gg hh ii jj kk ll mm nn oo pp qq rr ss tt uu vv ww xx yy zz

   a b c d e f g h i j k l m n o p q r s t u v w x y z

5. Keep your eyes on the following copy. Do not look at the keyboard and key all letters of the alphabet three times each backwards:

   zzz yyy xxx www vvv uuu ttt sss rrr

   qqq ppp ooo nnn mmm lll kkk jjj iii

   hhh ggg fff eee ddd ccc bbb aaa

6. Repeat step 5, but faster than the last time.

Appendix D - Keyboarding Touch System Improvement

7. Key each letter of the alphabet once backwards:

   z y x w v u t s r q p o n m l k j i h g f e d c b a

8. Think about the letters that took you the most amount of time to locate. Go back to the Skill Builder for those letters, and repeat those drills until you are confident about their locations. For example, if you have difficulty with the c key, practice Skill Builder 3 again.

Timed Writing

Prepare to take the timed writing, page D-10, according to your teacher's directions.

1. Get ready by:
   a. Clearing your desk of everything except your book and a pencil or pen.
   b. Positioning your keyboard and book so that you are comfortable and able to move your hands and fingers freely.
   c. Keeping your feet flat on the floor, sitting with your back erect.

2. Take a two-minute timed writing, page D-10, now according to your teacher's directions.

3. Calculate your Words A Minute (WAM) and Errors A Minute (EAM) scores using the instructions on the timed writing progress chart, page D-11.

4. Record the date, WAM, and EAM on the Skill Builder 6 line.

5. Repeat the timed writing as many times as you can and record each attempt.

SKILL BUILDER 7

Your Goal – Improve your keying techniques—which is the secret for improving your speed and accuracy.

Teamwork
• You may want to ask a classmate or your teacher to record your scores.

What To Do

1. Rate yourself for each item on the Keyboarding Technique Checklist, page D-12.

2. Do not time yourself as you concentrate on a single technique you marked with a "0." Key only the first paragraph of the timed writing.

3. Repeat step 2 as many times as possible for each of the items marked with an "0" that need improvement.

4. Take a two-minute timed writing. Record your WAM and EAM on the timed writing progress chart as 1st Attempt on the Skill Builder 7 line. Compare this score with your base score.

5. Look only at the book and using your best techniques, key the following technique sentence for one minute:

   . 2 . 4 . 6 . 8 . 10 . 12 . 14 . 16

   Now is the time for all loyal men and women to come to the aid of their country.

6. Record your WAM and EAM on the 7 Technique Sentence line.

7. Repeat steps 5 and 6 as many times as you can and record your scores.

Appendix D - Keyboarding Touch System Improvement

SKILL BUILDER 8
Your Goal – Increase your words a minute.

What To Do

1. Take a two-minute timed writing.
2. Record your WAM and EAM scores as the 1st Attempt on page D-11.
3. Key only the first paragraph only one time as fast as you can. Ignore errors.
4. Key only the first and second paragraphs only one time as fast as you can. Ignore errors.
5. Take a two-minute timed writing again. Ignore errors.
6. Record only your WAM score as the 2nd Attempt on page D-12. Compare only this WAM with your 1st Attempt WAM and your base score WAM.

Hot Tip
- You can now key letters in the speed line very well and with confidence. Practicing all of the other letters of the alphabet will further increase your skill and confidence in keyboarding.

Get Your Best WAM

1. To get your best WAM on easy text for 15 seconds, key the following speed line as fast as you can, as many times as you can. Ignore errors.

       . 2   . 4   . 6   . 8   . 10

   now is the time, now is the time, now is the time,

2. Multiply the number of words keyed by four to get your WAM (15 seconds x 4 = 1 minute). For example, if you keyed 12 words for 15 seconds, 12 x 4 = 48 WAM.
3. Record only your WAM in the 8 Speed Line box.
4. Repeat steps 1–3 as many times as you can to get your very best WAM. Ignore errors.
5. Record only your WAM for each attempt.

SKILL BUILDER 9
Your Goal – Decrease errors a minute.

Hot Tip
- How much you improve depends upon how much you want to improve.

What To Do

1. Take a two-minute timed writing.
2. Record your WAM and EAM as the 1st Attempt on page D-12.
3. Key only the first paragraph only one time at a controlled rate of speed so you reduce errors. Ignore speed.
4. Key only the first and second paragraphs only one time at a controlled rate of speed so you reduce errors. Ignore speed.
5. Take a two-minute timed writing again. Ignore speed.
6. Record only your EAM score as the 2nd Attempt on page D-12. Compare only the EAM with your 1st Attempt EAM and your base score EAM.

Appendix D - Keyboarding Touch System Improvement

Get Your Best EAM

1. To get your best EAM, key the following accuracy sentence (same as the technique sentence) for one minute. Ignore speed.

   Now is the time for all loyal men and women to come to the aid of their country.

2. Record only your EAM score on the Accuracy Sentence 9 line.
3. Repeat step 1 as many times as you can to get your best EAM. Ignore speed.
4. Record only your EAM score for each attempt.

SKILL BUILDER 10

Your Goal – *Use the touch system and your best techniques to key faster and more accurately than you have ever keyed before.*

Hot Tip

• You may want to get advice regarding which techniques you need to improve from a classmate or your teacher.

What To Do

1. Take a one-minute timed writing.
2. Record your WAM and EAM as the 1st Attempt on the Skill Builder 10 line.
3. Repeat the timed writing for two minutes as necessary to get your best ever WAM with no more than one EAM. Record your scores as 2nd, 3rd, and 4th Attempts.

Assessing Your Improvement

1. Circle your best timed writing for Skill Builders 6–10 on the timed writing progress chart.
2. Record your best score and your base score. Compare the two scores. Did you improve?

   WAM   EAM
   Best Score   ___   ___
   Base Score   ___   ___

3. Use the Keyboarding Technique Checklist on page D-12 to identify techniques you still need to improve. You may want to practice these techniques now to increase your WAM or decrease your EAM.

Appendix D 11

Appendix D - Keyboarding Touch System Improvement

Timed Writing

Every five strokes in a timed writing is a word, including punctuation marks and spaces. Use the scale above each line to tell you how many words you keyed.

```
        .     2     .     4     .     6     .
If you learn how to key well now, it

    8    .    10    .    12    .    14    .    16
is a skill that will help you for the rest

        .    18    .    20    .    22    .    24    .
of your life.  How you sit will help you key

 26    .    28    .    30    .    32    .    34    .
with more speed and less errors.  Sit with your

 36    .    38    .    40    .    42    .    44
feet flat on the floor and your back erect.

    .    46    .    48    .    50    .    52    .
To key fast by touch, try to keep your

    .    54    .    56    .    58    .    60
eyes on the copy and not on your hands or

    .    62    .    64    .    66    .    68    .    70
the screen.  Curve your fingers and make sharp,

       .    72    .
quick strokes.

       74    .    76    .    78    .    80    .
Work for speed first. If you make more

     82    .    84    .    86    .    88    .    90
than two errors a minute, you are keying too

      92    .    94    .    96    .    98    .    100
fast. Slow down to get fewer errors.  If you

      .    102    .    104    .    106    .    108
get fewer than two errors a minute, go for

      .    110
speed.
```

Appendix D - Keyboarding Touch System Improvement

Timed Writing Progress Chart

Last Name: _____ First Name: _____

Instructions:

Calculate your scores as shown in the following sample and footnotes (a) and (b). Repeat timed writings as many times as you can and record your scores for each attempt.

Base Score: Date ___ WAM ___ EAM ___ Time ___

Skill Builder	Date	1st Attempt		2nd Attempt		3rd Attempt		4th Attempt	
		WAM (a)	EAM (b)	WAM	EAM	WAM	EAM	WAM	EAM
Sample	9/2	22	3.5	23	2.0	25	1.0	29	2.0
Introduction									
6									
7									
8					-----				
9					-----				
10									
7 Technique Sentence									
8 Speed Line		-----		-----		-----		-----	
9 Accuracy Sentence			-----		-----		-----		-----

(a) Divide words keyed (44) by 2 (minutes) to get WAM (22).

(b) Divide errors (7) by 2 (minutes) to get EAM (3.5).

Appendix D - Keyboarding Touch System Improvement

Keyboarding Technique Checklist

Last Name: _____   **First Name:** _____

Instructions:

1. Write the Skill Builder number, the date, and the initials of the evaluator in the proper spaces.
2. Place a check mark (✓) after a technique that is performed satisfactorily. Place a large zero (0) after a technique that needs improvement.

Technique													
Skill Builder Number:	Sample												
Date:	9/1												
Evaluator:	SL												
Attitude													
1. Enthusiastic about learning	✓												
2. Optimistic about improving	✓												
3. Alert but relaxed	✓												
4. Sticks to the task; not distracted	✓												
Getting Ready													
1. Desk uncluttered	✓												
2. Properly positions keyboard and book	✓												
3. Feet flat on the floor	✓												
4. Body erect, but relaxed	0												
Keyboarding													
1. Curves fingers	0												
2. Keeps eyes on the book	✓												
3. Taps the keys lightly; does not "pound" them	0												
4. Makes quick, "bouncy," strokes	0												
5. Smooth rhythm	0												
6. Minimum pauses between strokes	✓												

Appendix E - Ten-Key Numeric Touch System Improvement

The touch system means striking the 0 through 9 keys of the 10-key pad without looking at the keyboard. Keep the index, middle, and ring fingers over the 4, 5, and 6 keys. See Figure E-1. Strike keys with a quick, light, rhythmic stroke.

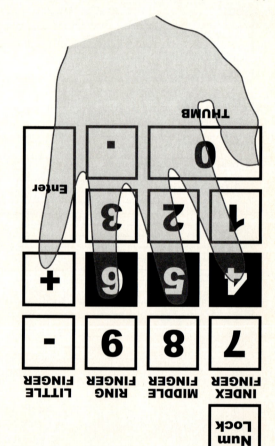

Figure E-1 The 4, 5, and 6 keys are the home row keys

You can improve your 10-key pad skill by practicing the following problems each day.

1.	2.	3.	4.	5.	6.	7.	8.	9.	10.
444	456	565	477	47	416	41	771	4	584
555	456	564	777	74	15	414	141	671	888
666	654	465	444	765	145	511	141	147	855
	654	546	456	675	146	516	717	751	568
	564	654	744	45	64	474	46	854
	564	464						446
								646
								658

11.	12.	13.	14.	15.	16.	17.	18.	19.	20.
2	882	1,257	969	7,259	504	40	146	76	678,091
25	522	85	936	948	400	12	729	67,290	542
682	252	5,128	663	9,631	605	205	358	819	7,891
265	258	426	396	1,654	406	578	708	37	46,720
285	858	82	639	548	506	63	160	8	501,348
548	852	452	993	2,468	540	719	249	25,469	6,493
8	285	867	363	723	604	643	630	8,514	18,379
42	558	761	396	3,975	605	98	549	1,043	205

Appendix F - Models for Formatted Documents

This section contains examples of documents you will use in your business, career, personal, and school life now and in the future.

The documents are in popular formats being used today; however, these are not the only formats. For example, a business letter in block format has all parts of the letter beginning at the left margin. A business letter in modified block format has the date, close, writer's name, and title at the center of the page and the paragraphs might be indented one-half inch.

The following documents are illustrated:

		See page
1.	Letter	
	a. business	F-2
	b. personal	F-3
	c. personal-business (2-page)	F-4
2.	Agenda	F-6
3.	Itinerary	F-7
4.	Memorandum	F-8
5.	Minutes	F-9
6.	Reference list	F-10
7.	Report	F-11
8.	Resume	F-12
9.	Topic outline	F-13
10.	Envelope guide	F-14
11.	State abbreviations	F-14

BUSINESS LETTER

Left and right margins one inch

Business letterhead
Sturduant Marketing Group
231 Topeka Lane
Kalamazoo, MI 49002-2300
616-555-3475
Sturduant@inet.com

Date September 14, 200—

[3 – 8 blank lines to center letter vertically]

Address
MR. JAMES BEST
BEST ENTERPRISES
513 THAYER AVENUE
KALAMAZOO, MI 48004-5100

Salutation Dear Mr. Best

Subject line NEW MARKETING INFORMATION

Body The brochure, *Marketing Guides*, is enclosed. This publication has helped many of our clients, and it should help you make successful marketing decisions.

Close Sincerely

Signature *John P. Williams*

[3 – 4 blank lines to center vertically]

Writer John P. Williams
Title Manager

Keyer's initials cw

Enclosure notation Enclosure

Appendix F 2

PERSONAL LETTER

Left and right margins one inch

Return	2184 Candy Lane
address	Jackson, MI 39290
Date	April 18, 200–

[3 - 8 blank lines to center letter vertically]

Salutation	Dear Aunt Terri
	I'm writing you this letter on the new computer my parents just bought.
Body	Thank you for the beautiful sweater you sent for my birthday. It matches my navy blue skirt and fits perfectly.
	I appreciate your thoughtfulness and hope to see you on Memorial Day.
Close	Love
Signature	*Michelle*

[3 - 4 blank lines to center vertically]

Writer	Michelle
Postscript	P.S. I'm learning how to format letters in my computer class. What do you think about the way this letter is formatted?

PERSONAL-BUSINESS LETTER, Page 1

Left and right margins one inch

Return address   947 Thompson Street
Springfield, IL 62780

Date   May 20, 200—

[3 - 8 blank lines to center vertically]

Address   MS. JANET HUMPHREY
PERSONNEL DIRECTOR
LAIR & KRAMER, INC.
P.O. BOX 2892
SPRINGFIELD, IL 62708-9591

Salutation   Dear Ms. Humphrey

xxxxxxxxxxxxxxxxxxxxxxxxxxxxxxxxxxxxxxxxxxxxxxxxxxxxxxxx
xxxxxxxxxxxxxxxxxxxxxxxxxxxxxxxxxxxxxxxxxx.
xxxxxxxxxxxxxxxxxxxxxxxxxxxxxxxxxxxxxxxx:

Enumerated items   1. xxxxxxxxxxxxxxxxxxxxxxxxxxxxxxxxxxxxxxx

2. xxxxxxxxxxxxxxxxxxxxxxxxxxxxxxxxxxxxxxx
xxxxxxxxxxxxxxxxxxxxxxxxxxxxxxxxxxxxxxxxxxxxx

3. xxxxxxxxxxxxxxxxxxxxxxxxxxxxxxxxxxxxxxx
xxxxxxxxxxxxxxxxxxxxxxxxxxxxxxxxxxxxxxxxxxxxx
xxxxxxxxxxxxxxxxxxxxxxxxxxxxxxxxxxxxxxxxxxxxx

Body   xxxxxxxxxxxxxxxxxxxxxxxxxxxxxxxxxxxxxxxxxxxxxxxxxxxxxxxx
xxxxxxxxxxxxxxxx

xxxxxxxxxxxxxxxxxxxxxxxxxxxxxxxxxxxxxxxxxxxxxxxxxxxxxxxx
xxxxxxxxxxxxxxxxxxxxxxxxxxxxxxxxxxxxxxxxxxxxxxxxxxxxxxxx
xxxxxxxxxxxxxxxxxxxxxxxxxxxxxxxxxxxxxxxxxxxxxxxxxxxxxxxx
xxxxxxxxxxxxxxxxxxxxxxxx

xxxxxxxxxxxxxxxxxxxxxxxxxxxxxxxxxxxxxxxxxxxxxxxxxxxxxxxx
xxxxxxxxxxxxxxxxxxxxxxxxxxxxxxxxxxxxxxxxxxxxxxxxxxxxxxxx
xxxxxxxxxxxxxxxxxxxxxxxxxxxxxxxxxxxxxxxxxxxxxxxxxxxxxxxx
xxxxxxxxxxxxxxxxxxxxxxxxxxxxxxxxxxxxxxxxxxxxxxxxxxxxxxxx

Bottom margin one inch

Appendix F 4

PERSONAL-BUSINESS LETTER, Page 2

Left and right margins one inch

Second-page heading
Ms. Janet Humphrey
May 20, 200–
Page 2

xxxxxxxxxxxxxxxxxxxxxxxxxxxxxxxxxxxxxxxxxxxxxxxxxxxxxxxxxxxxxxxxxxxxx
xxxxxxxxxxxxxxxxxxxxxxxxxxxxxxxxxxxxxxxxxxxxxxxxxxxxxxxxxxxxxxxxxxxxx
xxxxxxxxxxxxxxxxxxxxxxxxxxxxxxxxxxxxxxxxxxxxxxxxxxxxxxxxxxxxxxxxxxxxx
xxxxxxxxxxxxxxxxxxxxxxxxxxx

Close Sincerely

Signature *Kent R. Kimbrell*

[3 – 4 blank lines to center vertically]

Writer Kent R. Kimbrell

Enclosure notation Enclosure: Financial Report

AGENDA

Left and Right margins one inch

PRESCOTT INDEPENDENT SCHOOL DISTRICT
Agenda for Board of Trustees Meeting
7:00 p.m., Thursday, October 22, 2001

I. Verification of quorum and that meeting notice was posted in the required time and manner

II. Approve minutes for September 21, ---- meeting

III. Approve the Tax Report for August ----

IV. Committee Reports
  A. Curriculum
  B. Textbooks
  C. Construction
  D. Building Maintenance

V. Old Business
  A. Maintenance Contracts
  B. Cafeteria

VI. New Business
  A. Recognition of students participating in School Clean-up Week
  B. Short-term Borrowing

VII. Next Meeting, Thursday, November 19, ----

Appendix F 6

ITINERARY

Left and right margins one inch

ITINERARY
Natalie Burns

Monday, September 30
New York to Miami

6:50 a.m.	Leave New York La Guardia on Universal Airlines flight 232.
9:30 a.m.	Arrive at Miami International. Take Courtesy Van to Swifty Rent-a-Car lot to pick up rental car. Drive to the Ocean Inn on 1911 Palm Street.
10:45 a.m.	Meet Jacob Triste for brunch at Ocean Inn Restaurant.
1:00 p.m.	Go with Jacob to tour Technics Plant, Winchester Circle.
3:30 p.m.	Check in to Ocean Inn.
5:30 p.m.	Reception for Austin Arthur in Ocean Inn Green Room.
6:30 p.m.	Attend awards dinner.

Tuesday, October 1
Miami

9:00 a.m.	Attend seminar "The Future of Computer Technology" at Ocean Inn.
11:30 a.m.	Lunch with John Watkins, Jasmine Garden, 1907 Palm Street.
1:00 p.m.	Resume seminar "The Future of Computer Technology."
7:00 p.m.	Dinner with Shaltheimers at their home, 8654 West Ocean Drive.

Wednesday, October 2
Miami

7:00 a.m.	Breakfast meeting with Conner Hill, Bagel Mania, 6797 Jester Street.
9:00 a.m.	Attend seminar "Multimedia Exchange" at Ocean Inn.
11:45 a.m.	Lunch meeting with Riley Group at Cocoa Castle, 2100 Palm Street.
1:00 p.m.	Attend seminar "Doing Business on the Internet."
6:30 p.m.	Dinner with Uncle Joe and Aunt Ellen at Sam's Seafood, 5643 Tree Circle.

Thursday, October 3
Miami to New York

9:30 a.m.	Check out of hotel.
10:30 a.m.	Return rental car.
11:15 a.m.	Leave Miami International Airport on Universal Airlines flight 319.
2:10 p.m.	Arrive at New York La Guardia Airport.

MEMORANDUM

Left and right margins one inch

To: All employees
From: Jamie Smith
Date: November 10, 200—
Subject: Daily file backup

As discussed in the staff meeting on Thursday, files must be backed up daily using the BestBackup software. Here is the procedure for backing up files:

1. Start the BestBackup software.
2. Key your user ID number.
3. Key your password.
4. Choose Select from the File menu and highlight the directories to back up.
5. Choose Begin Backup from the Action menu.
6. Make sure the directories to back up are listed in the Files box.
7. Choose OK.
8. When files are backed up, the message "Backup Complete" will appear.
9. Choose Exit from the Action menu.

If you have any questions regarding this procedure, please call me at 555-9012.

Appendix F 8

MINUTES

Left and right margins one inch

Central High School Music Club
Minutes of the Business Meeting
October 5, 200–

The meeting was called to order at 4:30 p.m. in Room 109. President Alex Anson opened the meeting.

ATTENDANCE — Members present were Michelle Atbury, Justin Baker, Erin Campbell, Elizabeth Denton, Tess Edwards, Gabby Gomez, Karri Jackson, Cecily James, Katie Johnson, Austin Jones, Chris Kelly, Ben Mason, Angela Romero, Mitchell Smith, and Kelly Williams.

MINUTES APPROVED — The minutes of the September 4 meeting were approved.

COMMITTEE REPORTS — Justin Baker, treasurer, reported the balance in the REPORTS bank account is $117.32.

Mitchell Smith, membership chairman, reported that the club has 25 members—four more than last year. He reminded members to pay their dues by October 15.

Angela Romero reported on programs planned for the year. She gave everyone a calendar of events. She reminded everyone about the fall music festival at City College. Members will meet Saturday, **October 20**, at the City College Music Building at 7:15 p.m. to attend the performance of "College Life."

OLD BUSINESS — Chris Kelly reported on the club's fall fundraiser, which will be with Universal Music Sales. Members will receive their catalogs next week so they can begin selling the music cassettes and compact discs. The club's goal is to raise $700. The club will get $5 from each sale. To reach the goal, each member must sell at least five items.

NEW BUSINESS — Elizabeth Denton described a service opportunity for the club. The City Children's Home needs entertainment for a party in December. She moved that the club provide the entertainment. Cecily James seconded the motion. The motion passed. Elizabeth volunteered to organize the entertainment.

ANNOUNCEMENTS — The next meeting will be November 2 at 4:30 p.m.

The meeting was adjourned at 5:15 p.m.

Respectfully submitted,

Erin Campbell

Erin Campbell

REFERENCE LIST

Reader's Choice Book List

Hartley, Fred, and Family. *The Teenage Book of Manners...Please!* Westwood, New Jersey: Barbour Books, 2005.

Temple, Todd. *Answers to Everything.* Nashville, Tennessee: Oliver-Nelson Books, 2005.

Temple, Todd. *How to Become a Teenage Millionaire.* Nashville, Tennessee: Oliver-Nelson Books, 2006.

REPORT

Left and right margins one inch

Teenagers and Alcohol

"Spank them moderately and send them to church and don't give them anything to drink until they're over 18, and that's about all we can say." This advice was given by the Associated Press to parents of teenagers regarding the topic of alcohol. The facts have shown, however, that this is not all parents can say or do. Some people believe that talking to children about alcohol will make them curious and more prone to using alcohol. But studies have shown that children who receive frank information about the dangers of alcohol are less likely to want to try it. Education is the key to alcohol prevention.

To prevent teenagers from becoming involved with alcohol, they must first be informed about alcohol and taught basic principles and morals. Without strong beliefs about why they should not use alcohol, it will be harder for them to resist the temptation.

What Shall We Tell Them?

Young adults must know that alcohol acts as a depressant of the nervous system and brain. They need to be taught, when they are still very young, that alcohol is harmful to their bodies and to their minds. Addeo and Addeo state in the book *Why Our Children Drink* that youth must also know that, contrary to what advertisers would like us to believe, "...drinking doesn't make a person sexier, taller, stronger, older, more sophisticated or more popular, unless he's impressing the wrong people to begin with." After youth are presented with pertinent facts, it should be easier for them to make responsible decisions.

"Teenagers and Alcohol" report was adapted from an essay by Jennifer Simek, a student at Monterey High School, Lubbock TX. This essay won the Lubbock Lion's Club Annual Drug Prevention Essay Contest.

RESUME

Appendix F 12

KENT R. KIMBRELL
947 Thompson Street
Springfield, IL 62780-9047
217-555-9613

GOAL   A word processing position with a growth-oriented company.

WORK EXPERIENCE

Assistant to the Receptionist, Business Department
Melrose Junior College, Springfield, Illinois; August 19 -- to present
Duties: Use computer to help receptionist enter data, file, greet visitors, and answer the telephone.

Recreation Assistant, Springfield Elementary School
Summer ----
Duties: Helped teach sports to fourth grade students.

Cashier, Flick Video, Springfield, Illinois
January ---- to July ----
Duties: Greeted and helped customers and operated cash register.

Student Assistant, Ropes High School, Ropesville, Texas
September ---- to May ----
Duties: Filled out, delivered, and filed student passes.

EDUCATION

West Side High School, Springfield, Illinois
Expected graduation: May 31, ----
Grade Average: B (3.5)
Business Subjects: Accounting, Office Administration, Keyboarding
Machines Operated: Electronic typewriter, microcomputer, transcribing machine, calculator

EXTRACURRICULAR ACTIVITIES

Secretary, Future Business Leaders of America, Fall ---- to present
National Honor Society, Fall ---- to present
Band, Fall ---- to present

REFERENCES

Furnished upon request

TOPIC OUTLINE

Left and right margins one inch

RECYCLING IN THE USA

I. RECYCLING
   A. Why recycle?
      1. Save landfill space
         a) Landfill space is becoming scarce
         b) Recycled items do not take up space in the landfills
      2. Conserve natural resources
         a) Recycling paper products saves trees.
         b) Recycling aluminum saves energy that would be used to make new aluminum.
      3. Avoid pollution
         a) Oil dumped down sewers, in alleys, and in landfills contains toxic substances which contaminate water underground and on the surface.
         b) Oil kills freshwater organisms that fish eat.
         c) Litter is ugly and can be hazardous.
   B. What items can be recycled?
      1. Aluminum cans
         a) Food and beverage containers
         b) Pet food cans
      2. Newspapers
      3. Plastic
         a) Containers marked PET 1
         b) Containers marked HDPE 2
      4. Glass
         a) Clear
         b) Green
         c) Brown
      5. Tin
         a) Food and beverage containers
         b) Pet food cans
      6. Used oil

II. RECYCLED PRODUCTS
   A. Are the products made from recycling any good?
      1. Recycled aluminum cans are melted down, flattened into a sheet, and made into new cans with no loss in quality.
      2. Rerefined oil is as good or better than new oil.
      3. Recycled paper is used to make many high-quality paper products including games, puzzles, and copy paper.
   B. How can I purchase recycled paper products?
      1. Look for products made or packaged in recycled materials.
      2. Ask retailers to carry products that are made from recycled materials.

Appendix F 13

Models for Formatted Documents

Appendix F 14

STATE ABBREVIATIONS

Alabama ..... AL	Kansas ..... KS	Ohio ..... OH
Alaska ..... AK	Louisiana ..... LA	Oklahoma ..... OK
Arizona ..... AZ	Maine ..... ME	Oregon ..... OR
Arkansas ..... AR	Maryland ..... MD	Pennsylvania ..... PA
California ..... CA	Massachusetts ..... MA	Puerto Rico ..... PR
Colorado ..... CO	Michigan ..... MI	Rhode Island ..... RI
Connecticut ..... CT	Minnesota ..... MN	South Carolina ..... SC
Delaware ..... DE	Mississippi ..... MS	South Dakota ..... SD
Dist. of Columbia ..... DC	Missouri ..... MO	Tennessee ..... TN
Florida ..... FL	Montana ..... MT	Texas ..... TX
Georgia ..... GA	Nebraska ..... NE	Utah ..... UT
Guam ..... GU	Nevada ..... NV	Vermont ..... VT
Hawaii ..... HI	New Hampshire ..... NH	Virgin Islands VI
Idaho ..... ID	New Jersey ..... NJ	Virginia ..... VA
Illinois IL	New Mexico ..... NM	Washington ..... WA
Indiana ..... IN	New York ..... NY	West Virginia ..... WV
Iowa ..... IA	North Carolina ..... NC	Wisconsin ..... WI
Kentucky ..... KY	North Dakota ..... ND	Wyoming ..... WY

* Key addressee notations such as HOLD FOR ARRIVAL or PERSONAL in ALL CAPS.

** Key mailing notations such as SPECIAL DELIVERY and REGISTERED in ALL CAPS.

ENVELOPE GUIDE

John Addison
1538 Hazelhurst Ave.
Austin, TX 78746-1298

* ADDRESSEE NOTATION

2 inches

MS. JANE PARKER
SUNBELT PRODUCTS, INC.
10442 METRIC BLVD.
FT. WORTH, TX 76155-3498

2.5" small envelope
4.0" large envelope

** MAILING NOTATION

Appendix G - Task Filenames and Descriptions

Introduction Unit

Part	Filename	Description	Page #
1	Schedule Memo	Word document	11
	April Schedule	Excel workbook	17
	April Work Sched	Excel workbook	17

Word Unit

Part	Filename	Description	Page #
1	Time Plan	Document	5
	Spelling List	List of commonly misspelled words	10
	IW Task1-10	Advertisement	13
	Time Management Seminar	Advertisement	13
2	IW Task2-1	Agenda for trip	23
	NYC Agenda	Agenda for trip	23
	IW Task2-6	Business Letter	29
	NYC Letter	Business Letter	29
3	IW Task3-1	Research paper – Financial Planning for Teenagers	40
	Financial Planning	Research paper – Financial Planning for Teenagers	40
	Financial Planning Title	Cover page for research paper	51
4	IW Task4-1	Research paper – Financial Planning for Teenagers	59
	IW Task4-1a	Cover page for research paper	59
	Financial Title 2	Cover page for research paper	59
	Financial Planning Final	Research paper – Financial Planning for Teenagers	59
	IW Task4-4	Paycheck – Income and deductions	64
	Outline	Paycheck – Income and deductions	64
	IW Task4-5	Table – Computer equipment	66
	Equipment	Table – Computer equipment	66
	IW Task4-6	Memo with table – Voting Precincts	67
	Voting Memo	Memo with table – Voting Precincts	67
5	IW Task5-1	Newsletter for PTA	80
	PTA Newsletter	Newsletter for PTA	80
	IW Task5-5	Wedding Invitation	85
	Wedding2	Wedding Invitation	85
	Park Map	Drawing of directions to park	88
	IW Task 5-10	Business report with chart and graphics	92
	Organization Chart	Business report with chart and graphics	92
6	AW Task6-1	Company history	4
	Norton History	Company history	4
	AW Task6-3	Company benefits	7
	Norton Benefits	Company benefits	7
	AW Task6-7	Company directory	12
	Norton Directory	Company directory	12

(continued on next page)

Appendix G - Task Filenames and Descriptions

Appendix G.2

Part	Filename	Description	Page #
7	IT Memo	Professional memo template	20
	Norton Template	Letterhead template	21
	Norton Letter	Company letter	22
	Resume	Entry-level resume	23
	AW Task7-5	Application letter for resume	25
	Application Letter	Application letter for resume	25
	Envelopes	Create envelopes	27
	Labels	Create labels	28
8	AW Task8-1	E-mail document	36
	IT Recruiting	E-mail document	36
	AW Task8-2	Report with comments and changes	37
	IT Comments	Report with comments and changes	37
	AW Task8-5	Report with comments and changes	40
	IT Report Merge	Merged reports	40
	AW Task8-6	Web page	42
	Norton Jobs Web Page.htm	Web page	42
	AW Task8-7	Web page with a hyperlink	44
	AW Task8-7a	Company history	44
	Norton Product List	Company product listing	44
	Norton History	Company history	44
	Norton History Web Page.htm	Web site	44
	Norton Web Site	Web site with hyperlinks	45
9	Sullivan Achievements	Achievements for resume	53
	AW Task9-2	Sales production table	54
	Sales Leaders	Sales production table	54
	AW Task9-3	Product sales sheet	55
	Product Sale	Product sales sheet	55
	AW Task9-3a.xls	Spreadsheet	55
	Product Spreadsheet	Spreadsheet of Products	55
	AW Task9-4	Employee responsibilities	57
	Norton Expectations2	Employee responsibilities	57
	Norton Poster	Characteristics for good working relationships	58
10	Exercise	Outline	71
	Employee Handbook	Master document	73
	Norton Letter	Subdocument for master document	75
	Norton History	Subdocument for master document	75
	Norton Benefits	Subdocument for master document	75
	Your Responsibilities	Subdocument for master document	75
	Norton Products	Subdocument for master document	75
	Philosophy	Subdocument for master document	74

Appendix H - Application Filenames and Descriptions

Introduction Unit

Part	Filename	Description	Page #
1	April Schedule	Excel workbook	11
	April Work Sched	Excel workbook	17
	Schedule Memo	Word document	17

Word Unit

Part	Filename	Description	Page #
1	IW App1-1	Flyer for lecture	14
	Study Skills Lecture	Flyer for lecture	14
	Thank You Letter	Thank you letter to speaker	15
	IW App1-3	Checklist for language workshop	16
	SLW Checklist	Checklist for language workshop	16
	IW App1-4	Flyer for golf tournament	18
	Golf Tournament	Flyer for golf tournament	18
	IW App1-5	Pamphlet for career placement center	20
	Job Interview	Pamphlet for career placement center	20
	IW App1-6	Guide for telephone etiquette	21
	Telephone	Guide for telephone etiquette	21
2	Guidelines	Guidelines for proofreading documents	32
	IW App2-2	Handout - Body language in job interview	34
	Body Language	Handout - Body language in job interview	34
	IW App2-3	Business letter for client	35
	Business Letter	Business letter for client	35
	IW App2-4	Report using thesaurus	36
	Museum	Report using thesaurus	36
	IW App2-5	Minutes of business meeting	37
	Marina Minutes	Minutes of business meeting	37
3	IW App3-1	Certificate for employee of the month	52
	Certificate	Certificate for employee of the month	52
	IW App 3-2	Guidelines for proofreading documents	53
	Guidelines	Guidelines for proofreading documents	53
	IW App3-3	Wedding invitation	54
	Wedding	Wedding invitation	54
	IW App3-4	Copy for Web page	55
	Realtors Online	Copy for Web page	55
	IW App3-5	Copy for brochure	56
	Camp	Copy for brochure	56
4	IW App4-1	Table with shipping rates	70
	Shipping Rates	Table with shipping rates	70
	IW App4-2	Guidelines for proofreading documents	72
	IW App4-2a	Text used in Guidelines Final document	72
	Guidelines Final	Guidelines for proofreading documents	72

(continued on next page)

Appendix H - Application Filenames and Descriptions

Part	Filename	Description	Page #
	Agenda	Meeting agenda	75
	Resume	Resume for high school graduate	76
	IW App4-5	Table - Baseball schedule	77
	Baseball Schedule	Table - Baseball schedule	77
5	IW App5-1	Newsletter for animal shelter	93
	PAWS Newsletter	Newsletter for animal shelter	93
	Holiday Invitation	Invitation to office holiday party	95
	House Sale Poster	Poster for sale of house	96
	Key Financial Diagram	Diagram of financial portfolio	97
	Key Cover Letter	Cover letter for financial diagram	98
Simulation	Association Letter	Letter for fund raiser	100
	Camper Table	List of children's names and ages	102
6	AW App6-1	Employee responsibilities	13
	Norton Expectations	Employee Responsibilities	13
	AW App6-2	Restaurant menu	15
	Bagel Menu	Restaurant menu	15
	AW App6-3	Document about good diet	17
	Diet	Document about good diet	17
7	BSA Letter	Professional letter	29
	AW App7-2	Mail merge letter	31
	BSA Merge Letter	Mail merge letter	31
	Catering Template	Letterhead template	33
	Catering Letter	Business letter	34
8	AW App8-1	Pamphlet	46
	Checking Account	Pamphlet	46
	Sullivan Web Page.htm	Personal Web page	48
	AW App8-4	Web page with hyperlink	50
	AW App8-4a	Performance schedule	50
	Schedule Web.htm	Web page with hyperlink	50
	Theater	Web page with hyperlink	50
9	Sullivan References	References for resume	64
	AW App9-2	Checking account pamphlet	65
	Checking Account2	Checking account pamphlet	65
	AW App9-3	Letterhead	66
	Shipping Letter	Letter	66
	AW App9-3a	Table	66
	Shipping Table	Linked table	66
	AW App9-4	Newsletter	68
	Hampton Hills Newsletter	Newsletter	68
10	Ergonomics	Outline	79
	Security Manual	Master Document	80

Appendix H 2

Appendix I - E-mail Writing Guides

Because e-mail (electronic mail) is fast and inexpensive, it is rapidly replacing paper mail throughout the world. Electronic messages are usually less formal and more direct than paper messages.

The following guides will help you send effective personal and business e-mail messages.

A. Administration and Mechanics
   1. Try to reply to important e-mails promptly.
   2. Use "high importance" and "low importance" to help the recipient prioritize messages.
   3. Use the flag that reminds you to follow up on a message.
   4. Do not open attachments from senders you do not know.
   5. Use antivirus software.

B. Prepare to Write
   1. Limit your message to only one topic. Record the topic in the Subject line as concisely as possible.
   2. For very important or lengthy e-mails, write down the purpose of your e-mail and an outline of the major points before you key the message.

C. Write
   1. Write concise, clear sentences.
   2. Use active rather than passive sentences.
   3. Use a separate paragraph for each thought.
   4. If there are attachments, mention them within the message.
   5. Use the last paragraph to emphasize your major point, ask for action, and/or end courteously.

D. Be Cautious About
   1. Excessive use of all caps, bold, and italics.
   2. Excessive art, fonts, animated images, wallpaper.
   3. Bombarding recipients with unsolicited messages.
   4. Spreading viruses. Delete unsolicited attachments.

E. Edit
   1. Edit to be sure all of your information is accurate and complete.
   2. Use your computer's spell and grammar check.
   3. Before clicking Send, remember that your message represents you and can be archived by the recipient or easily forwarded to other people.

Appendix I - E-mail Writing Guides

F. Proofread
1. Proofread and revise if necessary to:
   a. Accentuate the positive.
   b. Change an excessive number of "I's" to "you's."
   c. Make the message personal but not overly friendly.
   d. Delete excess words.
   e. Recast words to make the message clearer and more concise.
2. Use bold, underline, italic, and color to emphasize items; but don't overemphasize.
3. Verify that an attachment is actually attached.

G. Edit and Proofread Again—and again if necessary!

H. After Sending
Continue to improve your e-mail messages so that you will benefit from and enjoy corresponding with a wide variety of people and organizations.

Appendix J - Letter Writing Guides

The following outline will help you write personal, personal-business, and business letters.

A. Planning the Letter You Will Write
   1. Responding to a letter
      a. Read the letter you will respond to.
      b. Underline important points to answer.
      c. Write key words in the margin.
   2. Originating a letter
      a. List the result(s) you want the letter to achieve.
      b. Write an outline of the letter to achieve the result(s).

B. Getting Started with the Opening Paragraph
   1. Effective letter writing is careful "talking" to the recipient on paper instead of face to face. Write the first paragraph as if you were talking face to face with the recipient using your best language. The opening paragraph should be no more than two concise sentences.
      a. Responding to a letter: "talk" in writing about the first item you wrote in the margin for step A, 1, c above.
      b. Originating a letter: "talk" in writing about the first item you wrote in the outline for step A, 2, b above.
   2. Some "easy getting started" words that are appropriate for many letters
      a. "Here is…"
      b. "Thank you for…"
      c. "Please…"
      d. Tell what you can do for your reader.

C. Middle Paragraph(s)
   1. Concise, clear sentences in brief paragraphs.
   2. Only one thought in each paragraph.
   3. If you can't get started or get "wound up in words"
      a. Relax; clear your mind of everything else.
      b. Ask yourself, "Exactly what do I want my reader to know?"; your answer is the paragraph.

Appendix J - Letter Writing Guides

   4. Eliminate trite (dull, meaningless) phrases, such as
      a. "This is in reply to..."
      b. "We regret to inform you..."
      c. "I have received your letter." (your reader knows you received her or his letter because you're answering it).

D. Last Paragraph (which could be the most important part of your letter)
   1. Write a thought that makes it easy for your reader to act, such as "A stamped, addressed envelope is enclosed..."
   2. Resell the topic of your letter using different words or a different approach; many letters are sales letters—if you're not selling a product or a service, you're selling yourself.
   3. Be courteous:
      a. "Thanks for..."
      b. "You can depend on me to..."

E. Edit and Proofread
   1. Are all facts included?
      a. Responding to a letter: did you include all of the key words you wrote in the margin for step A, 1, c?
      b. Originating a letter: did you include all of the thoughts in the outline you wrote in step A, 2, b?
   2. Is all information complete and accurate?
   3. Use spell check and check for all errors by proofreading.
   4. Revise if necessary to:
      a. Accentuate the positive and eliminate the negative.
      b. Change an excessive number of "I's" to "you's."
      c. Make the letter friendly.
      d. Delete excess words.

F. Edit and Proofread Again (and yet again if necessary)

G. After Sending
   Continue to improve your writing so you will benefit from and enjoy corresponding by letter.

Appendix J 2

Appendix K - Proofreader's Marks

Always proofread a document while it is still on the screen and corrections are easy to make. Use a spell checker when possible, but remember that spell checkers will not find some errors such as homophones (*to* instead of *two*) and proper names.

For important documents, it is wise to proofread the paper printout. You can use the proofreader's marks below on your own paper or your instructor can use the symbols to indicate corrections you should make.

Change	Proofreader's Mark	Corrected Draft	Final Draft
Abbreviate	⬭	The (United States) constitution is fair.	The U.S. constitution is fair.
Align			
Left	[	[Save the file.	Save the file.
Right	]	]Save the file.	Save the file.
Center	][	]Save the file.[	Save the file.
Bold	~~~~~	Laptops are Here!	**Laptops are Here!**
Capitals			
Uppercase	≡	Jamie found hal.	Jamie found Hal.
Lowercase	/	Jamie Found Hal.	Jamie found Hal.
Delete	⌒	Print one ~~more~~ copy.	Print one copy.
Delete and insert	⌒	Print the ~~final~~ *another* draft.	Print another draft.
Insert			
Apostrophe	⌄	Stacy's computer.	Stacy's computer.
Comma	⌄	Hal, Seth, and Jo are here.	Hal, Seth, and Jo are here.
Hyphen	⌃	Key a two-page resume.	Key a two-page resume.
Letters or numbers	⌃	He is study*ing* math.	He is studying math.
Period	⊙	Mr. James is smart.	Mr. James is smart.
Quotation marks	⌄⌄	She said, "Delete this file."	She said, "Delete this file."
Word	⌃	Restart *the* computers.	Restart the computers.
Ignore Correction (Stet)	...	May is my ~~favorite~~ month.	May is my favorite month.
Italicize	*ital*	*Save As* is a magazine.	*Save As* is a magazine.

Appendix K 1

Proofreader's Marks

Appendix K - Proofreader's Marks

Change	Proofreader's Mark	Corrected Draft	Final Draft
Paragraph Start	¶	¶Liz wants to make three As.	Liz wants to make three As.
Run together	⌒	Al and Ty play baseball. Jan and Sue play soccer.	Al and Ty play baseball. Jan and Sue play soccer.
Spacing			
Delete space	⌒	The paper tray⌒is full.	The paper tray is full.
Insert space	#/	I am studying for a#test.	I am studying for a test.
Vertical			
Double space (1 blank line between text)	DS	Texas Tech University DS] Administrative Office	Texas Tech University Administrative Office
Triple space (2 blank lines between text)	TS	Texas Tech University TS] Administrative Office	Texas Tech University Administrative Office
Spell in full			
Word or number	○	Clay lives on Main (St.) Spot had (5) puppies.	Clay lives on Main Street. Spot had five puppies.
Transpose			
Letter	∽	Turn on the mu sc.	Turn on the music.
Word	⌒	Stereos can be easily used.	Stereos can be used easily.
Underline	—	Save As is a magazine.	Save As is a magazine.

Appendix K 2

Appendix L - The Microsoft® Office Specialist Correlation

The logos on the cover of this book *Microsoft Office Word Applications* and on the last page of this appendix, indicate that the book is officially certified by Microsoft Corporation at the core user skill level for Office XP in Word. This certification is part of the Microsoft Office Specialist program that validates your skills as knowledgeable of Microsoft Office.

The following grids outline the skills and where they are covered in this book.

Microsoft Word 2003 Core

Code	Skill Set and Skills Being Measured	Introduction or Advanced Book	Word Page #	Task or Application
W2002-1	**Inserting and Modifying Text**			
W2002-1-1	Insert, modify, and move text and symbols	Introduction	11, 27, 31, 16, 18, 20, 32, 37	T1-8, T2-5, T2-8, A1-3, A1-4, A1-5, A2-1, A2-5
W2002-1-2	Apply and modify text formats	Introduction	40, 42	T3-1, T3-2
W2002-1-3	Correct spelling and grammar usage	Introduction	25, 29, 30, 32, 35, 36, 37	T2-3, T2-6, T2-7, A2-1, A2-3, A2-4, A2-5
W2002-1-4	Apply font and text effects	Introduction Advanced	43, 44, 52, 53 42	T3-3, T3-4, A3-1, A3-2 T8-6
W2002-1-5	Enter and format Date and Time	Introduction	30, 35, 37	T2-7, A2-3, A2-5
W2002-1-6	Apply character styles	Introduction Advanced	43, 53 4, 15	T3-3, A3-2 T6-1, A6-2
W2002-2	**Creating and Modifying Paragraphs**			
W2002-2-1	Modify paragraph formats	Introduction	46, 47, 48, 53, 54, 55, 81, 93	T3-6, T3-7, T3-8, A3-2, A3-3, A3-4, T5-2, A5-1
W2002-2-2	Set and modify tabs	Introduction	66, 70, 76	T4-5, A4-1, A4-4
W2002-2-3	Apply bullet, outline, and numbering format to paragraphs	Introduction Advanced	64, 75 71, 72, 79	T4-4, A4-3 T10-1, T10-2, A10-1
W2002-2-4	Apply paragraph styles	Introduction Advanced	51 5, 15	T3-9 T6-2, A6-2
W2002-3	**Formatting Documents**			
W2002-3-1	Create and modify a header and footer	Introduction	61, 72	T4-3, A4-2
W2002-3-2	Apply and modify column settings	Introduction Advanced	80, 93 8	T5-1, A5-1 T6-4
W2002-3-3	Modify document layout and Page Setup options	Introduction	13, 46, 60, 61, 72, 75, 76	T1-10, T3-6, T4-2, T4-3, A4-2, A4-3, A4-4
W2002-3-4	Create and modify tables	Introduction Advanced	67, 68, 69, 77 53, 54	T4-6, T4-7, T4-8, A4-5 T9-1, T9-2
W2002-3-5	Preview and Print documents, envelopes, and labels	Introduction Advanced	9, 13, 14, 15, 20 27, 28	T1-6, T1-10, A1-1, A1-2, A1-5 T7-6, T7-7
W2002-4	**Managing Documents**			
W2002-4-1	Manage files and folders for documents	Introduction	23	T2-1
W2002-4-2	Create documents using templates	Advanced	20, 21, 22, 29, 33, 34	T7-1, T7-2, T7-3, A7-1, A7-3, A7-4
W2002-4-3	Save documents using different names and file formats	Introduction	5, 14, 15, 20	T1-2, A1-1, A1-2, A1-5

T = Task   A = Application   Example: T1-2 = Part 1, Task 2

(continued on next page)

Appendix L - The Microsoft® Office Specialist Correlation

Microsoft Word 2003 Core, continued

Code	Skill Set and Skills Being Measured	Introduction or Advanced Book	Word Page #	Task or Application
W2002-5	**Working with Graphics**			
W2002-5-1	Insert images and graphics	Introduction	82, 83, 87, 89, 90	T5-3, T5-4, T5-6, T5-7, T5-8, T5-9, A5-1, A5-2, A5-3, A5-5
		Advanced	91, 93, 95, 96, 98 57, 58, 63	T9-4, T9-5, T9-10
W2002-5-2	Create and modify diagrams and charts	Introduction	92, 97	T5-10, A5-4
W2002-6	**Workgroup Collaboration**			
W2002-6-1	Compare and Merge documents	Advanced	40	T8-5
W2002-6-2	Insert, view, and edit comments	Advanced	39, 46, 47	T8-4, A8-1, A8-2
W2002-6-3	Convert documents into Web pages	Advanced	42, 44, 45, 48, 50	T8-6, T8-7, T8-8, A8-3, A8-4

T = Task   A = Application   Example: T1-2 = Part I, Task 2

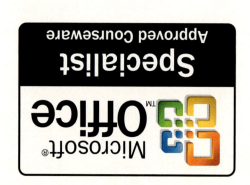

Appendix M - Start-Up Checklist

MICROSOFT OFFICE 2000

Hardware: Minimum Configuration
- ✓ PC with Pentium processor
- ✓ 32 MB RAM
- ✓ Hard disk with 200 MB free for typical installation
- ✓ CD-ROM drive
- ✓ VGA monitor with video adapter
- ✓ Microsoft Mouse, IntelliMouse, or compatible pointing device
- ✓ 9600 or higher baud modem
- ✓ Printer

Hardware: Recommended Configuration
- ✓ Pentium PC with greater than 32 MB RAM
- ✓ Super VGA 256-color monitor
- ✓ 28,800 baud modem
- ✓ Multimedia capability
- ✓ For e-mail, Microsoft Mail, Internet SMTP/POP3, or other MAPI-compliant messaging software

Software
- ✓ Windows 95, 98, or NT Workstation 4.0 with Service Pack 3.0 installed
- ✓ For Web collaboration and Help files, Internet Explorer 5 browser or Windows 98

MICROSOFT OFFICE XP

Hardware: Minimum Configuration
- ✓ PC with Pentium 133 MHz or higher processor. Pentium III recommended.
- ✓ RAM requirements:

  - Windows 98 and Windows 98 Second Edition – 24 MB of RAM plus 8 MB for each application running simultaneously.
  - Windows Me, Windows NT Workstation 4.0, or Windows NT Server 4.0 – 32 MB of RAM plus 8 MB for each application running simultaneously.
  - Windows 2000 Professional – 64 MB of RAM (128 MB RAM recommended), plus 8 MB for each application running simultaneously.

Appendix M - Start-Up Checklist

✓ Hard disk with 245 MB free for typical installation
✓ CD-ROM drive
✓ Super VGA monitor with video adapter, (800 x 600) or higher-resolution, 256 colors or more required.
✓ Microsoft Mouse, IntelliMouse, or compatible pointing device
✓ 14,000 or higher baud modem
✓ Printer

Hardware: Recommended Configuration
✓ Pentium III PC with 128 MB RAM or higher.
✓ 56,000 baud modem
✓ Multimedia capability
  • Accelerated video card
  • Audio output device
✓ For e-mail, Microsoft Mail, Internet SMTP/POP3, or other MAPI-compliant messaging software

Software
✓ Windows 95, 98, Me, or NT Workstation 4.0 with Service Pack 6.0 installed, or Windows 2000
✓ For Web collaboration and Help files, Internet Explorer 5 browser or Windows 98

Glossary

A

alignment - How text is positioned between margins.

application letter - A letter sent with a resume to introduce a person to a prospective employer and request an interview.

AutoComplete - Suggests the entire word after keying the first few letters.

AutoCorrect - Corrects common spelling and grammatical errors as you key text.

AutoFormat As You Type - Automatically applies built-in formats to the text you type.

automatic grammar checking - Identifies grammatical errors as you key your text by underlining them with a wavy green line.

automatic spell checking - Identifies spelling errors as you key your text by underlining them with a wavy red line.

AutoText - Stores frequently used text so you do not have to re-key it each time.

B

bookmark - A place marker that identifies text for future reference.

borders - Lines that are placed around text for emphasis or decoration.

bullet - A character or symbol placed before text, usually in a list, to add emphasis.

C

character style - Character style dictates the appearance of text. Character style options such as font type, font size and color can only be selected from the Font dialog box and the Borders and Shading dialog box.

clip art - Graphics that are already drawn and available for use in documents.

clipboard - A temporary storage place in the computer's memory.

collapse subdocuments - Hides the contents of the subdocuments and displays them as hyperlinks.

continuous section break - A mark indicating the beginning of a new section. It does not begin a new page.

copy - To place a copy of the selected text on the Clipboard while the original text remains in the document.

cross-reference - Text that refers you to another part of the document for further information.

cut - To remove selected text from the document and place it on the Clipboard.

D

desktop publishing - The process of combining text and graphics to create attractive documents.

destination file - The recipient file that receives information from a source file.

drag and drop - A quick method for copying and moving text a short distance.

E

E-mail - The use of a computer network to send and receive messages.

Expand subdocuments - Displays the contents of the subdocuments.

F

find - Command that searches a document for every occurrence of a word or phrase keyed in the Find what box.

first line indent - First line is indented more than the following lines.

font effect - Formatting feature that enhances text.

font size - Size of keyed character determined by measuring the height of characters in units called points.

font style - Formatting feature that changes the appearance of text such as bold, italic and underline.

fonts - Designs of type.

footer - Text that is printed at the bottom of the page.

footnote - Text printed at the bottom of a page, used to document quotations, figures, summaries, or other text that you do not want to include in your main text.

Format Painter - Feature that applies format attributes such as fill color, font size and line color from an object or text to any selected object or text.

formatting - Arranging the shape, size, type, and general make-up of a document.

Glossary

G

graphics - Pictures that help illustrate the meaning of the text or that make the page more attractive.

grouping - Working with several objects as though they are one object.

H

header - Text that is printed at the top of the page.

highlight - Emphasizes important text by shading it with color.

hyperlinks - Underlined and colored text that links you to a different location on your document, or to an external location, such as a Web page.

I

indent - The space placed between text and a document's margins.

indent from both margins - All lines are indented on both sides of the paragraph.

integration - Combining more than one program to complete a project.

L

landscape orientation - Page orientation in which the document is wider than it is long.

leader - A line of periods or dashes that precedes a tab.

line spacing - The amount of space between lines of text.

linked object - An object created in a source file and inserted into a destination file. Changes made in the source file are reflected in the destination file.

M

mail merge - Combining a document with information that personalizes it.

margins - Blank spaces around the top, bottom, and sides of a page.

master document - A file containing links to separate document files.

O

outline numbered list - A list with two or more levels of bullets or numbering.

overtype - Allows you to replace existing text with the new text that is keyed.

P

page break - Separates one page from the next.

paragraph style - Paragraph styles dictate the appearance of a paragraph. Paragraph style options such as alignment, indents, and spacing can be selected from the Font, Paragraph, Bullets and Numbering, and Tab dialog boxes.

paste - To copy text from the Clipboard to the location of the insertion point in the document.

portrait orientation - Page orientation where the document is longer than it is wide.

print preview - Allows you to view a document as it will appear when printed.

R

redo - Command that reverses an Undo action.

replace - Command that replaces a word or phrase in the Find what box with another word or phrase in the Replace with box.

resume - Presents a person's qualifications for a job in a concise form.

S

section - A part of a document with different formatting characteristics than other parts of the document.

selecting - Highlighting a block of text.

selection box - Box placed around a group of objects so that all objects included in the box will be selected.

selection rectangle - The box that appears around a graphic when you select it.

shading - Adding colors or grays to emphasize text.

sizing handles - The small squares that appear on the selection rectangle that allow you to resize a graphic.

Glossary

sort - Arranges a list of words or numbers in ascending order (A to Z; smallest to largest) or in descending order (Z to A; largest to smallest).

source file - The origin or source for information inserted into a destination file.

spelling and grammar checker - Checks for spelling and grammar errors in a document after you finish keying.

style - A predefined set of formatting options that have been named and saved.

subdocument - A separate file contained in a master document.

T

table - An arrangement of data in rows and columns, similar to a spreadsheet.

tabs - Mark the place the insertion point will stop when the Tab key is struck.

template - A file that contains page and paragraph formatting and text you can customize to create a new document similar to, but slightly different from, the original.

text animation - Calls attention to text by creating movement within or around text.

theme - A preformatted design applied to a Web page to change its appearance without changing the content.

thesaurus - A feature for finding a synonym, or a word with a similar meaning for a word in your document.

U

underline style - Formatting feature you can apply to text.

undo - Command that reverses a recent action.

V

vertical alignment - How text is positioned between the top and bottom margins of a document.

W

Web page - A document created with HTML (Hypertext Markup Language) that can be viewed by a Web browser.

Web site - A collection of related Web pages connected with hyperlinks.

Wizard - Microsoft tool that helps you set up and design documents.

word wrap - A feature that automatically wraps words around to the next line when they will not fit on the current line.

Index

Introduction Unit = IN; Word Unit = IW

A

Active sentence, IW-37
Active window, IW-59
Add Favorites dialog box, IN-24
Address bar, IN-22–24
Alignment, IW-47
    button, IW-40
    vertical, IW-51
All caps, IW-43
Antonym, IW-30
Application, IN-28
    quit, IN-16
    start, IN-16
AutoComplete, IW-26
AutoCorrect, IW-24, IW-29
AutoCorrect Options dialog box, IW-27–28
AutoFormat As You Type, IW-24
AutoFormat Table, IW-77
AutoRecover, IN-9
AutoShape, IW-97
AutoText, IW-26

B

Backspace, IW-9
Bold text, IW-40, IW-43
Border, IW-82
    See also Page Border; Shared border
Borders and Shading, IW-69, IW-81
Break. *See* Page break
Browser. *See* Web browser
Bullet, IW-40, IW-64
Bulleted list, IW-64–65

C

Cells
    align text in, IW-69
    merge, IW-69
Change
    border color, IW-69
    bullet character, IW-72
    case of selected text, IW-45
    column width, IW-69
    font size, IW-42
    font style, IW-43
    line color, IW-90
    line spacing, IW-46
    line style, IW-90
    margin setting, IW-46
    object color, IW-90
    row height, IW-69
    underline style, IW-44
Chart
    organizational, IW-92
    See also Organization charts
Click and Type, IW-54
Clip art, IW-83–84
    defined, IW-82
    edit, IW-83
    resize, IW-83
    select, IW-83
Clipboard, IW-11
Close
    document, IN-9–10
    Word, IW-9
Close preview, IN-10
Collegeview.com Web site, IN-23
Column
    change width, IW-69
    insert, IW-68
    select, IW-68
Column dialog box, IW-80
Computer work habits, IN-29
Context Sensitive Help, IN-10
Copy, IW-89
    drag and drop text, IW-12
    Word, IW-11
Copy and paste between documents, IW-59
Create
    columns, IW-80
    new folders, IW-23
    numbered or bulleted list, IW-64
    outline numbered list, IW-64
    table, IW-67
Customize Toolbar dialog box, IN-24
Cut, IW-86
    Word, IW-11

D

Data
    share, IW-100
Date and Time dialog box, IW-30
Default, IN-15
Delete
    in Word, IW-9
Demote item. *See* Indent
Desktop Publishing, IW-79–98
Destination file, IW-100
Diagram, IW-97
Diagram Gallery dialog box, IW-92
Dial-up access, IN-24
Dictionary, IW-29
Document, Windows 2000, IN-7
Document, Word, IW-58–78
    Copy and paste between, IW-59
    opening existing, IN-7
    page break, insert, IW-60
    switching between, IW-59
    view, IW-4
Drag and drop
    defined, IW-12
    in Word, IW-12
Drawing
    add text to, IW-91
    edit, IW-89
    See also Object
Drawing toolbar, IW-87

Introductory Index 2

E

Edit
  clip art, IW-83
  drawing object, IW-89
  Word, IW-3–21
Emboss font effect, IW-43
Emoticon, IW-34
End-of-the-file marker, IW-4
Engrave font effect, IW-43

F

Favorites, IN-24
File menu, IN-7
Fill Color button, IW-90
Find and Replace dialog box, IW-31
  wildcard, IW-32
Find command, IW-31
First line indent. *See* Indent
Folder, IW-23
Font
  color, IW-40, IW-42
  defined, IW-40–41
  dialog box, IW-42
  effect, IW-43
  sans serif, IW-53
  serif, IW-53
  size button, IW-40–42
  size not listed, IW-102
  style, IW-43
Font Dialog box, IW-40–41
Font effect, IW-43
Footer, IW-61. *See also* Header and Footer
Format
  defined, IW-40
  document in columns, IW-80
Format menu
  text and paragraphs, IW-39–57
  text, IW-39–57, IW-80
  change case, IW-45
Format Painter, IW-45
Formatting document, IN-29
Formatting toolbar, IN-5, IW-40–44, IW-51
Full screen, IN-10

G

Grammar check, IW-5, IW-37
  AutoCorrect, IW-24
  automatic, IW-5, IW-25
  limitations, IW-29
  passive and active sentences, IW-37
Graphic. *See* Drawing

H

Handle, IW-83
Hard break. *See* Page Break
Header, IW-61. *See also* Header and Footer
Header and Footer
  toolbar, IW-61–62
Help, IN-12–13, IN-29
Hidden font effect, IW-43
Highlight, IW-44
Highlight text, IW-40
Hyperlink, IN-23
  defined, IN-23

I

Icon, IN-5, IN-28
Indent
  from both margins, IW-48–50
  buttons, IW-40
  decrease, IW-64
  demote item, IW-75
  first line, IW-48–50
  increase, IW-64
  promote item, IW-75
Indents and Spacing tab, IW-46
Insert
  chart, IW-92
  clip art, IW-82
  column, IW-68
  line between columns, IW-80
  pyramid diagram, IW-97
  row, IW-68
  text box, IW-91
Insertion point, IN-5, IW-4
  move in Word, IW-7
Insert Table dialog box, IW-67
  defined, IW-100
Internet, IN-20–26
  add Favorites, IN-24
  connecting to, IN-21–22
  dial-up access, IN-24
  direct access, IN-24
  hyperlink, IN-23
  Internet Service Provider, IN-22
  search, IN-22
  start page, IN-21–22
  URL, IN-23
Internet Explorer, IN-21–22
Internet Service Provider, IN-22
Italic text, IW-40, IW-43

K

Keyboarding. *See* Keying
Keying, IN-28
Key text, IW-5

L

Landscape orientation, IN-10–11, IW-13
Language, IW-30
Line between box, IW-80
Line spacing, IW-40, IW-46
Line Style button, IW-90
Link, IN-13. *See also* Hyperlink

M

Magnifier, IN-10
Margin, IW-46
Menu, IN-5–6
  basic, IN-6
  expanded, IN-6
  help, IN-12, IN-18
Menu bar, IN-5, IW-4
Microsoft Office Specialist Certification, IN-28
Microsoft Web site, IN-4
More Buttons list, IN-6
Move
  drag and drop text, IW-12
  object in Word, IW-89
My Recent Documents (Windows XP), IN-7

N

New Office Document dialog box, IN-4
Normal view, IW-6
Numbered list, IW-64–65
Numbering button, IW-40

O

Object
    add color, IW-90
    change line style, IW-90
Office Assistant
    defined, IN-15
    Troubleshoot Help, IN-19
    turn off, IN-12
Open
    existing document, IN-7
    file from application, IN-4
    Word, IW-4
Organizational chart, IW-92
Orientation, IN-10–11, IW-13
Outline font effect, IW-43
Outline numbered list, IW-64
Outline view, IW-6
Outlook, IW-14
Overtype, IW-10

P

Page Border, IW-85–86
Page break, IW-60, IW-72
Page Number button, IW-61–63
Page Setup, IW-46
Page Setup dialog box, IW-13
Paragraph dialog box, IW-47
Passive sentence, IW-37
Paste, IW-89
    Word, IW-11
Picture, IW-82
Plagiarism, IN-26
Portrait orientation, IN-10–11, IW-13
Print
    in Word, IW-5
Print layout view, IW-6
Print preview, IN-10–11, IW-13
Promote item. *See* Indent
Pyramid diagram, IW-97

Q

Quit applications, IN-16

R

Readability statistics, IW-32
Rectangle, selection, IW-83
Redo command, IW-10
Replace, IW-31
Resize clip art, IW-83
Row
    change height, IW-69
    change width, IW-69
    insert, IW-68
    select, IW-68
Ruler, IN-10, IW-4

S

Sample pages, IN-30–32
Sans serif font, IW-53
Save, IW-5
    AutoRecover, IN-9
    name file, IN-9
Save As dialog box, IN-9, IW-5
Scroll bar, IN-5, IW-4
Secretary's Commission on Achieving Necessary Skills (SCANS), IN-28
Select
    clip art, IW-83–84
    defined, IW-8
    text, IW-9
Serif font, IW-53
Shading, IW-81
Shadow, IW-43
Shortcut, IN-4
    grammar, IW-35, IW-37
    to open recently used files, IN-7
    Thesaurus, IW-36
Show/Hide command, IW-55
Shrink to fit, IN-10
Small caps font effect, IW-43
Soft break. *See* Page Break
Sort, IW-66
Source file
    defined, IW-100
Spacing, IW-55
Spell check
    AutoCorrect, IW-24
    automatic, IW-5, IW-25
Spelling and Grammar dialog box options, IW-29
Spelling and Grammar tab, IW-25
Standard toolbar, IN-5, IW-4
Starting application, IN-4
Start page of Internet browser, IN-21–22
Status bar, IN-5, IW-4
Strikethrough, IW-43
Style, IW-51
Style and Formatting button, IW-51
Style box, IW-40
Subscript, IW-43
Superscript, IW-43
Synonym, IW-30, IW-36

T

Table
    AutoFormat, IW-77
    border, IW-69
    center, IW-68
    defined, in Word, IW-67
    format, IW-68
    insert, IW-67
    merge cells, IW-69
    modify, in Word, IW-69
    revise, IW-68
    shading, IW-69
Table Properties, IW-68–69
Tabs
    common, stops, IW-66

Introductory Index 4

U

Underline, IW-43, IW-44
Undo command
  Word, IW-10
Universal Resource Locator, IN-23
URL. *See* Universal Resource Locator

V

Vertical alignment, IW-51
View
  change, in Word, IW-6
  outline, IW-6
  Print layout, IW-6
  ruler, IN-10
  Web layout, IW-6

W

Web browser, IN-21-22
  Add Favorites, IN-24
  address bar, IN-22
  start page, IN-21-22
Web layout view, IW-6
Web toolbar (Office XP), IN-21-22
Wildcard, IW-32
Word features, IW-22-37
Word opening screen, IN-5
  end-of-the-file marker, IW-4
  formatting toolbar, IN-5, IW-4
  insertion point, IN-5, IW-4
  menu bar, IN-5, IW-4
  ruler, IW-4
  scroll bar, IN-5, IW-4
  standard toolbar, IN-5, IW-4
  status bar, IN-5, IW-4
  taskbar, IN-5, IW-4
  task pane (Office XP), IN-5
  title bar, IN-5, IW-4
Word wrap. *See* Wrap text
World Wide Web, IN-21-22
Wrap text, IW-5

Tabs dialog box, IW-66
Taskbar, IN-5, IW-4, IW-59
Task pane, IN-5
Tasks, IN-28
Text, IN-28
  color. *See* Color
  position in spreadsheet, IW-25
  wrap. *See* Wrap text
Text box, IW-91
Thesaurus, IW-30
  synonym, IW-36
Title bar, IN-5, IW-4
Toolbar, IN-5-6
  defined, IN-5
Type styles, IN-28
Typing. *See* Keying

Index

Word Unit = AW

A

Accept Change button, AW-38
Align
    objects, AW-66
Animation
    add text to, in Web page, AW-42–43
    text, AW-42–43
Application letter, AW-25-26
Ascending order sort, AW-12
AutoFit, AW-53

B

Bookmark, AW-76
Borders and Shading button, AW-53
Break. *See* Page break
Bullets and Numbering, AW-8, AW-62

C

Calculation. *See* Formula
Carbon copy (CC), AW-21
CC. *See* Carbon copy
Cells, merge in table, AW-53
Center button, AW-54
Center table, AW-54
Change
    character styles inside comments, AW-39
    font on envelope, AW-27
    line color, AW-60
    line style, AW-60
    pagination, AW-9
    product number label, AW-28
    See also Resize; Revision marks
Character style
    apply, AW-4
    change inside comments, AW-39
    create, AW-4
    defined, AW-4
    verify, AW-7
Clear
    formatting, AW-4
Clip art
    insert, AW-57
    insert, in template, AW-21
Collapse button, AW-71–72
Collapse subdocument, AW-71, AW-74
Color
    Highlight button, AW-19
Column
    setting, AW-8
Comments, AW-37
    balloons, AW-37
    edit, AW-39
    insert, AW-39
    print with, AW-38
    view, AW-37
Compare and Merge Documents, AW-40–41
Continuous section break, AW-8

Copy
    Excel worksheet into Word, AW-55
    object, AW-59
Create
    character style, AW-4
    cross-reference, AW-77
    envelope, AW-27
    label, AW-28
    master document, AW-73
    outline, AW-71
    paragraph style, AW-5–6
    subdocument, AW-71
    table, AW-53
    table of contents, AW-78
    Web page using templates, AW-44
    Web site using Web Page Wizard, AW-45
    See also Insert
Cross-reference, AW-77
Customize
    bulleted list, AW-62
    toolbar, AW-66
Custom toolbar, AW-67

D

Data
    sort, in table, AW-54
Demote button, AW-71
Descending order sort, AW-12
Deselect object, AW-59
Destination file, AW-55
Distribute horizontally, AW-66
Distribute vertically, AW-66
Document, Word
    sort text in, AW-12
Documents, Word
    compare, AW-40–41
    merge, AW-40–41
    send by e-mail, AW-36
    working with long, AW-70–81
Document Template, AW-22
Drag object, AW-59
Drawing toolbar, AW-58

E

Edit
    comments, AW-39
E-mail
    defined, AW-36
    send documents by, AW-36
Envelope, AW-27
Envelopes and Labels dialog box (Office 2000), AW-27–28
Expand
    outline, AW-71–73
    subdocument, AW-74
Expand button, AW-71
Extension .doc, AW-21

Index

Advanced Index 2

F
Fill color, add, AW-60
First line indent. *See* Indent
Flip object, AW-62
Font
  change on envelope, AW-27
Footnote, AW-10–11
Format
  table, AW-54
Formatting, AW-4
Formula
  add, to table, AW-54

G
Gridlines
  hide, in table, AW-53
Grouping, AW-61
Group objects, using a selection box, AW-61

H
Hard break. *See* Page Break
Heading
  move down one level in outline, AW-71
  move up one level in outline, AW-71
Hide
  gridlines in table, AW-53
Highlight button, AW-17
Horizontal alignment, AW-57
Hyperlink
  defined, AW-44
  insert, AW-44
Hyperlink dialog box, AW-44

I
Indent, AW-17
Index, AW-79
Index and Tables dialog box, AW-78
Insert
  addresses stored in Outlook, AW-27
  bookmark, AW-76
  clip art, AW-57
  comments, AW-39
  cross-reference, AW-77
  footnote, AW-10–11
  hyperlink, AW-44
  index, AW-79
  revision marks, AW-38
  row in table, AW-53
  subdocument, AW-71
  table, AW-53
  WordArt, AW-63
  See also Create
Insert subdocument button, AW-75
Insert WordArt button, AW-62

K
Keep lines together, AW-9
Keep with next, AW-9

L
Label, AW-28
Labels tab, AW-28
Layered objects, change order of, AW-61
Letters and Mailings dialog box (Office XP), AW-26–28
Line and Page Break tab, AW-9
Line Color button, AW-60
Line Style button, AW-60
Link. *See* Hyperlink
Linked object, AW-55

M
Mail merge, AW-25–26
Mail Merge Wizard, AW-25–26
Master document
  create, AW-73
  defined, AW-73
  save, AW-75
Merge
  cells in table, AW-53
  documents, AW-40–41
Minus symbol (-), AW-71
Move
  object behind another, AW-61
  object in front of another, AW-61
Move Down button, AW-71–72
Move Up button, AW-71–72

N
New Comment button, AW-39

O
Object
  align, AW-66
  change order of layered, AW-61
  copy, AW-59
  deselect, AW-59
  distribute, AW-66
  drag, AW-59
  flip, AW-62
  group, AW-61
  layered, AW-61
  linked, AW-55
  move, behind another, AW-61
  move, in front of another, AW-61
  paste, AW-59
  resize, AW-59
  rotate, AW-62
Open
  Drawing toolbar, AW-58
  Resume Wizard, AW-23–24

Index

Reviewing toolbar, AW-37
See also Start
Orphan, AW-9
Outline, AW-71–72
Outline View, switch to, AW-71–72
Outlining toolbar, AW-71–72
Outlook
    insert addresses stored in, AW-27
Oval button, AW-58

P

Page break, AW-9
Page break before, AW-9
Pagination, controlling, AW-9
Paragraph mark, AW-5
Paragraph style, AW-5–7
Paste, object, AW-59
Paste Link button, AW-55
Paste Special dialog box, AW-55
Plus symbol (+), AW-71
Preview
    document as Web page, AW-42–43
Print
    with comments, AW-38
        envelope, AW-27
        label, AW-28
Product number box, AW-28
Professional Memo template, AW-20
Promote button, to move heading, AW-71
Promote item. *See* Indent
Protect document command, AW-38

R

Rectangle button, AW-58
Remove subdocument button, AW-75
Resize object, AW-59
Resume Wizard, AW-23–24
Reviewing toolbar, AW-37
Revision marks, AW-38
Rotate object, AW-62
Row, insert in table, AW-53

S

Save
    with .doc extension, AW-21
    document as Web page, AW-42–43
    master document, AW-75
Section, AW-8
Section break, continuous, AW-8
Select
    objects, AW-61
Selection box, AW-61
Send to Back, AW-61
Send to Front, AW-61
Show/Hide button, AW-5
Soft break. *See* Page Break

Sort
    data in table, AW-54
    lists, AW-12
Source file, AW-55
Start
    mail merge wizard, AW-25
    See also Open
Subdocument, AW-71, AW-73
    collapse, AW-74
    create, from existing document, AW-75
    create, from Outline heading, AW-74
    defined, AW-73
    expand, AW-74
    move, AW-75

T

Table, AW-52–55
    add formula to, AW-54
    center, AW-54
    create, AW-53
    format, AW-54
    hide gridlines in, AW-53
    insert, AW-53
    insert row in, AW-53
Table of contents, AW-78
Table Properties, AW-53
Template, AW-19–22
    create document using original, AW-22
    create original, AW-21
    create Web page using, AW-44
    defined, AW-20
    insert clip art, AW-21
    Professional Memo, AW-20
    use existing, AW-2
Templates on Microsoft.com, AW-21
Text
    color, AW-19
    highlight, AW-19
    sort, in Word document, AW-12
    wrap. *See* Wrap text
Text animation, AW-42
Theme, AW-42–43
Tracked changes option, AW-38

U

Untracked changes, AW-38
U.S. Labor Department, Bureau of Labor and Statistics Web page, AW-40

V

View
    comments, AW-37
    switch to Outline, AW-71

Index

W

Web page, AW-42–45
  create, using templates, AW-44
  defined, AW-42
  preview document as, AW-42–43
  save document as, AW-42–43
  Web Page Wizard, AW-45
Web site
  create using Web Page Wizard, AW-45
  defined, AW-45
Widow, AW-9
Widows/Orphans check box, AW-9
Wizard, AW-23–26
  defined, AW-23
  mail merge, AW-25–26
WordArt
  insert, AW-63
Word wrap. *See* Wrap text
Workgroup collaboration, AW-36–41
  accept changes, AW-38
  comments, AW-37
  compare documents, AW-40–41
  defined, AW-37
  edit comments, AW-39
  insert comments, AW-39
  merge documents, AW-40–41
  opening reviewing bar, AW-37
  print with comments, AW-38
  Protect Document command, AW-38
  send documents by e-mail, AW-36
  track changes, AW-38
  view changes, AW-37
Worksheet
  copy Excel, into Word, AW-55
Wrap text, AW-57

Y

Yung-lo ta-tien (Great Canon of the Yung-lo Era), AW-73

Experience Office for the Future!

Our exciting new Microsoft® Office Applications books provide everything needed to master Microsoft Office suites. These materials work with Office 2000, Office XP, Office 2003, and future versions of Office. These books include:

NEW! **Microsoft Office Applications,** Introductory, by Pasewark and Pasewark

75+ hours of instruction

- 0-619-05599-5 Introductory Text, Hard Top-Spiral Cover, Easel Back, 4-color
- 0-619-05589-8 Introductory, Supplement for Office 2000 Step-by-Step Instructions
- 0-619-05524-3 Introductory, Supplement for Office XP Step-by-Step Instructions
- 0-619-05590-1 Introductory Annotated Instructor Edition, Hard Top-Spiral Cover
- 0-619-05576-6 Instructor Resources CD-ROM, includes testing software
- 0-619-05577-4 Review Pack (Data CD)

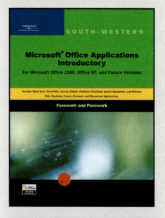

NEW! **Microsoft Office Applications,** Advanced, by Pasewark and Pasewark

75+ hours of instruction

- 0-619-05500-6 Advanced Text, Hard Top-Spiral Cover, Easel Back, 4-color
- 0-619-05592-8 Advanced, Supplement for Office 2000 Step-by-Step Instructions
- 0-619-05527-8 Advanced, Supplement for Office XP Step-by-Step Instructions
- 0-619-05593-6 Advanced Annotated Instructor Edition, Hard Top-Spiral Cover
- 0-619-05576-6 Instructor Resources CD-ROM, includes testing software
- 0-619-05577-4 Review Pack (Data CD)

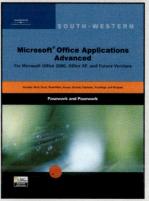

NEW! **Microsoft Office Word Applications,** by Pasewark and Pasewark

35+ hours of instruction

- 0-619-05528-6 Textbook, Soft Top-Spiral Cover, Easel Back, 4-color
- 0-619-05576-6 Instructor Resources CD-ROM, includes testing software
- 0-619-05577-4 Review Pack (Data CD)

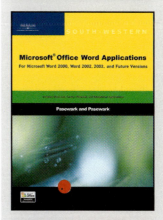

NEW! **Microsoft Office Excel Applications,** by Pasewark and Pasewark

35+ hours of instruction

- 0-619-05525-1 Textbook, Soft Top-Spiral Cover, Easel Back, 4-color
- 0-619-05576-6 Instructor Resources CD-ROM, includes testing software
- 0-619-05577-4 Review Pack (Data CD)

Join Us On the Internet

www.course.com